Evolution
of
International
Management
Structures

Edited by
Harold F. Williamson

Evolution
of
International
Management
Structures

*A Joint Publication
of the University of Delaware
and the
Eleutherian Mills–Hagley
Foundation*

University of Delaware Press

This volume is the edited proceedings
of a conference on the evolution of
international management structures,
which was held May 4–6, 1972.
The conference was sponsored by
the University of Delaware and the
Eleutherian Mills–Hagley
Foundation.

University of Delaware Press,
Newark 19711

International Standard Book Number:
0-87722-101-4
Library of Congress Catalog Card
Number: 74-83671

Printed and distributed for the University
of Delaware Press by Temple University
Press, Philadelphia, Pennsylvania 19122

Contents

Contributors

Robert T. Averitt
Smith College

Alexander Billon
University of Delaware

Alfred D. Chandler, Jr.
Harvard University

Wolfram Fischer
Free University of Berlin

John Kenneth Galbraith
Harvard University

Vsevolod Holubnychy
Hunter College
City University of New York

Herman E. Krooss
New York University

James M. Laux
University of Cincinnati

Peter Mathias
All Souls College
Oxford University

Hugh T. Patrick
Yale University

Hans A. Schmitt
University of Virginia

Barry Supple
University of Sussex

Mira Wilkins
University of Massachusetts

Charles Wilson
Cambridge University

Kozo Yamamura
University of Washington

Editor's Introduction

One of the most striking economic features of the twentieth century has been the emergence of multiproduct, multifunctional and multinational industrial enterprises. Reactions to this development have been mixed. Most observers agree that these organizations have played a significant role in the mobilization and administration of the extensive resources and advanced technologies needed for the mass production of goods and services that are characteristic of the more advanced industrial economies. To some, the multinational corporations hold the key to the future economic growth of the underdeveloped countries. Others, including J. K. Galbraith, argue that the emergence of the modern large-scale corporation has significantly modified and distorted the operation of the market economy; that governments in the new industrial states can only be understood in light of the needs and goals of these industrial giants. In his book, *The American Challenge*, J. J. Servan-Schreiber expressed concern over the possibility of an industrial power—exceeded in size only by the United States and Russia—emerging in Europe and dominated by large American corporations. Spokesmen from other parts of the world have expressed similar concern over the potential or actual influence of international corporations on the economic and social life of their respective countries.

Because of the growing interest in the subject and its significance, the University of Delaware and the Eleutherian Mills–Hagley Foundation decided to cosponsor a conference that would consider the growth and development of large-scale enterprises, both internationally and in the major economically advanced countries. A group of scholars, selected on the basis of their specialized research and publications were invited to prepare papers and to serve as commentators. Invitations to participate in the conference were also extended to a group of business historians and business school faculty with an expressed interest in the topic and to representatives from the business community with first-hand experience in the management of large-scale industrial enterprises.

To ensure meaningful comparisons, participants were asked to consider how closely the growth and changes in the management structures of large-scale enterprises in various countries followed the American experience as outlined by Alfred D. Chandler, Jr. in his *Strategy and Structure: Chapters on the History of Industrial Enterprise*. In this volume Professor

Chandler provides an illuminating account of the emergence of large-scale industrial enterprises in the United States, including such giants as Du Pont, General Motors, Standard Oil of New Jersey and Sears Roebuck. His special interest was focused on the relationships between the management strategies adopted by large American companies and the changes in their respective management structures.

Strategy, as used by Professor Chandler in his analysis, has to do with the determination of the basic long-term goals and objectives of an enterprise and the courses of action adopted for the allocation of the resources necessary for achieving these objectives. Structure he defines as the design of the organization through which the enterprise is administered. It covers the lines of authority and communication among the executives and the nature of the information and data that flow through these lines of communication and authority. He points out that as long as business units produced (or distributed) a limited number of products or services for a limited number of markets, as was the situation in the United States until well into the nineteenth century, there was little need for an elaborate management structure. Typically, the entrepreneurial decisions involving the organization's long-run strategy as well as the tactical decisions affecting its short-term operations were made by one top executive, or at the most a small group.

By the turn of the century, however, this situation had begun to change with an increase in the number of large-scale industrial enterprises. Their emergence was largely the result of a self-generating drive, prompted by a growing management awareness of the needs and opportunities for more profitable employment of existing or expanding resources created by the expanding U.S. economy. This led to the adoption of more elaborate managerial structures which, in turn, required new or at least refashioned management structures if the enlarged and more complex enterprises were to be operated efficiently. The result, as far as the great majority of large-scale enterprises in the United States were concerned, was the adoption of a management structure under which the top executives retained responsibility for the strategic or entrepreneurial decisions of the organization, but delegated responsibility for tactical or operating decisions to divisional or departmental heads.

Professor Chandler's account of the American experience suggested that the following questions would be appropriate for consideration by the conference. First, how and when did large-scale industrial enterprises emerge in the major industrialized countries outside the United States, more specifically Great Britain, France, Germany, Japan, and the Soviet Union? Second, how, when, and where did multinational organizations emerge? Third, to what extent did the evolution of these enterprises follow the American model where changes in the economic and social environment stimulated changes in management strategies and, in turn, in management structures? Finally, what effects have these developments had or are they likely to have on the economic, social, and political life of the areas under consideration?

As had been anticipated by the Planning Committee, a lack of data and a time constraint made it impossible for the conference to consider more than a limited number of the topics suggested by these questions. Members of the Committee were, however, gratified by the extent to which the historical approach contributed to a better understanding of the subject. By comparing the development of industrial enterprises in the various settings, it was possible to indicate how cultural and economic factors influenced their size, their methods of recruiting personnel, and their ways of making decisions.

As had also been anticipated by the conference planners, the exchange of ideas and experiences between the academic and the business participants in the conference contributed much toward a more realistic interpretation of the processes and problems involved.

Two general conclusions emerge from the conference. It was clear from the material presented, for example, that aside from the Soviet Union, the large multifunctional industrial enterprise has become the dominant decision-making unit in the world's technologically advanced economies. (Even the Soviets appear to be under considerable pressure to develop some functionally equivalent type of decision-making institution.) It became equally clear that although the large-scale organizations have contributed significantly to economic growth and development, their size and influence on the economy and their reluctance to accept responsibility for solving the increasingly acute ecological problems associated with their operations, strongly suggest the need for greater social control over their activities.

It should be emphasized that the various participants in the conference were by no means in complete agreement in respect to the nature, causes and public policy implications of these developments. A vigorous debate emerged, for example, over the degree to which the authoritarian tradition has continued to be a characteristic of the management of large-scale German companies. There were differences of opinion over the question of how far businessmen in France were willing to sacrifice profits to maintain their corporate independence. Disagreement was voiced regarding the assumption that the consensus method of making decisions was a unique product of the Japanese culture. To some, the British experience suggested that, contrary to Professor Chandler's model, structural changes had frequently preceded rather than followed changes in strategy. A number of the participants were of the opinion that the extent to which large organizations could control prices and markets had been greatly exaggerated.

But these disagreements served less to confuse than to clarify the issues involved. By suggesting potentially productive areas for research they contributed significantly to the major goal of the conference sponsors, which was to stimulate further consideration of this important subject.

Evolution of International Management Structures

1. The Structure of the Firm and the Structure of the Industry: A Study in Industrial Development

JOHN KENNETH GALBRAITH

In the conventional view of economic life, there is a tendency to regard the participants as broadly homogeneous. Many individuals and firms share the tasks of production. Some are large, some are small; but all are motivated by the same purposes and are subject to the same constraints. All firms seek to maximize their profits; all are subordinate to the command of the market. Some firms (and some trade unions) somewhat modify the homogeneity and symmetry of this system by their power to control the supply, and therewith the prices, of what they sell. They possess monopoly power—a notably wicked thing. But even the monopoly is subject to the ultimate power of the consumer. It is concerned to maximize its profits. The consumer, by his purchases, determines where maximum profits are to be made. The consumer and the market remain in control.

In the last two or three years, I have been seeking to develop a view of the modern industrial economy which abandons this assumption of homogeneity. It divides the modern economy into two parts—that of the few large firms which I call the planning system, and that of the many small firms which I call the market system. What separates the two parts is the susceptibility of a particular task to being performed by organization. The singular feature of the firms in the planning system is complex organization. The feature distinguishing the market system is the continuing need for a dominant role by a single individual or entrepreneur.

I believe this new view of the modern economy gives a much better insight into the way it functions—and the way it fails to function—than the more traditional theory. There is a tendency for scholars so to favor their own thoughts. My purpose in this lecture is first to give you an outline of this bimodal theory of the modern economic system. Then I shall go on to see, with you, what it explains. In this effort, I am summarizing a long and fairly complex book which I hope to publish next year. All who follow perfectly what I say in this lecture are exempt from the need to buy the book.

The two systems into which, for the purposes of analysis, I divide the modern industrial economy are, in their contribution to total output, about equal in size. What I have denoted the market system consists, in the

United States, of between ten and twelve million small firms—service establishments, small retailers, handicraft and small manufacturing concerns, artists, lawyers, physicians and the like. The planning system consists of the one thousand to two thousand great corporations—the economy of General Motors, Ford, General Electric, IBM, General Dynamics.

The market system consists, as I have said, of firms performing those economic tasks that do not lend themselves to accomplishment by organization. A variety of factors exclude or make uneconomic the use of organization in economic life. Four of special importance are as follows:

1. Organization is difficult if the activity is geographically dispersed and unstandardized as to task. Such is the case with much agriculture, most repair services, much retailing. Because of geographical dispersion, supervision of the working force is difficult. Because tasks are unstandardized, it is difficult to set performance norms. So the individual is able to set his own pace—which is normally slow. The energy, both mental and physical, that he puts into the job is considerably increased if he is subject to the incentive system of the independent entrepreneur; if he gets the rewards of his own diligence and intelligence, and—what may be more important—if he suffers personally for their absence. All of this is to say that the firm that consists of an individual or is under the eye of an individual has advantages over more organized effort.

2. Organization is difficult and frequently impossible where the service depends for its value on the interaction of personality—when, in the purest sense of the term, it is a *personal* service. A lawyer, psychiatrist, priest—as in other times, the body servant, or in other places, the prostitute—sells some aspect of his, or her, personality or person. Here, an organization has no advantage—or is irrelevant.

3. Organization is invariably difficult where the service or product has major artistic content. The artist, unlike the scientist or engineer, does not work well as a member of a team. He does not share his art with others; he must be in command of the whole task. This is recognized in everyday language. A man who fits badly into an organization is usually described as being "too much of an artist."

4. Organization is at a disadvantage in the very considerable number of cases where the individual exploits himself or his family or his immediate employees. In organization, men work to rule and for specified pay. The individual entrepreneur—the small commercial farmer for example—can work himself (and his family and, on occasion, his few employees) as hard and as long as he wishes and for as little pay as he wishes. Thus he survives where organization could not.

For these four reasons: geographical dispersion of unstandardized tasks, essential interaction of personality, artistic constraints, self-exploitation—organization cannot function successfully. The firm remains identified with individual personality—and thus remains small. Being small, it is without power. It is subject to movements in prices and costs and consumer choice which it can do little to control. It remains subordinate to the market. In this way, the market system survives in the modern industrial economy. I turn now to what I have called the planning system.

This planning system in the United States consists of some two thousand large manufacturing, transport, power, utility, communications, and merchandising firms. These contribute around 40 percent of gross national product—about the same as the market system. (The rest comes from the state.) In other industrial societies—France, Britain, Germany, Italy, Japan—the position is roughly comparable if state-owned corporations are assigned to the planning system.

   The firm in the planning system is highly organized; this is its central feature. Not only do its tasks lend themselves well to organization—to the mass deployment of workers—but there is also organization for management, or command. In the management, no individual can possess more than a fraction of the information that is required for important decisions. So, when fully developed, the firm is guided collegially by a complex organization for sharing and using the information of numerous individuals. This guiding organization—engineers, scientists, plant managers, sales managers, marketing specialists, advertising managers, controllers, lawyers—I have called, with some acceptance, the technostructure. In this firm, power passes to those who have and share information. Those who do not have such information are helpless. Or, if they intrude, being uninformed, they are dangerous. So they are excluded. Such is the fate of the owner or the shareholder. Not being a participant in the collegial process, he cannot influence its decision. He is a threat to the enterprise if he tries. (The dispersion of stock ownership in the modern corporation and the habit of giving proxies to the management further reduces his power.) So, in the large, fully mature corporation—such firms in the United States as General Motors, General Electric, United States Steel Corporation, Standard Oil of New Jersey—the power of the technostructure, so long as the firm is making a reasonable minimum of earnings, is plenary. The nominal representatives of the stockholder sitting on the board of directors will often have the illusion of power. They ratify decisions with appropriate ceremony. They speak with the solemnity that is always induced by association with large sums of money. They are treated with deference. Their practical power is not negligible but nil. In the smaller corporations with less fully developed technostructures—more common in France, Britain, Italy and the Low Countries—power may still remain with the stockholder, although this ordinarily requires active participation in the management. But in all cases in all countries, as the corporation matures the tendency is for power to pass from the stockholder to the technostructure.

The point is an essential one. In the ultimate evolution of the industrial enterprise, power does not rest with the capitalist. It resides with organization, with the industrial bureaucrat. Many people seek to keep the power of the capitalist alive. The modern radical, like the older socialist, needs the capitalist as an enemy. The economist needs him as the profit-maximizing pivot of his system. The modern manager needs him as the cover for his personal power. To challenge such a formidable opposition must seem quixotic. But the point is a vital one. We understand very little of modern industry unless we see that, at the higher stages of development, power passes, and passes irrevocably, from the capitalist to the industrial bureaucrat.

Power having passed to the technostructure, the latter uses it to advance its own interests. On this point—that self-interest is still pursued in economic life—I am wholly orthodox. Since the firm is large and powerful, its power is great.

In the capitalist firm the capitalist was assumed, I believe rightly, to maximize the profits of the enterprise. In the market system, this remains the basic motivation—no other is consistent with survival. The technostructure has as its first interest the need for a secure minimum of earnings. This keeps the stockholders quiet and ensures the autonomy of the technostructure and thus its power—and survival. Its interest is therefore better served, not by the greatest possible earnings but by the greatest possible growth. Earnings accrue to the stockholders to whom the technostructure is no longer beholden. The benefits of growth, in contrast, accrue directly to the technostructure, and increase the responsibility and thus the salaries and perquisites of the members of the technostructure. Growth improves opportunity for promotion and thereby income. The larger the firm, the more power that is exercised collegially by the technostructure. Power, as always, is a source of prestige. It makes more effective the pursuit of other goals.

I do not suggest that growth is the only goal of the technostructure. It has a strong technical orientation. It may, within limits, make technical innovation a goal in itself. And although it does not maximize earnings, the ability to increase earnings from one year to the next remains an important index of success. But, given the necessary minimum of earnings, it is the dominant motivation. A healthy rate of growth, as it is called, is the basic index of success.

I come now to the reasons why I have designated this part of the economy the planning system. Unlike the firm in the market system, which responds passively to the message of the market, the technostructure is active in pursuit of its goals. Being large, the firm has the power to control its prices—as the firm in the market system does not. The planning system has similar influence over its major costs. It actively seeks to influence consumer behavior in its own behalf, and to this task it brings the vast resources and talent of modern advertising and salesmanship. And it shapes public attitudes and state policy in accordance with its needs. This last deserves a special word.

There is little that is devious, corrupt, or wicked in the way the planning system influences the state. The membership of the technostructure comprises the most affluent, reputable, and substantial element in the national community. It is, in the common phrase, "the establishment." What it regards as good, the reputable philosophers, the press, and the politicians regard as good. To be an advocate of its needs marks a man as reliable and reputable. The goals of the technostructure and the planning system tend, accordingly, to become the goals of the state. The technostructure, as I have noted, values growth. Largely for this reason, economic growth has become a prime goal of the modern state. The technostructure has a strong technical orientation. Largely for this reason, technical innovation has become coordinate with human progress.

The technostructure has other advantages in its relation to the modern state. The public bureaucracy, not the legislature, is increasingly the locus of public power. The corporate bureaucracy has great advantages in dealing with the public bureaucracy—there is, indeed, a relationship of reciprocal advantage between the two. In the United States, the large weapons firm persuades the air force to want the products it can supply. The air force in turn persuades the firm to supply what it wants. This inter-bureaucratic symbiosis is a unique feature of the planning system at its highest level of development. The individual farmer or merchant from the market system and the public bureaucracy cannot sit down together and work things out to mutual advantage. But the doors are always open to the large corporation. The president of General Motors has a prescriptive right to see the President of the United States. The president of General Electric has a similar right to see the Secretary of the Air Force. The president of General Dynamics can always see a general. The farmer or small businessman has no similar access to the bureaucracy. Only an organization can deal effectively with another organization.

We see that the firm in the planning system exercises power in its own right—over prices, costs, the consumer. It also exercises power that it derives from the state. It is power so exercised—by human agency as distinct from the market—that makes accurate my designation of this part of the economy as the planning system.

The distinction just developed—the two parts of the modern economy, each operating under its own dynamic—brings both the nature and the problems of the modern economic system into focus. Let me now turn to what is so revealed. I shall concentrate primarily on the problems of the modern economic society. This is not because, by nature, I prefer gloom. The technical achievements of modern economic society are not in doubt. Where the technostructure is highly developed they are very great. (They can, in a sense, be too great. Overdevelopment in this part of the econ-omy—an overdevelopment that reflects the power of the technostructure in pursuit of its goals—is the counterpart of deficient or retarded develop-ment elsewhere in the economy.) It is only that it is better that we under-stand our faults than our virtues. We can be destroyed by our faults; virtue is not so dangerous. Let me list some of the problems that now oppress us and see how they may be understood in light of the analysis I have just offered.

1. The modern economic system is criticized for being unequal or ir-rational in its performance: It produces too many automobiles; too many cigarettes; too few houses; too few doctors. This is the most pervasive criticism. We now see how this is possible—and inevitable. Where the technostructure is powerful and highly developed and highly persuasive, there is strong development. Where the technostructure is undeveloped, where its capacity to persuade is slight, there is less development. This difference in performance is unrelated to the importance of the product. It is related to the different power of different technostructures or to the total lack of such power in the market system. Housing, health services, some forms of transportation have very poorly developed technostructures or are in the market system. We suffer especially from inferior develop-ment in these industries.

2. There is an instinct that the system has a special bias toward mili-tary technology and production, especially in the United States. This is hard to explain as the citizens' responses to perceived need. Military secrecy and the complexity of modern weapons make it impossible for the citizen or even the legislator to know what is being done. The present analysis shows that the weapons economy is the extreme case of the development of the technostructure—a development that is marked by what I have called bureaucratic symbiosis. Overdevelopment here, where the large weapons firms react symbiotically with the Pentagon, is entirely predictable.

3. One hears that modern *governments*, again most notably that of the United States, have got their priorities wrong. Too much is spent on industrial research and development, supersonic transport, space explora-tion, highway and airport development, technical education. These have ready access to public funds. Such elementary public needs as welfare,

sanitation, health care, ordinary education, police, museums, law courts and the like are starved. We see that this is not a random error. It is systemic. The planning system is powerful in the state. Public services that supply its needs are amply provided. Other public services, those for the market system or the citizen, are less amply provided—or are starved.

4. There is now much complaint that the modern economic system produces goods and renders services at a heavy or even intolerable cost in polluted air and water and damaged and corrupted landscape. This invites great public opposition. We see now the reason. The firm in the planning system pursues its own goals. It has an independent purpose; unlike the firm in the market system it is not subject to the command of the consumer. Its purpose may differ from those of the public. Specifically, the planning system wants growth; it does not want to be deterred by environmental considerations. The public, on the other hand, experiences the environmental damage and disharmony. It reacts accordingly and adversely. Thus the conflict between the planning system and the public over the environment.

5. It is held that many consumers' goods are without serious function or do not perform their function. Products, from detergents to cigarette filters to breakfast foods to new automobile models, are the objects of highly organized persuasion. On examination they turn out to be useless or unreliable as to performance. On this tendency, Ralph Nader has made his career and reputation. The present analysis also explains and sustains this criticism. The technostructure is concerned with growth, and sets prices that encourage growth. So the consumer is not exploited in the old sense. But technical virtuosity is greatly emphasized as a goal. It is associated, in turn, with the goal of growth. What counts is not whether the innovation serves a perceived need. What counts is whether it promotes sales and therewith the growth of the firm. Performance is secondary to what can be sold. Functionless innovation, if it lends itself to persuasion, may be as good for the growth of the firm as that which has function.

6. It is observed that even in the richest of modern economies many people continue to live a precarious existence. They do not share in the general affluence. Inequality, if anything, increases. This, too, the present analysis shows to be possible. The planning system has a stong technical dynamic based on high technical competence and strong state support; the market system has not. The planning system has strong control over its prices and consumer responses; the market system has no such control. In the planning system, firm rules govern wages and hours of work; in the market system, some survive because they can reduce their wage (or that of others) and increase hours of work. A strong tendency for incomes in the two parts to diverge is hardly surprising. And the greater power of the planning system to set prices and costs means, *pari passu*, that it can

set prices and costs for the market system to which it is juxtaposed. To an important degree, the planning system is able to exploit the market system.

7. It is noticed that the modern economic system has a strong tendency to inflation. This, too, is explained. Orthodox fiscal and monetary policies still work in the market system. Here their effect on market demand brings a prompt effect on prices. But the planning system, we have seen, has power over its prices. Accordingly, it has power to resolve its conflicts with its labor force by conceding increases and passing the costs on to the public. In the planning system, monetary and fiscal policy run afoul of the power of the technostructure to control its prices and its use of this power to pass on wage costs. Here these traditional defenses against inflation work badly if at all.

8. Increasingly it is held that modern industry is bureaucratic and unresponsive to public will. Considering its massive organization, and its pursuit of goals that are its own, this criticism is hardly surprising.

The question remains: To what lines of practical action does this view of the economy lead? Here I must abbreviate; I must leave something for the book that is to come. But let me list the major practical consequences —seven in all.

First, we must be clear that the modern economy has no inherent tendency, as it develops, to perfect itself. The most important imperfection is the unequal development of the economy. This, in turn, leads us to a new view of social action and of socialism. The socialist has always been attracted, instinctively, to the positions of power in the economy, where he expects to find exploitation. But exploitation in the classical sense is not, we have seen, the problem. In the positions of power neither workers nor consumers are abused. It is the positions of weakness in the economy that are now the problem. Therefore, the theater of social action must be in these areas of weakness. The first concern must be not with the commanding heights but with the abysmal swamps. The pressure of need has in fact run counter to ideology in these matters, since it is with housing, hospitals, health care, urban transportation, urban services and agriculture that modern social action has been greatly concerned. The weakness of these industries—their lack of a developed technostructure—has already forced the pace of social action.

Second, the problem of the overdeveloped technostructure must, nonetheless, be a subject of profound public concern. We must recognize that we get weapons, automobiles, highways, space travel in their present abundance not because we want or need them but because the planning system has the power to obtain them. This fact must be kept urgently in mind in the allocation of public resources. The problem of the modern legislature is to allocate resources in accordance with the public need as opposed to the power of the planning system. If legislatures respond to the planning system, they will (as now) reinforce the positions of abundance in the economy. Only if they resist technocratic need and respond to the differing public need will they effectively enhance economic and public well-being.

Third, we must recognize that the environmental problem involves a fundamental conflict between the purposes of the planning system and the public interest. This means that cosmetic action—measures designed to internalize external diseconomies and so add them to the price of goods—will not serve. Firm parameters must be established defining the public interest in the environment. Production and consumption must, henceforth, be within those parameters. In everyday language, what industries may do to air, water, and landscape will have to be far more rigorously defined than in the past. And increasingly there will be kinds of production and consumption—damaging chemicals, automobile use in large cities, air travel over metropolitan areas—which will have to be controlled or forbidden.

Fourth, in the United States, a new look at military expenditures in the modern state is obviously indicated. In the past, these were imagined to serve the public interest. They reflect, in fact, bureaucratic symbiosis and the purposes of the planning system.

Fifth, much stronger measures to correct economic inequality are called for than in the past. The tendency is not to reduction of inequality; it is to increasing disparity between the industrial and the market systems. Public measures for the protection of prices and wages in the market system are essential. So, and even more important, is the recent move to establish a minimum guaranteed income—a way, in effect, of putting a floor under incomes in the market system. So are steps to decrease inequality within the corporate bureaucracy.

Sixth, a new view of macroeconomic policy is obviously required. Orthodox fiscal and monetary policy will no longer ensure stable prices at full employment. The planning system, as an inherent feature, has the power to defeat such measures. This means that public intervention on wages and prices *in this part of the economy*—where a strong technostructure faces a strong union—is the only alternative to inflation. Mr. Nixon, not an original student of these ideas, accepted this conclusion. It is worth noting that the controls he invoked apply rather specifically to the planning system.

Seventh, we must recognize that the tensions associated with organization are not accidental and evanescent. The technostructure requires a massive educational apparatus to sustain it; its substitution of an educated for an uneducated proletariat is, perhaps, its greatest achievement. But education, with its emphasis on personality, and the technostructure, with its intellectual disciplines, are uneasy companions. Not surprisingly, the tension is greatest in the universities where the disciplines of the techno-structure, as also its truths, come increasingly into question. Over the longer period this means that more and more people are going to be forced to face the choice between the pecuniary rewards of organization and the lesser discipline of a lower and simpler standard of living. One already sees young people making this choice—opting for fewer goods and more freedom. It is, we may suppose, only a beginning.

In the years following World War II, when the goals of the technostructure were accepted without question as the goals of the society and when economic growth in particular seemed to be the solution for all public ills, economists in the industrial countries came imperceptibly but very definitely to the conclusion that most of the problems of their subject matter had been solved. Mathematical refinement of existing models was now the need. The age of major structural reform was over. The concept of a bimodal economy—and the principal consequence, which is the sub-stitution of the goals of the planning system for those of the public— shows how wrong this estimate was. It shows also how many other ideas, from the traditional view of socialists to the neo-Keynesian views on fiscal and monetary policy, must be revised. In economics, the age of thought, I am happy to advise you, is not yet over.

2. Time's Structure, Man's Strategy: The American Experience

ROBERT T. AVERITT

My thesis is a rather straightforward one. The long-run dynamics of an economic system may best be understood as an evolutionary process. Economic institutions—households, business firms, governments—adapt to their environment. But in adapting, they change that environment. To understand the logic of institutional movement, we must try to decode the system's laws of transformation. I shall contend that the evolution of the American economic system is best understood in the context of economic development. During our industrialization drive, extending from the 1840s until the 1920s, the U.S. economy took its signals in major part from the logic of economic development. Since the concept of *time* is central to an understanding of the developmental process, it must occupy a prominent place in our theory.

Economic development has continued in America since the 1920s, but the content of the development thrust has shifted during the past generation from mechanical to chemical and electronic processes. This shift subjects development to an ecological flaw and thus threatens its integrity. At the same time a growing labor force, appearing at a time when workers producing goods continue to enjoy substantial productivity gains, is producing a dual, imbalanced economy. In the industrial, goods-producing sectors, highly paid, productive workers turn out an abundance of goods, their quantity limited only by the size of their market. By contrast, the service sector employs workers enjoying fewer productivity gains and, in general, lower pay. The labor-saving nature of goods production pushes a growing percentage of our expanding labor force into service work at a time when goods abundance is lowering the marginal utility of goods by comparison with services. Since economic development, with its stress on productivity gain, is a heavily goods-oriented phenomenon, this, too, threatens the integrity of economic development as a core process in the American economy.

Finally, the increasing complexity of our economic system, its modern inability to provide full employment in the private sector, the demand for general economic regulation, and the lessons of our wartime experience impelled Americans to turn to government for economic direction at the system level. But government has a logic of its own quite different from that informing a business system. I shall contend that a business-oriented system is an essentially open system, while the predilection of government is toward system closure. As the imperatives of government rise to dominate over the logic of business and economic development, the American system begins to move away from its traditional openness. The movement from a system characterized by development and openness to one tending toward government domination and closure is evolutionary in character. The point of this paper is to distinguish evolutionary time from biological and mechanical time. I do believe that systems evolution can be understood, and that Professor Chandler's work can be evaluated by placing it inside this broad theoretical frame.

A THEORY OF SYSTEMS EVOLUTION

To use the term evolution in relation to economic institutions is—to speak metaphorically—to borrow images about change from biology and, hence, to enter the dialogue about necessity and chance in living systems. Since there is no accepted, deterministic law of evolution, numerous interpretations abound and compete. To read nature's movement through time, man must examine not only nature, but himself. He is the one introducing the concept of time. Is there any proof of time apart from man's stream of consciousness, from his awareness and the corresponding awareness of consciousnesses like his that time is real? Time is very real, indeed, for man, but for nature, too? Evolution escapes the easier mechanics of our understanding, for the issue of time itself is being judged by our consciousness *in medias res.*

Georgescu-Roegen asserts in *The Entropy Law and the Economic Process* that it is from physics, not biology, that we are supplied with the only clear example of an evolutionary principle: the second law of thermodynamics, also called the entropy law.[1] The numerous efforts of social scientists to find an evolutionary principle based on impressionistic criteria suffer because scientific testing is impossible. The most common criteria used to determine evolutionary movement—the direction of time's arrow —are (1) changes in the complexity of organization, and (2) a gain or loss in control over the environment. A third criterion, that of shifts in humanitarian consciousness, defines evolutionary progress as a social order less given to superstition, less tolerant of cruelty—an expansion of human consciousness based on the assumption that life's purpose is harmony and survival. Most analysis of economic phenomena attempts to illustrate evolutionary progress by grounding its proof on the first two criteria, increased complexity of organization and a greater degree of environmental control.

We are all familiar with cyclical, repetitive, biological time, the time of generations and of seasons. We are also familiar with hierarchical, progressive time, the mechanical time of clocks and calendars. Repetitive, biological time and linear, mechanical time are major props for our orientation in the world. But evolutionary, entropic time is a stranger to our common understanding. The second law of thermodynamics deals with the unidirectional movement of all known forms of energy, a unique flow from a higher to a lower level, illustrated by the proposition that heat always moves from hotter to colder bodies. The discovery of entropy in the universe creates a crisis for the physical laws of mechanics, for they are grounded on the possibility of reversibility. A mechanical action can be reversed. An entropic action cannot.

Reversibility, reducing all phenomena to locomotion, omits the question of evolutionary time and addresses itself to the domain of Newton's law of inertia. Its successes underlie the story of the rapid industrialization of the modern period. Equations made invariant to evolutionary time ground our understanding in predictable, communicable, empirical habits and grant man his sovereignty and control over nature. The standards of objectivity and positivism, the assumption that scientific knowledge deals only with phenomena that are "real," that go on irrespective of whether they are observed or not, could be demonstrated in repeatable experiments, in a public and practical technology that turns its hypotheses and theories into products.

Clarity and utility recommend the mechanical model. We expect to find mechanical order in nature, but nature seems orderly only when its modes of being can be grasped analytically, and then controlled, by man. Progressively the extension of the scientific paradigm, its success ramifying into every area of knowledge, has moved us beyond a mechanical control of nature through reversible structures whose locomotion can be constantly speeded up, to an interaction with nature, literally acting into, and tampering with, the biologically timed rhythms of nature's ecology. A manless nature is unimaginable today for the power of our man-made tools literally discloses the structure of nature at the level of the quantum of action and indeterminacy, making the mechanical behavior of inert matter appear to be only a surface illusion.

I have organized a model of economic development and the institutions stabilized and formulated in its evolutionary path around the concept of three modes of time: (1) biological, (2) mechanical, and (3) evolutionary-entropic time. I have written not with an eye to the event level of this process—its history is well recorded—but to its structural or theoretical character.

Consider, then, for emphasis that from the 1840s to the 1920s, the American economy's evolution was predominantly informed by the laws of economic development, operating in a context of an abundant nature and energized by capitalistic, market-oriented assumptions. During the generation extending from the twenties through the fifties, the economy experimented, often simultaneously, with systems based upon consumerism (emphasizing consumer credit), welfare capitalism, and military capitalism. By the 1960s it was clear that the logic of state direction threatened ascendancy as the economic system's dominant element. As with development capitalism during the years of its triumph, we are discovering in the 1970s that public revelations of the state's critical flaws cannot alone undermine the workings of a logic that is achieving overdomination.

THE LOGIC OF ECONOMIC DEVELOPMENT

What we call economic progress can be divided into two types—economic growth and economic development. Economic growth, as I use that term, can be defined as an increase in output gained with standard production techniques within the confines of the existing mode of economic organization. It involves doing what is already being done, but doing more of it with greater efficiency. Economic growth is a short-run concept. It occurs when an economic system becomes more fully employed; it results from using the present mix of economic inputs more effectively. The contemporary theory of economic growth springs largely from the writings of John Maynard Keynes and his followers.

Economic development is a process of structural change. Economists use the term most often when referring to the transformation of an underdeveloped economy into a developed one, for it is here that the structural changes are the most visible and dramatic. But development continues in advanced economies as well. Indeed, the cultural resistances to development are usually weakest where past development has been extensive and prolonged. Development is a long-run phenomenon, requiring the adoption of new skills, the accumulation of new knowledge, the use of new commodities, the creation of new materials, new markets, and new organizational forms.

The first principle of economic development can be stated as follows: development in an economic system is largely achieved by increasing the average velocity of production per unit of labor-time. The quantity of labor-time available to an economic system during a given period is relatively fixed. If population size and composition are stable, the labor force can be expanded when wives, children, and those adults beyond retirement age are induced to take employment. Additional labor-time can also be squeezed from a static population by extending the length of the work day. But attitudes toward working wives, child labor, retirement age, and a standard work day are culturally determined. They usually change slowly.

It may be possible for an economic system to attract a large number of new immigrants, thus increasing the pool of labor-time by expanding the labor force. If the enlarged labor supply is kept fully employed, output will rise; but unless development occurs, output per worker may not increase. Immigration stimulates economic growth, but not development, when full employment is maintained.

The logic of economic development can best be understood by using *time* as a core concept. In a state of absolute underdevelopment, human lives and economic activity are caught in the ecological rhythm of biological time. Men take their sustenance from their surroundings in the form of food, shelter, and clothing without consciously altering the ecological balance. We have been progressively freeing ourselves from the rhythm of biological time for several centuries.

Mechanical, clock time is a device fostering economic development, a contradiction of the psychological nature of human time. The acceptance of clock time as a social sanction displaces time from the psyche of the person and places it in the public domain. To go on the hour standard is to go on the economic standard—to switch to labor savings time. The mechanical hour allows the reduction of individuals to a common denominator so that their activities can be made additive and aggregative for purposes of social movement. Clock time is spatialized time, rendering it visible, tangible, substitutable, public. Clock time is reversible time. In fact, it reverses itself every twelve hours. Because human time and energy are not naturally or inevitably economic, the mechanical hour in a mechanical age is alienating for those caught in its grip.

So long as men and their culture remain on the biological level, economic development is stymied. Nature's biological clocks were not set by man, and we speed their movement with great difficulty and with considerable risk. Even in an economic system as developed as that of the United States, major sectors of the economy retain significant biological time-constraints. On the most progressive farm it still takes a season to grow a crop. Let us call those industries where output is strongly conditioned by the passage of biological time, the *primary sector*. An underdeveloped economy is characterized by the fact that most work time is spent in the primary, biologically oriented sector. Development in an agricultural economy consists of shifting labor-time away from primary pursuits, thus escaping nature's slow pace.

The heart of the development enterprise resides in the *secondary sector*. Here the velocity of production is determined by mechanical, chemical, or electrical (including electronic) factors. Even the most primitive economy provides the characteristics necessary to sustain social life—food, shelter, clothing, transportation, communication. But when the commodities providing these life-support services are largely produced in the secondary sector, freeing their generation from biological constraints, the velocity of production can be increased, bringing the development multiplier into play.

If we assume that the building of an Egyptian pyramid required the work of fifty thousand men for twenty years, while a skyscraper of comparable size can be built by five thousand workers in six months, the ratio of construction workers is 10 to 1; but taking time into account, the ratio becomes 400 to 1. It took four hundred times as much food, clothing, and shelter to sustain the pyramid work force as it takes to maintain our hypothetical skyscraper labor. This enormous saving assumes no increase at all in productivity in the primary sector. Much of the affluence derived from economic development springs from the operation of this development multiplier.

The final sector is the tertiary one, where output is limited by the use of relatively unaided human skill. The *tertiary sector*, like the primary, offers only limited possibilities for production acceleration. A major factor depressing the profitability of mechanized agriculture is the idle time of expensive farm machinery. And so it is in the tertiary industries. The healing time of the human body is heavily determined by biological rhythm, even when the sick are subjected to mechanical, chemical and electronic treatment. And as in agriculture, the idle time of expensive equipment in modern hospitals is a major factor in escalating hospital costs.

As in health, so in education. The human mind acquires knowledge and skills through time; the maturation process is speeded up with considerable difficulty and within narrowly confined limits. We can enjoy massive health and education facilities, but the high velocity of genuine mass production cannot be fully realized in either the primary or the tertiary sectors.

Clearly the secondary sector, particularly its manufacturing, communications, and transportation components, is central to economic development. Within manufacturing, the key industries of machinery (including electrical), steel, nonferrous metals, transportation equipment (including aircraft and automobiles), chemicals (particularly industrial chemicals), rubber products, petroleum refining, electronics, and instruments are pivotal. Taken as a whole, the secondary sector forms a distinct power-metal-science system sustained by mass-merchandising, large-scale finance, and modern transportation and communications facilities. Major inputs include the basic energy resources of coal, petroleum, natural gas, and falling water, as well as the industrial metals—iron ore, copper, aluminum, lead, zinc, tin, and nickel. During the American industrialization drive, expanding productive capacity with rising labor productivity in the secondary sector contrasted sharply with relatively modest advances in the primary climate-soil-topography system and in the tertiary sector specializing in human services.[2]

TRANSMITTING THE DEVELOPMENTAL IMPULSE

Originally the American productive mode was almost exclusively primary and tertiary. Primary production was meshed with the ecological cycle of climate, soil, and animals, with tertiary production dependent on the relatively unaided use of human hands working with simple tools. Then handicraft work began to transfer into the mechanizing secondary sector. Labor productivity began to rise in a few scattered industries, spreading through emulation and by way of backward and forward linkages. (Chandler: "Then in the late 1840s and 1850s factory production began for the first time to be significant in the making of sewing machines, clocks, watches, ploughs, reapers, shoes, suits and other ready-made clothing, and guns and pistols for commercial use.")[3]

If, for example, the new textile mills could produce serviceable cloth quickly and in abundance, they could stimulate a mass market for raw cotton. A dramatic rise in the velocity of cloth production disturbed the existing equilibrium along the cotton-cloth-clothing nexus. Bottlenecks occurred on both the input and output side, generating a strong economic impulse for innovations such as the cotton gin and the sewing machine. Even as early as the time of the introduction of the cotton gin, the bottleneck was clearly centered in the labor-intensive, time-consuming process of cotton planting and picking. When the introduction of the mechanical cotton picker suffered a delay, cotton growers were encouraged to seek very low-cost (per unit of work) but dependable labor for their operations.

A single time-intensive link in the productive chain can significantly retard the development thrust for the entire sequence. Seen in this theoretical way, low-cost labor in Southern cotton fields—slavery and share-cropping—provided a partial substitute for innovation in an operation fully integrated into a technical sequence undergoing uneven technical advance. Furthermore, wages in textile mills were low, allowing large productivity gains to be converted into low, market-stimulating prices and high profits. Textile profits could then be used—and were—to expand modern textile facilities, and for investment in other promising industries. In the middle phase of American industrial development the captains of finance provided an important link between industries ripe for productivity improvement.

The acceleration of production in a linked industry has its impact on the forward (output) side as well. To cite a modern example, the assembly line production of automobiles created a substantial market for high-ways and gasoline. Growing demand for these complementary goods in turn stimulated capital-intensive innovations in road building and in the discovery, refining, and long-distance piping of petroleum.

The suburbanization of cities, creating a central city ghetto surrounded by affluent suburbs, was a second-order consequence of development in the automotive complex. Here we have a classic case of a new industry with an old characteristic (transportation) having very strong develop-mental linkages. (Chandler: "By 1925 an industry that had barely existed in 1900 ranked first in the value of its product, the cost of its materials, the volume added to manufacture, and wages paid. Moreover it became overnight a major market for steel, rubber, plate glass, aluminum, nickel, tin, copper, felt, leather, paint, and other products. The new market in turn encouraged technological and distribution innovations in these indus-tries.")[4]

The fragmented markets in biological and handicraft articles progres-sively gave way to a series of industries undergoing industrial acceleration, linked to one another through technical sequences, common technical problems, shared financial flows, improved channels of communication and transportation, and through an increasingly national labor market. The high-velocity industries continually expanded their output, markets, and influence. Many of them provided major markets for one another. They became organized by corporate giants, enterprises I have called center firms. (Chandler: "The United States pioneered in the techniques of mass production and mass distribution precisely because the giant, consolidated, integrated enterprise replaced the small family-owned and managed single-function firms and associations and combinations of these firms.")[5] As atomistic production units gave way to center firms, so in time the center labor supply became organized by large trade unions. The bifurcation of power in the labor market and the disruptive conflicts of interest that occasionally erupted finally induced state regulation of indus-trial relations.

Collective bargaining between center unions and center firms first Balkanized the labor market, with individual unions continually improv-ing the terms of employment within their respective territory. Strong competition in the remainder of the economy prevented noncenter labor from realizing comparable improvements. Finally, the American labor market was transformed into a dual structure.[6] The working poor are compressed into such low-productivity sectors as nursing homes, laundries and cleaning services, hospitals, hotels and motels, gasoline service sta-tions, and retail food stores. The state is now pushed to move directly into the labor market with legislation designed to generalize the standards and benefits realized in the center through collective bargaining.

Consumption in a Developing Economy

Economic development is achieved through the use of capital-intensive, high-speed, time-saving production techniques. But the productivity of industry is limited by the extent of the market. Mass- and process-produced goods cannot be created in a market economy unless they can be sold. What kinds of goods have enjoyed the highest demand since the twenties? Again the answer lies in time-saving, both on the production side (cutting the real cost of the goods to the consumer) and in consumption, freeing the consumer's limited time for other activities.[7]

Consumption, like production, demands time—a limited resource. The level of household consumption is limited both by the availability of money income and of time. With affluence, the income constraint decreases in importance. But even in the wealthiest household the consumer has a fixed time constraint, the twenty-four hour day. True, it is possible to "buy time" in a limited way. One can trade money for time by hiring a cook, a housekeeper, or a baby-sitter. The time available to a given household can be marginally increased by buying the time of other households. But as average income rises while the productivity of household help remains constant, the price of household service moves rapidly upward. Most households must put their own time into consumption—shopping, cooking, sitting with their own children, tending their own gardens. Consumption-time is subject to very limited productivity increases.

American consumers have sought choice as well as time-saving. Goods, like those useful human acts we call services, also provide a service of more or less durability. When we purchase a car, we are not buying so many pounds of steel and plastic, but highly flexible transportation service. When the car will not start, we still own the steel and plastic, but we have lost that which we bought, transportation. In a time-scarce society, affluent consumers are constantly trying to buy the generalized characteristic of choice. The choice between brands of the same product is petty choice. Given the consumer's time and information constraint, the level of petty choice can easily be excessive, a nuisance rather than a joy. Automobiles, television sets, and telephones have an enormous appeal because the consumer controls the duration, and to a large extent the content, of their use. The auto can take us down the block, to Miami or Montreal. Television can provide a current sports event or a silent film of the twenties. To a significant extent it is the user who chooses.

Understandably, harried Americans have stressed the consumption time-saving goods, particularly when they embody a high choice component. Classified according to time, most goods fall into one of three general categories: (1) high time-cost in production and consumption (live theater, education, medical care); (2) high time-cost in production but low time-cost in consumption (hand-made jewelry, hand-painted china); and (3) low time-cost in production and in consumption (packaged foods, wash-and-wear synthetic clothing, automobiles, laundry detergents, television).

Mass- and process-produced goods, with low time-costs per unit in production *and* low consumption time-costs, form the basis of the American style of life. The list includes breakfast cereals, television, automobiles, petroleum, synthetic fabrics, and electricity. Television sets are mass-produced while television programs are process-distributed. Enormous time-saving can be achieved by letting the message travel while the recipient stays at home. Velocity is increased by sending the message instead of moving the viewer. The cost per viewer of producing and broadcasting a popular television show approaches zero. Time-saving products interact in interesting ways. Automotive, petroleum, and breakfast cereal firms are major sponsors for television productions, so that time-saving products finance television, a time-saving medium.

Advertising may reinforce our time-consciousness, but it does not create it. Using a four-digit industry classification containing 348 industries ranked in terms of labor productivity (using value added per employee as a measure of productivity), I prepared Table 1 listing the productivity of the top seven industries in terms of advertising expenditures with their percent of total advertising expenditure in six media during the first six

TABLE 1

PRODUCTIVITY RANK AND ADVERTISING

4-digit industries	Percent of total advertising expenditure, first six months, 1971	Rank in value added per employee
Soap and detergents	14.97	2
Pharmaceutical preparations	11.91	8
Motor vehicles and parts	9.50	0
Toilet preparations	8.02	4
Cereal preparations	7.77	7
Cigarettes	6.13	3
Flavorings	3.18	1

SOURCES: A list of the advertising expenditures of 100 leading advertisers during the first six months of 1971 was taken from *Advertising Age*, October 4, 1971, p. 66. Individual listed firms were then placed in the industry classification where their advertising expenditures are concentrated. Personal judgment was sometimes involved in this process, but no reasonable allocation would have changed the results significantly. Data on rank in value added per employee for 1963 was obtained from *Concentration and Productivity* by Betty Bock and Jack Farkas, Studies in Business Economics No. 103 (National Industrial Conference Board, 1961), appendix C–1.

months of 1971 (the media are magazines, newspaper supplements, network television, spot television, network radio, and outdoor advertising). The results are striking. The top seven advertisers are industries ranking no lower than eighth in productivity with the single exception of automobiles. Over half of the total advertising expenditure during the first half of 1971 in the six major media was made by firms in industries ranking no lower than eighth in productivity in a set of 348 industries. Clearly the major advertisers are capital-intensive, high-productivity firms attempting to maintain a profitable volume of sales.

Conventional demand theory asserts that purchase decisions are based on price ratios between goods and on the individual preference pattern of the consumer. But in an advanced economy, consumers tend to select goods with prices reflecting low labor-time per unit and requiring the least time-expenditure during consumption. Industrial development demands a corresponding pattern of goods consumption. To repeat, the common denominator between developmental patterns of production and consumption is to be found in the element of time.

The Ecological Flaw of Contemporary Development

Two major strategies of economic development are *displacement* and *substitution*. Textiles and soap provide excellent examples of economic displacement. American cotton and wool consumption declined from over 5 billion pounds annually to about 4 billion between 1948 and 1968. During the same period the use of noncellulose synthetic fibers rose from near zero to 3.5 billion pounds a year.

Cotton and wool are natural fibers produced in the biological sector. The postwar shift in textile production from biological to nonbiological products is a straight-line continuation of the core process of economic development. Primary sector products are being displaced by secondary sector outputs where the potential for high-speed operation is greatly enhanced. The displacement of soap by detergents provides a parallel case. Soap production fell from 3 billion pounds in 1946 to 1 billion in 1968. Synthetic detergents increased during the same period from near zero to almost 2 billion pounds.

Detergents can displace soap, and synthetic fibers can displace natural fibers, because they share fundamental service characteristics. In the same way aluminum and plastic can partially displace steel. But development also proceeds through the substitution of one service characteristic for another. Much of the advance in food processing and packaging has reduced spoilage and waste, the major losses that occur between farmer and consumer. Improved packaging, transportation, refrigeration, and product quality have enormously increased the yield of consumable farm output from a given harvest. Product-saving innovations have provided perfect substitutes for additional agricultural products. Transportation, packaging, and refrigeration do not share service characteristics with food, but they do decrease the system's reliance on a biological process by shifting work to the secondary sector.

While development has always operated through displacement and substitution, since World War II it has taken a new turn. During the nineteenth century and the first third of the twentieth, displacements generally took the form of replacing human and animal toil with mechanical devices and inanimate energy. In a mechanical era, the machine-tool industry provided a pool of skills and technical knowledge employed throughout the mechanizing economy. After World War II, the industrial catalytic function shifted from machine tools toward the chemical and electrical (including electronic) industries. Synthetics progressively replaced natural fibers, rubber, soaps and fertilizers. Once horses and mules were displaced by mechanized devices, chemical fertilizers moved in to replace the lost manure.

We are now discovering that our postwar pattern of development contains a tragic ecological flaw. The natural polymers in cotton and wool are constituents of the soil ecosystem. They mold and decay, forming humus that contributes to the soil's fertility. But synthetic polymers are outside the biological cycle. They can only be destroyed through burning —a polluting process—or they accumulate as permanent rubbish on the land and in the sea. Similarly, the disintegration of soap does no damage to the environment, while the dumping of detergents into our inland streams and lakes causes significant environmental stress. Furthermore, the increased output of synthetic organic chemicals requires a heavy power input and often results in the intrusion of mercury into our surface waters.

Each pound of aluminum requires about 29,860 Btu's of power for its production compared with 4,615 Btu's per pound of steel. Disposable containers, such as nonreturnable bottles, also fall outside the ecosystem's automatic recycling process in addition to demanding a heightened energy expenditure in their production. The pattern of displacement during the past generation has been strongly counterecological. The postwar increase in negative second-order consequences is of the utmost economic significance, for it strikes at the heart of economic development. When the social cost of further development exceeds the social benefits, we can no longer further our affluence by speeding up production. The development multiplier seems to be turning cancerous.[8]

THE DISCOVERY OF NATURE'S STRUCTURE

The developmental success of American capitalism is squarely based upon the abundance of this continent's physical endowment and the progressive use of an intellectual process known as the *economy of thought*. Thought is economized by illuminating the structure of a phenomenon, as opposed to its content. Contemporary examples abound. Men once associated raw food with nutrition. We now know that what the human body needs is a series of balanced elements—vitamins, minerals, proteins, and so on—contained in things we classify as food. With this sort of knowledge we can produce a perfectly balanced and nutritious diet in a highly compact form, eliminating the extraneous, bulky elements present in ordinary food stuffs. Energy provides another familiar example. Until quite recently everyone assumed that energy was distinct from matter. Now we know that $E = mc^2$, that is, we know that energy and matter are an identity given a proper context. We have the formula for converting one into the other under ideal conditions. The progressive economy of thought enlarges an economy's production options. Wood supplied 90 percent of the inanimate energy consumed in the United States during the nineteenth century, largely because it was virtually free. Now coal, hydroelectric power, fossil fuels and nuclear reactors provide most of our energy. Had we not progressively diversified our energy generation, moving from the heat of burning wood to the more efficient heat of fossil and nuclear fuels, we would have experienced an energy constraint on our economoc development. We were successful in escaping this bottleneck because we were able to divorce the *content* of a single source, wood, from the *structure* of an essential resource, energy.

When structure can be separated from content in this manner, we have exposed the skeleton of nature's coding system responsible for the appearance of type and species in the world. The biological order is thus exposed and placed in a threatened position. The ecosystem is at the mercy of man's economy of thought. As the development process compels an increasingly rapid use of nature's resources, their conversion into goods generates negative externalities. When production acceleration overburdens the capacity of the ecosystem to decompose waste, or when the waste is not ecologically decomposable, the social cost of production begins to grow more rapidly than its social benefits. Since the key to development is an increasing flow of goods, the pollution of the environment threatens development at a vital point. There are a number of techniques for reducing pollution's impact, but there is no way to remove it as a counterforce to development as an unlimited process.

The Industrial Bias

The logic of economic development demands that society invest in its superior economic agents—in those industries, business firms, and individuals who are best, most promising, in productivity. Productivity has a social dimension. Its gains are personalized, localized only to the extent that its monetary rewards are kept in the family. The automobile workers experience a rise in productivity of 5 percent. Having done so, they are judged to merit at least a corresponding wage increase. But the American economic system is one of significant productivity differentials. How, for example, does one calculate output per man-hour of a teacher or hospital employee or a ballerina? Workers in the human services fall in the category Adam Smith called "unproductive but useful."

Market-generated price signals reward technological innovation, capital accumulation, economies of scale—techniques of labor-time conservation. In short, a market system has a strong industrial, secondary sector bias. Markets are often praised as facilitators of free exchange, but their major social benefit is the incentives they provide for development. Development demands diversion of economic activity toward the secondary, and away from the primary and tertiary sectors. But what happens to the service worker? With productivity, however measured, relatively fixed, does he experience real income erosion as wages in the progressive sector rise? Or does his income rise with the general trend, forcing accelerating costs, and potential bankruptcy, on his service employer?

What actually occurs is a compromise between the two extremes. Wages do rise in the sectors of constant or lagging productivity growth, but they tend to lag behind those in the dynamic sectors. There is a consistently widening gap between the incomes of workers producing high-speed goods and those with comparable skills in low-productivity industries. The consumer is faced with rising real costs in the service sector, creating a price structure strongly favoring the purchase of mass-produced goods over direct services.[9] Economic development generates a pattern of materialistic consumption, a pervasive social "preference" for goods over services. Americans are materialistic only because they inhabit an industrialized economy. As incomes rise, the desire for services grows. Yet the developmental process that boosted incomes does so by increasing the productivity of labor in goods industries, thus lowering the comparative price of goods. By comparison, service prices, reflecting the cost of less productive workers, cannot but rise. Still the need for services grows, necessitating a massive shift of work-time into the less productive tertiary sector. Even in secondary sector firms, nonproduction workers increase as a percentage of all employees. Thus it is that economic development ultimately becomes a self-retarding process.

Mass Unemployment and the Keynesian Solution

Federal economic policy before the First World War can best be summarized as one providing restrained environmental support. Although government was active in adding new territory and in making the existing territory more accessible (canals, railroads), between the 1840s and

World War I, market forces were usually strong enough, except during the Civil War, to generate a high level of employment when accompanied by a limited array of public underpinnings including the judicial enforcement of private contracts and a relatively open immigration policy. Major spurts of investment were followed by recessions, but new, profitable opportunities were always opening up. This was the era of the entrepreneur, the captain of industry, of finance, and of commerce, taking his signals from the market, borrowing and accumulating money, buying materials, hiring men, selling products, reinvesting profits, or failing in these efforts and falling back into the ranks of the hired, perhaps to try again.

But like homo sapiens, a creature first caught in the ecological web of nature but evolving into its major force, a relatively small number of the more successful entrepreneurial firms, using such corporate techniques as internal financing and finally decentralization, emerged from the economy's high-speed industries to become a supraenvironmental influence. These firms slowly but surely assumed a symbiotic relationship with the American social environment, emitting strong environmental signals as well as receiving them. Between World War I and the depression, a new politics emerged, creating what we now call the Progressive Era. Progressive reformers had a variety of goals, but the most prominent were to impose rural, small-town morals on an urbanizing society (prohibition), to aid the casualties of industrialism (the ghetto poor, female factory workers, and the working child), and to bring to government (urban and national) and to public utilities the rationality of professional management emerging in the business community.

Legislation could not long sustain an outmoded moral code, social work could not eliminate the ghetto or abolish discrimination against women, but a more active conception of the state began to gain grudging acceptance among the less conservative members of the business community. Confronted for the first time with the prospect of an active peace-time state, sophisticated business leaders soon perceived that economic regulation need not serve exclusively the purposes of the radicals. In dealing with an active state, business representatives suffered from numerical inferiority, but they had the advantages of wealth, legal advice, and the cultural support of a national ideology that considered the nation's astonishing economic development its most important achievement.

By the 1930s, it was abundantly clear that spontaneous market forces were no longer sufficiently strong or dependable to employ the American labor force fully under the existing distribution of property, income, and productivity. (Chandler: "The leveling off of demand in the 1920s and its collapse in the 1930s demonstrated the inability of the mass-production, mass-distribution economy to maintain its momentum. The resulting sharp and severe economic depression also made clear that only the federal government was in a position to act as a regulator and pacesetter for the economy as a whole.")[10] The federal government began tentatively to experiment with a new type of economic encouragement—fiscal stimulation. Keynesian ideas took root in this fertile climate, gaining prominence first in the economic literature and then in political practice. Put simply, the Keynesian lesson teaches that employing the labor force is simply a matter of spending sufficient money. There exists some level of total spending that will employ all but a few of those seeking work. Until the 1920s, the requisite expenditure level often occurred spontaneously in the process of development. Now, however, full employment could no longer be assured; this, too, must be added to government's economic agenda.

The new public responsibility quickly generated a policy crisis. If a major portion of the flow of full employment funds must emanate from government, what should it buy? When public spending finances potentially profitable work performed in the public sector, government is competing with business. If money is simply given to the poor as a right of citizenship, a new market for goods and services is created, but such a program might also dim the incentive of the nation's underclass for performing the economy's low-productivity, poorly paid drudge work. Even rebuilding the decaying core of the older cities touches upon property rights and vested interests at every turn.

The solution has taken several forms. Private producers can be subsidized, particularly when they are "overproducing." Farm subsidy programs were designed to funnel cash payments to farm owners, thus increasing their income without affecting the incentive of their employees. Since farmers are in a biological industry, their subsidy helps to reduce the system's strong industrial bias. The very young (education, aid to dependent children) and the very old (social security) can be subsidized without harming worker incentive. By subsidizing education and medicine, government is providing aid to a nonsecondary sector, providing additional redress against the system's industrial leanings.

But the major solution was a familiar one. Having a democratic political system, Americans assumed that their government was free of the age-old military infection so virulent among strong governments. It was not so. As the national income began to tilt away from households toward government (since 1939 the share of national income available for household spending has fallen by about 10 percent, while the military budget increased its share by approximately the same percentage), the military sector began, for the first time, to establish itself on a permanent basis. The traditional government preference for military goods to further national prestige, and thus the prestige of its national leadership, demonstrated once again that militarism knows no boundaries of race, color, creed, income level, or national origin.

Money spent on the military (and on space) does not depress business in the beginning; indeed it stimulates certain key sectors. Defense-oriented industries include aircraft and missiles, communications equipment, ship-building and ordnance, instruments, electronic components, metalworking machinery, and office and computing machines. Employment for many highly skilled workers is defense-related. Over 40 percent of the nation's aeronautical engineers and airplane mechanics have defense jobs; over 20 percent of our physicists, patternmakers, sheet metal workers, electrical engineers, and mathematicians do defense work; military jobs employ more than 10 percent of our radio and television mechanics, general mechanics, machinists, industrial engineers, metallurgical engineers, purchasing agents, technicians, tool and die workers, and metalworking assemblers.[11]

Military production, like development, has an industrial bias. During the early industrialization phase in the United States, military demand provided important technological stimulation. Manufacturing with inter-changeable parts originated in the defense sector. During mobilization, military firearms are produced in large quantities. They are easily standardized. The personal preference of individual users is of no consequence. The assurance of large output levels justifies the introduction of costly, specialized machines capable of achieving low unit costs at high outputs. Precision manufacture is essential if the weapons are to be easily assembled. Interchangeability is equally important to the producer of the firearm and to its user, since it facilitates repair and maintenance in the field. But the dynamic technology of modern military research and development has changed all that, reducing the importance of mass production in favor of high-technology prototype and small batch output.

Still, although the new technology of war attenuates the link between research and productivity gains, and even though the economy has moved beyond the possibility of developmental stimulus from government contracts for standardized products, defense expenditures do aid in absorbing manpower. Military service and defense-related employment can rise without loosening the psychic link between income and work. During the wars, hot and cold, of the 1950s and 1960s, the total number of persons in the labor force disengaged from productive economic activity (the unemployed and those in defense jobs) fluctuated between ten and thirteen million persons, averaging about one worker in seven.

This diversion of labor-time was less harmful than the redirection of those activities containing an economy's genetic code, research and development. (Chandler: "The investment in research and development and in the technical skills and equipment that can handle a range of products within a comparable technology is a far more meaningful index of economic growth in a highly urban and industrial nation than is the output of steel, meat, or even automobiles.")[12] From our early days, the American trump in international markets has rested on superior productivity. During most of our industrialization drive, Great Britain's economic lead seemed imposing. The United States was sparsely populated, with substantial distances between population centers. The British had a comparatively large, compact population, providing an easily accessible domestic market of considerable dimension. In addition, the British Commonwealth afforded the mother country a valuable source of raw materials and an extensive outlet for finished goods. The labor force also had a superior supply of skilled craftsmen.

But development allowed the United States to fill the gap. Mass production, the standardization of parts, and a host of labor-substituting and product-displaying devices enabled the United States to surpass Great Britain by the First World War. World War II solidified American gains by instigating war capitalism, with its emphasis on round-the-clock production, while subjecting major portions of British, German, French, Russian, and Japanese industry to military devastation. With its productive capacity enhanced by the war, the United States stood alone during the 1950s as the world's ultimate industrial power and would meet no challenge for industrial goods in international markets until the 1960s, when German and Japanese rebuilding would allow a renewal of international competition.

The United States chose to spend the postwar decades building a military establishment and fighting two additional wars. The pre-eminent American superiority in industrial productivity allowed American key industries to pay wages several times those paid to corresponding workers in Europe and Japan, while the nation's research and development capabilities, the original source of our productivity differential, became heavily engaged in military-industrial pursuits. As the modern European and Japanese capacity began to make itself felt in traditional markets, the American advantage in trade began to shift to defense-related industries. By the 1970s, three decades of specialization in military technology began to take a toll. Unionized workers in key industries continued to demand wages consistent with continued productivity gains, even as employment shifted to low-productivity tertiary areas and technological break-throughs became concentrated in nonconsumable military products. Now multinational corporations are accelerating their transfer of new productive capacity from the high-unit-cost homeland.

THE OPEN BUSINESS SYSTEM

An economic system organized along business lines is a relatively open one. Business firms use information generated by the market to repair failures in their operations and to restore their health. The complexity of a business organization's internal structure is a function of the permissiveness, the richness, of its environment. In *Strategy and Structure*, Professor Chandler documents the creation of highly complex internal mechanisms within major business firms during the zenith of American economic development.[13] Between the 1920s and 1960, with the exception of the depression years, center business flourished in an environment including high incomes generated by war, preparation for war, the process of suburbanization, and the displacement of natural materials with synthetics. One is tempted to label the past two decades the last great developmental boom for the United States.

We have seen that a developing economy evolves according to a program or blueprint. The essence of this movement is from the biological and handicraft industries toward secondary sectors, activating the development multiplier. In other words, a developing economy minimizes labor-time per unit of output. Every living system has a binding structure, a means of enforcing the logic of the process, superintending the rules by which subsystems and components interact. In the American case this set of rules is codified in the pecuniary logic of the market mechanism. A total social system also includes critical but nondominant subsystems, with parasitic and symbiotic relationships, carrying out those social functions that the dominant subsystem (business during development) omits. These include government (law and order, enforcement of contracts) and households (the locus of consumption time, the producers of the next generation).

In a healthy society, the subsystems are integrated to form self-regulating components capable of reproduction by a culturally prescribed formula. The offspring of two households form a new household, two business firms merge to create a single firm. There are, of course, restrictions. In many states first cousins cannot form a new household; large firms in the same industry are generally prohibited from merging. American firms have been growing larger, American households smaller.

Living systems demand a supportive environment. In biological systems, variations of temperature, air pressure, hydration, atmospheric oxygen content, or intensity of radiation outside a narrow range (that common to the surface of the earth) produce stress taxing the organism's capacity to adjust. The same is true of a business system. For example, a healthy business community needs a viable household sector. The two are in a symbiotic relationship. They are linked through production and consumption, through work-time and consumption-time. Both thrive in a relatively open system, emphasizing the importance of information-flow, the free use of voice, the availability of exit.[14] An open system stresses the flexibility of boundaries and the importance of contacts between subsystems and between units of a given subsystem. Not so for government. While the essence of a healthy business-household system is information, voice, and exit, the propensity of government runs toward manipulation and control.

Business must adjust to its environment. Left to their own devices, business firms will enter into and exit from a given industry or country as the market situation demands. The employees of a business firm are free to exit at will. Business firms maintain only a limited interest in their suppliers and customers. The attention of both customer and supplier is focused on a third thing, the object or direct service being transferred. The primary concern of business is not with the personal characteristics of the person, his behavior or beliefs, so long as these do not affect the objective transaction. There are, to be sure, lapses from this norm, but to the extent that private employers and sellers stress uncritical loyalty, national origin, race, creed, or sex, they are violating the logic of the marketplace, and are subject to the penalties of that violation.

THE CLOSED SYSTEM OF GOVERNMENT

Governments tend to seek domination within a closed system. They seek security and survival not through heavy reliance on accuracy of information and flexibility of response, but within the authoritarian mold of shaping the environment to an ideal image. A market system can certainly coexist in a world inhabited by non-market systems. Left alone, participants in the two systems are likely to generate a mutually beneficial flow of trade. But two or more powerful governments on the same planet seem automatically to become threats to one another. Governments seek safety through total defense. For the nation state, perfect security exists only when there is but one nation, or when a single nation controls other states through trusted regimes.

Governments inhabit a zero-sum universe. The growth of Russian influence in the third world is automatically seen as a decline in American influence. By contrast, business operates in a world infused with mutual benefit. When your business is good, my prospects tend to be bright. If your income is rising, my chances of selling to you are improved. When you are broke, my market is impoverished by your misfortune.

BUSINESS STRATEGY, BUSINESS STRUCTURE

One of the cardinal rules of ecology can be stated as follows: Any given resource base will support more living creatures if they are diversified into a multiplicity of divergent species. If one species lives on grass, but another on insects, the two species can fill the same territory without destroying their survival base. So it is with business firms. (Chandler: "The institutionalizing of the policy of diversification thus helps to assure continued production of new products to cut costs and raise the efficiency of American industry. Such a development is far more significant to the economy's over-all health than production increases in the older basic industries, such as metals and food.")[15] The major industrial firms in Chandler's study were, however, members of the same species. They faced a common market environment, they adopted similar strategies, and they evolved internal management structures bearing a strong family resemblance. Drawing energy from a common source, they face a common danger if the environment turns hostile.

The contemporary economy bears little resemblance to the expansive system fueled by the developmental impulse, a system we remember so fondly and so well. An economy dependent on perpetual government stimulation must adhere to government's priorities, the preparation for atomic, biological, and chemical warfare. Government scorns diversification among its corporate satellites, preferring instead the specialization of a Lockheed. In return, government promises that those who curry its favor shall be spared the peril of bankruptcy. Furthermore, government has usurped a major portion of the economy's diversification mechanism, its research and development. Once research and development activities are rationalized and institutionalized, they are made public, ready to be allocated by the system's dominant institutions to be used for the dominating priorities.

Forsaking the pressing problems of industrial bias and ecological imbalance, American government has used its post-industrialization ascendancy to direct research and development talents into military-space technology, weakening the vital link between innovation and social-economic improvement. This innovation-without-benefit is largely financed through the relative euthanasia of the household. Because of taxes and inflation, a married couple with two children earning $10,000 in 1949 had to earn $17,049 in 1970 to maintain their purchasing power. When a higher income is required to purchase the same basket of goods, the household falls behind, for a higher income puts the federal taxpayer in a higher tax bracket. When tax cuts are not rapid and systematic, inflation punishes the household sector but increases the federal revenue. Since households are the ultimate consumers of business firms outside the military-industrial complex, household euthanasia slowly strangles the private market.

True, government has also responded to industrial bias and ecological degradation. Leading primary industries (agriculture) and tertiary activities (education, health care) are partially subsidized. But if the system is to remain healthy, much of the subsidy must be *generated* within the secondary sector. (Forbes: "In the long run, much of the U.S. steel industry probably cannot survive without tariffs, quotas and possibly direct subsidies.")[16] Environmental protection inevitably raises costs, reversing the effect of productivity growth by lowering the value of output per man-hour. (Forbes: "Considering the vast and expensive pollution and ecology problems, the utility industry faces more of a burden than it has seen in decades.")[17]

Business diversification is an expansive response to a vigorous, expanding market. In a hostile business environment, survival calls for retrenchment. If my analysis is correct, if the contemporary American economy is moving away from its historical pattern, we might expect to see the reflections in new strategies and structures among major, bellwether firms. And so we do. (Forbes: "But prices are already sky high, and now there are price controls to contend with. Detroit, therefore, is reaching back into the factory to save dollars. The bywords: centralization, simplification, internationalization . . . the most dramatic example of the push to centralize production is probably General Motors. It is in the process of interring Alfred P. Sloan Jr.'s profit-center approach after more than forty-five years of use.")[18] Only a decade ago Professor Chandler was able to report that "the new organizational structure served General Motors well."[19] During the 1970s it can serve no more.

Folk wisdom warns against taking anything to an extreme, of the ruinous traits of intemperance, vaulting ambition, excessive pride: "There can be too much of a good thing." Any system following a single logic long enough ensures its own destruction. More is better than less, bigger is better, progress is inevitable in the long run, the invisible hand of the market insures that social benefits exceed social costs; all of these are members of the family of industrializing ideas. Perhaps they best summarize the order, precision, and material success of a well-remembered but departing American culture based on the developmental logic of intensified mechanical time. Evolutionary entropy grinds slowly, but it grinds exceedingly fine.

NOTES

1. Nicholas Georgescu-Roegen, *The Entropy Law and the Economic Process* (Cambridge: Harvard University Press, 1971).

2. My classification of economic sectors follows that in Martin Wolfe, "The Concept of Economic Sectors," *Quarterly Journal of Economics*, vol. 69, no. 3 (August 1955), pp. 402–20.

3. Alfred D. Chandler, Jr., "The Coming of Big Business," in Alfred D. Chandler, Jr., Stuart Bruchey, and Louis Galambos, eds., *The Changing Economic Order* (New York: Harcourt, Brace and World, 1968), p. 271.

4. Alfred D. Chandler, Jr., *Giant Enterprise: Ford, General Motors, and the Automobile Industry* (New York: Harcourt, Brace and World, 1964), p. xii.

5. Alfred D. Chandler, Jr., "The Coming of Big Business," p. 277.

6. For an extended discussion of economic dualism, see Robert T. Averitt, *The Dual Economy* (New York: W. W. Norton, 1968); a good discussion of dual labor markets is Peter B. Doeringer and Michael J. Piore, *Internal Labor Markets & Manpower Analysis* (Boston: D. C. Heath and Company, 1971), pp. 165–83; also see Barry Bluestone, "The Tripartite Economy: Labor Markets and the Working Poor," *Poverty and Human Resources*, vol. 5, no. 4 (July-August 1970), pp. 15–35.

7. For a fascinating discussion of consumption-time, see Staffan B. Linder, *The Harried Leisure Class* (New York: Columbia University Press, 1970).

8. My argument on this point follows that of Barry Commoner, "Economic Growth—A Biologist's View," *Monthly Labor Review*, vol. 94, no. 11 (November 1971), pp. 3–13.

9. For a brief, precise formulation of this proposition, see William J. Baumol, *Economic Dynamics* (3d. ed.) (New York: Macmillan Company, 1970), pp. 425–37.

10. Alfred D. Chandler, Jr., "The Coming of Big Business," p. 211.

11. Richard P. Oliver, "Employment Effects of Reduced Defense Spending," and Richard Dempsey and Douglas Schmude, "Occupational Impact of Defense Expenditures," *Monthly Labor Review*, vol. 94, no. 12 (December 1971), pp. 3–15.

12. Alfred D. Chandler, Jr., *Strategy and Structure: Chapters in the History of the American Industrial Enterprise* (New York: Doubleday & Company, 1966), p. 491.

13. *Ibid.*

14. For an analysis of the importance of voice and exit, see Albert O. Hirschman, *Exit, Voice, and Loyalty* (Cambridge: Harvard University Press, 1970).

15. Chandler, *Strategy and Structure*, p. 491.

16. *Forbes*, vol. 109, no. 1 (1 January 1972), p. 104.

17. *Ibid.*, p. 172.

18. *Ibid.*, p. 152.

19. Chandler, *Strategy and Structure*, p. 191.

Comment

Herman E. Krooss

I assume, of course, that all of you have very carefully read all of the papers prepared for this conference. You must have been impressed as I was by the variety of approaches, demonstrated not only by the cultures that were represented but also by the different authors. For example, Schmitt on Germany, *noblesse oblige* and the aristocracy; Yamamura with sociology and rank order; Mathias with lagging England once again. And here, Professor Averitt with biology and thermodynamics and things of that sort.

I think, of course, we were all very much impressed by Professor Averitt's paper. I found it especially awe-inspiring because he reduced ten dollars and sixty cents' worth of thermodynamics to thirty-three pages. That's a feat that leads me to believe that the possibilities of raising productivity in the service industries have been much underestimated.

Let me be the next to the last, or next to the first, to say that I found this paper tantalizing and exasperating. That's the case for almost all business theory. Tantalizing because so much of it is true, and exasperating because he doesn't tell me where business is going; what the structure and strategy are going to be like, so that I know which stocks to buy tomorrow.

If I interpret Professor Averitt correctly, he is saying among other things that (1) growth is an increase in production, (2) development is an increase in productivity, and (3) development proceeds in an evolutionary fashion from primary (extractive) to secondary (processing) to tertiary (service). This may also be looked upon as an evolution that first emphasizes goods and then time. Or this evolution may also be looked upon as a circular development in productivity—little productivity in the primary state, a great deal in the secondary state, and very little in the tertiary era. And it may be looked upon in yet a third way, as an evolution along the lines of Engel's law and Wagner's law. Now all of this, I think, is well known and almost universally agreed to by all economic historians. The case is slightly different with the implications that Averitt has made, and with the inferences that can be drawn from what he implied. He draws the dismal picture that is becoming increasingly fashionable: (1) ecological dangers in economic growth with the implication that social costs are exceeding, or at least beginning to exceed, social benefits; (2) an imbalance in the economy with high-paid goods producers and low-paid service workers; (3) inability of the private economy to produce full employment, which leads to (4) the necessity of government intervention. The government thereby takes on an existence of its own and with it a kind of goal system different from that of private enterprise. I don't know whether the conflict that this creates is irreconcilable or whether it can be solved in some fashion or other. All this leads Professor Averitt to say, "One is tempted to label the past two decades the last great development boom for the United States."

Now I submit that none of the four conclusions that are arrived at in this paper are indisputable, although I think some of them are more than most. For example, I do not think that anything in the past thirty years has proved that full employment cannot be produced by the private system. I don't think, incidentally, that service workers are being exploited. The last time that I looked at the figures they looked something like this. In the last ten years federal government salaries had gone up 51 percent, service workers 43 percent, trade workers 41 percent, manufacturing workers 37 percent, and transport workers 35 percent. In short it's just the other way around, that the goods-producing areas are not producing the same wage increases that the services are producing. And, of course, the service industries are not nearly so productive. They run 30 to 40 percent behind the goods-producing industries in terms of productivity.

But whether or not Professor Averitt's emphases and conclusions are true hardly matters. What does matter is that they are overwhelmingly accepted. And I think that most of them are accepted not only by laymen, but also by business people, which is, to my mind (purely subjective I admit) an extraordinarily depressing thought.

Now what does all this have to do with the evolving structure of management? Professor Averitt, if I read him correctly, concludes that the economy is moving away from its historical pattern, leading to new strategies and new structures. I am, however, a little confused about what these are. I suffer from chronic confusion, made acute by Professor Averitt's paper. I've no notion of where we're going, or at the moment of where we are. The nature of change is more complex than simple, and more discontinuous than continuous. Historically, changes in strategy and structure in the United States were a function of the entrepreneur adjusting to changing exogenous forces. Entrepreneurs tried to maximize profits within the restraints of social institutions and social values. In a production function it is not enough to talk about land, labor, capital, and business enterprise. There is room for the addition of two highly unquantifiable, highly abstract factors: social values and social institutions. I think this is demonstrated much better in the evolution of financial intermediaries than in the evolution of manufacturing. That is, all over the world, different types of values have produced different types of banking structures. Some have emphasized stability, some have emphasized growth, and some have tried to have both.

In the interest of fun and games I propose the following: that strategy and structure in terms of size, concentration, oligopoly, and managerial structure are little changed today from what they were in the 1920s. This does not mean, of course, that no significant change is in the offing. History is a process of change by jerks. That is, a series of shocks interspersed with a series of short-run adjustments. I am, of course, oversimplifying, but in view of the model used by Professor Galbraith, I think I can emulate my illustrious predecessor in inexcusable over-simplification.

Today's society is certainly in one of its periods of groping and confusion. Consider, if you will, that before the 1972 primary elections, many people announced that they were going to vote for McGovern or, if he did not run, for Wallace. Or consider that we don't know whether or not we really want a continuation of economic growth, or if we want to stop the war on poverty. We don't really know whether we want a higher gross national product or more pollution. And so forth and so on.

All values are certainly being challenged or, as I prefer to think, threatened. And economic values, as in every period of affluence, are being downgraded and treated patronizingly. The voices of authority have shifted from economics and history to sociology and behavioral science. If full-scale economic growth continues, I think the strategy and structure of business will be fundamentally influenced by a new set of exogenous factors adding to the three-level management which is still in its embryonic stage. I digress a moment to note that some of you will say, "If nothing has changed, what about maxiconglomerates?" Maxiconglomerates have not done well, and I think one reason is that that third level of management that Redlich and Chandler talked about in a recent article[1] has not been developed sufficiently or given enough thought.

The difficulty in most of the many conglomerates that have run into trouble is that there's no coordinating factor, and this is that third level of management. I think if the situation continues to develop, there will be a fourth level added, in the form of somebody in charge of social responsibility or, if you prefer, a consumer lawyer or somebody of that sort.

To some of us this is a terribly shocking possibility, but as Professor Averitt pointed out and emphasized, management is an adjustable factor. I think that it will adjust to what it thinks society's values are. The values that are now being stressed are in the realm of noneconomics. They are in the realm of social responsibility.

The educational process offers some evidence of the changing nature of values. Education once followed business. The appearance of the self-trained engineer in business was partly responsible for the birth of engineering schools in the middle of the nineteenth century. The appearance of the professional manager at the end of the nineteenth century (earlier in the railroads) was partly responsible for the professional business school. Now the academic business world has turned on its head and instead of following, it is leading the parade. I do not know if this trend will continue. The preference at the moment for "know what" instead of "know how" and the emphasis on behavioral science may reinforce the present slight tendency toward thinking more about social responsibility.

David Rockefeller, in one of his many speeches on the theme of the responsibilities of big business, remarked that criticism of business has changed and changed fundamentally. He said that the old indictment of business was that it was too big, and that was the only indictment and of course it was directed at big business. But now, he suggests, criticism is against business in general, not in terms of size but in terms of what business is doing.

There is no doubt that American productivity is falling behind; no doubt that we are becoming increasingly a service economy. There is no doubt that the government is increasingly an active rather than a passive force. There is little doubt in my mind that in the future these tendencies will grow stronger. As I have said, this is to me, as a business historian, an extremely depressing outlook.

NOTE

1. Alfred D. Chandler Jr. and Fritz R. Redlich, "Recent Developments in Business Administration and Their Conceptualization," *Business History Review*, vol. 25 (1961).

3. Conflicts of Function in the Rise of Big Business: The British Experience

PETER MATHIAS

Much of this paper is concerned with problems and conflicts of interest which arise between structure and objectives in large organizations—particularly those where size has led to a multiplicity of functions being controlled within the same enterprise. It should be said that size appears to give no necessary basis for success or efficiency. It may be a necessary condition for success in some fields—doubtless an increasing number of fields—of productive enterprise, but it is certainly not a sufficient condition either for success or for efficiency. Size may, however, raise the threshold of tolerance for inefficiency, and allow inefficiency to survive longer than in small organizations more sensitive to the pressures of the market. Equally, vertical integration, though building in problems associated with multifunctional enterprise, has clearly been as characteristic of very successful, as it has of unsuccessful, enterprise. In the abstract, removed from considerations of specific context, vertical integration, like size, in an enterprise, cannot be said to be favorable or unfavorable. As specific circumstances change, the appropriate boundaries for an enterprise will change. In this, as in so many other ways there is little which can be said about the structure of enterprise which has absolute validity *sub specie aeternitatis*. The problems concerning the appropriate boundaries of an enterprise, and the appropriate management structure in relation to those boundaries, are nevertheless among the most strategic which have to be faced. This is why a certain historical retrospect may be of relevance for the present—not by providing any specific guide to policy, but by widening the range of awareness of policy makers—as well as of intrinsic interest to historians of business.

MANAGEMENT STRUCTURE AND EARLY MULTIFIRM LATERAL MERGERS

This paper is not primarily concerned with the problems of organizational structure and efficiency in function which arise through expansion, whether by merger or growth, which does not involve the problems of vertical integration. "Lateral" growth which characterized the spate of cartels and multifirm mergers sweeping through the British economy in the latter years of the nineteenth century did, it is true, raise important structural issues of a related, if different, kind. The large multifirm mergers, in particular, could not avoid facing the implications of reorganization if functional efficiency were to be preserved—or regained. Lateral integration brought many production units and many selling units within the same ultimate control. Rationalization between units in a parallel relationship, hitherto competitive or at least "arm's length" to a degree, was the first potential gain. Overcapacity in relation to current levels of demand (which lay at the back of many of the problems of depressed prices and low profits which induced the mergers in the first place) invited the elimination of some capacity. The wide gap in efficiency and technology between plants revealed by the mergers further suggested that higher-cost plants could be closed or brought up to the level of the higher-productivity capacity. The opportunity also arose for regrouping specialist functions—research, advertising, property management, share-certificate registration, legal advice, negotiating for raw material purchasing, advertising, freight and railway rates, or the purchase of any inputs or services where advantage could be gained from exploiting the leverage that centralized bargaining made possible. Not least, a restructuring of top management was invited—and the creation of an appropriate central board which the merger itself made inevitable. The greater the restructuring of "line and staff" operations throughout the organization, the more effective the restructuring of productive capacity, selling organization, or any other sector of the group's activities was to be, then the more effective the central decision-making authority needed to be to reshape the structure as a whole and to recast the strategy of operations which the merger made possible.

But no merger tends to be better in result than its original motivations. The vast mergers characteristic of these decades were, on the whole, inefficient and unprofitable. By 1903, the Salt Union (1888), the United Alkali Company (1890), English Sewing Cotton (1897), the Calico Printers Association (1899), and the Associated Portland Cement Manufacturers (1900) all had assets of lower value than their issued capital, on very bad profit records. The only really successful large combination in Yorkshire textiles was said to have been the Bradford Dyers' Association, which brought thirty-five separate businesses together with a capitalization of £4.25 million in 1897. The scale of the management reconstruction required to fashion an effective—and rationalized—group from these amalgamations, which covered much of an industry, can be seen at once from the number of firms involved: the Salt Union: sixty-four firms (90 percent of the industry's capacity); the United Alkali Company: forty-eight firms (90 percent of capacity); Calico Printers Association: forty-six firms (85 percent of capacity); Associated Portland Cement Manufacturers: twenty-seven firms (45 percent of capacity); Bleachers Association: fifty-three firms (50–60 percent of capacity); British Cotton and Wool Dyers Association: forty-six firms (85 percent of capacity);

Yorkshire Woolcombers Association: thirty-eight firms; Fine Cotton Spinners and Doublers Association: thirty-one firms (40 percent of capacity).[1]
Yet these mergers were not characterized by vigorous restructuring. Indeed, if anything, their characteristic seems to have lain in the minimum
managerial restructuring necessary to give effective sanction to the attempt
to set more amenable prices, and to control sufficiently the level of output
of constituent parts to effect this. They were more in the nature of an
existing trade association given a single legal entity than they were effective operational units in a management sense. Many were, in fact, built
up from the ruins of unsuccessful trade associations, like the woolcombers,
the bleachers, and the dyers. The Calico Printers Association had its origin
encapsulated in the title.

Failure, or at the very least, inefficiency was built into these mergers
from their conception, and characterized by the failure to restructure
management according to the new logic of the larger grouping. They came
into existence to push up prices rather than to reduce costs; to make life
tolerable for the least efficient, highest cost member in the merger rather
than to prune such capacity out of existence. They floated off unrealistic
sums into the capitalization of the new entities as goodwill items in an
ocean of watered stock, which, with a pricing policy aiming to produce
dividends of 20 percent, became a guarantee for unprofitable business.
Unlike some cartel movements in "lateral" mergers in the United States
and Germany—which were inspired by certain defensive intentions, even
if they were not, in the event, as completely negative in operation as some
of the main British multifirm mergers—these ambitions were being pursued in a free-trade country. Imports negated pricing policies, more particularly when adverse trade conditions intensified competitive pressures
internationally as well as nationally. "The Calico Printers Association,"
ran a contemporary comment, "affords a spectacle of mismanagement
that is likely to become classic."[2] Like its fellows, this merger had been
contrived for the mutual benefit of the contracting parties. No public
watchdog guarded the establishment of monopoly in the United Kingdom
—at least through any effective statutory instrument. This came only after
1948, the common law alone standing against restraint of trade, though not
often invoked. No effective banking presence lay behind these British cartel-
mergers, comparable to that in Germany, which could have been an instrument for imposing managerial efficiency upon them; nor was there an organized shareholders' interest beyond that of the contracting parties (where
shareholding was identified with the existing managements). Company promoters, with interests in the actual flotation of the merger, planned these
reorganizations, self-inspired by the firms to keep them all in business,
including all the directors. "Since the combinations have been engineered

by the vendors we have large boards of directors to represent the interests of the combining firms—this is euphemistically called 'putting all the ability in the trade at the disposal of the new company.' "[3] The board of the Calico Printers Association, decided on this principle, contained no less than eighty-four directors—and the constituent companies were said to have an uncontrolled mob of 114 vendor-managers competing with each other out of jealousy or ignorance.

One of the first articulate essays in establishing a rational structure for such an agglomeration of firms came from the investigating committee appointed under the chairmanship of Charles Phillips of J. and P. Coats (a more successful textile merger which had established hegemony over another sector of the cotton trade) to sort out the mess. They proposed a small board of directors of six persons, supervising policy directives over a small executive committee of between two and four salaried senior officials not having departmental responsibilities within any subsection of the business. These "statesmen of the association" attended directors' meetings but had no vote. Beneath the executives came seven advisory committees, organized along functional lines, drawing their three to eight members from the ablest officials actively engaged in the business of the several branches—works production, pricing, trading, cloth buying, designs and styles, concentration, and drugs, stores, coal, etc. The executive committee was also served by a separate "group statistical department." In operation, the executive committee was to send to the chairman of each advisory committee a list of the subjects requiring attention (a member of the executive committee was present at the meetings of each advisory committee). The advisory committees "primarily decided" on the measures required and the executive committee then saw that they were carried into effect in the different companies and sectors of the business. But the executive committee could decline to accept the recommendations, whereupon the conflict of opinion went to the board of directors for decision (they received all the reports of the advisory committees). Thus the board of directors were to supervise, the executive committee was to administer, and the advisory committees advise, "whilst cooperating in the general control of the business and directing its policy." High in the order of priority for the new regime was to be the application of the "best chemical and mechanical science" through the establishment of a "central department of technical chemistry applied to calico printing." Modern technology in all its manifestations, whether applied science or an appropriate managerial structure, had been lacking. The Calico Printers Association did not change with dramatic speed, but at least it survived. The proposed new organizational structure raised as many questions as it answered, in terms of the report itself.

MANAGEMENT AND ACCOUNTING OBJECTIVES

One of the many issues raised (but not elaborated) was the nature of the information flowing in to the central management from the new statistical department. No management structure can be better than the information it receives. Decisions on where to expand, where to contract, criteria of successful or inadequate operations, must rest upon a diagnosis, and that diagnosis must rest, in turn, upon the flow of information. That flow of information is, in part, consequential upon the organizational structure of the enterprise. The identification of the information required, the conceptual formulation of accounting objectives and procedures, matched by an organizational context which makes them realizable in operational terms, are preconditions for effective management in the terms posited by the committee investigating the Calico Printers Association's failings.

In certain ways the cartel organization itself required statistical data which could help certain cost-accounting techniques. Membership dues for trade associations were usually based on annual output or labor employed or capital engaged—and comparability in accounting techniques was quickly demanded so that levies could be made upon a common basis. Where objectives of cartels were more ambitious—involving production quotas, pricing agreements, collective fines on excess profits for redistribution etc., then stricter accounting rules had to be laid down governing the separation of current accounts from capital accounts, depreciation rules, distribution of overhead expenses and all the other conventions which lay behind the concept of an annual profit. But accounting methods, at least those publicly advocated, did not provide much help. Company legislation had, indeed, specified increasingly detailed accounting techniques as the nineteenth century progressed but these were concerned almost exclusively with the problem of protecting investors against fraud and did not, even in result if not by intention, provide the concepts or the data which might serve as measures of efficiency.[4] The 1844 act required a "full and fair" balance sheet for public companies, with "true and full" accounts demanded by the 1845 act. Model articles were proposed in the 1856 act—which suggested independent auditors, dividends payable only out of profits, a double-entry bookkeeping system and a profit and loss account as well as a balance sheet. But such an ideal—itself fairly elemental—did not become mandatory because of the widespread opposition to the legal enforcement of "best-practice" techniques laid down in statutes. Not until 1900 was an annual audit made obligatory upon registered companies. More specific auditing techniques for separating capital and revenue accounts, distinguishing between productive and nonproductive capital, deciding the basis for the valuation of assets and the like were enforced on railway companies, and appropriate conditions were laid down for special types of incorporated enterprise, such as gas and electric companies or life insurance, also with the prime purpose of protecting investors. These categories of public utility investment, particularly railways, attracted more share capital from the general public than manufacturing industry (more particularly equity investment) which meant that each major fraud brought with its exposure demands for increased public regulation. Less public pressure was applied to increase the minimum accounting procedures for manufacturing industry; and the demands of the law in relation to public companies fell a long way short of the detailed regulations which some partnerships had instituted to regulate their internal financial procedures (a degree of sophistication over audit much encouraged by the *de facto* specialization between managing partners and sleeping partners, when large joint capitals were at risk).[5]

Accounting procedures to act as instruments for gauging economic performance would doubtless have evolved had the demand existed in industry. (The same might be said of applied science.) The discussions of the objectives of accounting methods in the pages of *The Accountant* do not suggest that there was a ready market; while handbooks of accounting and treatises on scientific management ignore the problems raised by the organization of the multiplant, multicompany or multifunctional enterprise. Most concentrate on the problems of accounting, quantification of information and efficiency within the single-plant, single-role enterprise. Garke and Fells, presenting what they asserted was the "first attempt to place before English readers a systematised statement of principles regulating factory accounts" in 1887, thought they had to make the case that accounts were needed for factories and warehouses, although acknowledged as necessary for mercantile transactions.[6] They go in some detail into questions of quantifying and monitoring current costs, depreciation techniques, revenue and capital accounts, sinking funds to debit revenue accounts for a fading asset, the incidence of taxation, fixed "establishment" charges and interest on capital. There is clear recognition of the problem of a surplus on current account being fictitious if balanced by a deterioration on capital account. The closest they get to cost accounting objectives is a brief discussion (pp. 62–63) that an analysis of the percentage of total costs of different processes will reveal the most strategic areas for economies and new methods—quoting Charles Babbage on the *Economy of Machinery and Manufactures* (of 1835!). The only mention of organizational or management structure comes under the heading of "miscellaneous" at the end of the book,[7] where they recommend that a staff organization chart, showing the relative rank of officials, be placed in a conspicuous position in the general offices—"some officials being disposed not infrequently to regard themselves as equal, if not superior, to men who are really their masters." In one of the most widely read contemporary treatises on "correct" commercial organization, Slater Lewis also concentrated on efficiency within the factory rather than on the most appropriate managerial structure for the large enterprise as a whole.[8] Assuming a single-plant, single-function engineering firm he takes everything for granted about a simple management hierarchy from chairman, managing director, director, manager, company secretary, auditor, accountant, cashier down to the junior correspondent clerk and gives more space to a discussion of good taste in the company's stationery than to organizational efficiency in the wider sense.[9] An equivalently narrow discussion of accounting methods for collieries avoided wider issues with the explanation: "Various enterprises sometimes associated with coal mining, including farms, brick-works, coke ovens, etc. have been omitted as beyond the scope of the present book."[10]

This tradition governed the technical bibliography on accounting generally.[11]

F. W. Taylor was very conscious of the importance of an efficient organization standing behind the factories, going out of his way to stress that a common failing of directors was that they could see the utility of up-to-date and efficient plant more readily than a good organization—by which he patently meant managerial structure. "The building up of an efficient organisation," he wrote, "is necessarily slow and sometimes very expensive. . . . There is no question that, when the work to be done is at all complicated, a good organisation with a poor plant will give better results than the best plant with a poor organisation."[12] He made a shrewd prophesy—the intimations of which are with us yet: "The writer feels that management is also destined to become more of an art, and that many of the elements which are now believed to lie outside the field of exact knowledge will soon be standardised, tabulated, accepted and used as are now many of the elements of engineering."[13] But he saw the problems of organization still within the assumptions of a single-plant operation. All his proposals for improving the efficiency of an enterprise lay at this level —scientifically timed piecework techniques on the floor of the shop, the efficient organization of tasks for the workmen, "functional foremanship," scientific selection of workmen, task management, and the like—within a factory of five hundred to one thousand employees, rather than with the structure of organization as such.[14]

If this was the current state of "best practice" technique in accountancy methods and scientific management—a virtual silence on the problems of organizing the large multifirm enterprise, we can see the confusion which beset many of these multifirm lateral mergers in some perspective. They were, of course, quite unrepresentative of the scale and differentiation of enterprise in productive industry as a whole—but so were the techniques being advocated by Taylor and others. But the fact that no mention is made of the basic analytical concepts of judging returns on capital in the operational form of assets owned or assets employed, or of the accounting unit to be determined in the light of the operations whose profitability was to be analyzed in this way, is more a reflection of the lack of demand from those organizations that—in principle—could have benefited from these techniques than it is an autonomous variable stemming from the lack of expertise among accountants. Accounting methods are, in the main, a dependent variable, responsive to need, despite the growing professionalization of this function in the later nineteenth century.[15]

If size and share of the market were no guarantees of success with multifirm lateral mergers, problems of organizational structure and management objectives applied no less certainly to growth which involved vertical integration. It was commonly said at the time that lateral mergers were for defense and monopoly; vertical integration was for efficiency. But problems of objectives and certain conflicts of interest were built into vertical integration which, though different from the problems of multifirm lateral mergers, were in some respects more elemental, being integral with the multifunctional nature of a vertically integrated enterprise. Although this section, because of shortages of space, concentrates on moves by manufacturers forward toward retailing (and by retailers back to manufacturing) equal ranges of arguments apply to moves backward to the ownership and control of inputs, transport, and raw materials.

The advantages to retailers and manufacturers in moving forward to the control of distribution and retail outlets by a manufacturer, and backward to the control of inputs by retailers or manufacturers have appeared very tempting *ex ante*; and the moves have often been taken as answers to present difficulties rather than with considered judgment about the new problems which the commitments revealed in due course. *Ex ante* there were many temptations to move forward. For a manufacturer of consumer goods, such as Clarks[16] in footwear, a minimal retailing presence gave information on costings, prices, and margins which allowed them an independent means of testing claims made by the independent distributors and retailers who took the bulk of their output. Being in direct touch with customers, the firm's shops allowed an important feedback in design, styles, fashion, and all the tricks which gave popularity to particular lines, provided that appropriate departments in the manufacturing divisions were alive to the opportunities and that a voice from the shops could make itself heard. (Both depended upon the appropriate managerial structure and the intentions of the central board planning relations between divisions.) The determining arguments were usually more specific than this. Senior management saw advantages mainly through the eyes of manufacturers. Factory interests looked to tied shops to take a higher volume, with greater unit orders, and at a more predictable level, than independent distributors and retailers on "arm's-length" terms. Production runs could thus be maximized and scheduled to the greatest advantages of the factories. Unit orders were greater than orders from retailers who divided their custom between many suppliers and delivery costs could be minimized. The "through-put" argument for the factories probably carried the most weight as a production argument for owning shops, but commercial considerations supported this in many cases. Where no powerful groupings existed in retailing the relevant lines, or where no legal restrictions prevented access to consumers, then such commercial arguments might not be so influential; but in other contexts they proved mandatory. The manufacturers of margarine in Britain in the early twentieth century all pressed forward to control retail outlets. Their product, being perishable, and in the mass, basic foodstuff market, demanded rapid, high-turnover selling, with efficient stock control—in short the multiple stores with regional and national chains of branches. Very high overheads in the factories required large, predictable sales. And when one of the small group of manufacturers began to buy into stores; and one main national store group (the Maypole Dairy Company selling one-third of the margarine in the land) set up its own manufacturing capacity a chain reaction quickly spread through the trade. If one main operator in an oligopoly situation adopted this strategy, then the others were almost bound to follow suit. The pricing objectives of the Lever, Jurgens, Vandenberg group in the 1920s were not so expected. Whereas a commonly voiced objective of vertical integration was that the resulting economies and efficiency would allow lower prices and extending trade, in this case the great hope was to buy out, or bankrupt, the Maypole Dairy Company (the price leader), then raise prices to a level which would allow profitable manufacture for the factories and make life tolerable for the small, independent (and higher cost) grocers who were now generally stocking margarine and of great importance to its makers.[17]

The brewing industry in England and Wales developed the most complete commitment to retailing during the nineteenth century—more than 85 percent of retail outlets in the country being owned by manufacturers in 1914—because very special conditions applied to the retail sale of alcoholic liquors. Indeed similar conditions had evoked a very similar response in London and provincial towns during the enghteenth century.[18] Restrictive licensing by the justices meant that, once a public house was tied to a brewer, the brewery had achieved a local monopoly. Other brewers could not open new competing outlets. When one brewer moved to tie local trade, therefore, competitors needed to take equivalent steps or be squeezed out. Competition continued to a degree, when the public was willing to walk to different public houses or when new licensing was taking place in a newly built-up area. Further reasons compounded the consolidation of the retail tie in the trade. When a publican left, restrictions on licensing put a very high cash premium on a licensed house which was quite beyond the pocket of an ordinary incoming publican, so that he would naturally turn for the capital to the person with the greatest interest in lending it to him—a brewer. The retailing of alcoholic drinks remained a less-differentiated form of selling—virtually a single-product operation—than most others, with great continuity in the style of products sold and the structure of demand, all of which encouraged stability and continuity in marketing structure. Integration of functions between manufacturing (including considerable backward integration to the control of a proportion of malting capacity) and retailing was more successful in the brewing industry than in most other industries, largely because of the uniquely restrictive legal controls over retailing. This has some relevance, doubtless, to the success of oil companies in integrating forward to control petrol stations. Ironically, it was from exactly such a long-standing successful tradition that the brewing industry became exposed to take-over threats in the late 1950s. Characteristically the capital assets of a brewing firm were by then predominantly in its real estate—the public houses— often much undervalued in its balance sheets and earning a very small return on assets as long as they remained tied outlets for the sale of the company's beer. They were seen only as a functional dependency of the factory—not as capital assets in their own right to be employed for maximizing returns, either in retailing or in the real-estate business. The invasion of the industry by real-estate interests and other "take-over" bidders, more aware of the capital assets and earning capacity of these sites than the brewers themselves, whose horizons of consciousness were still bounded by the limited business of making and selling beer and liquors, taught the industry certain elemental truths for the first time.

In the footwear industry the marketing reasons for controlling shops were not so clear-cut. A manufacturer such as C. and J. Clark Ltd., having built up their business on selling nationally branded lines, nevertheless found the reasons compelling. Trade was becoming more concentrated in "high-street" shopping. The major presence in shoe retailing in the high street were general multiple/department stores and the chains of multiple shoe shops, particularly those of the British Shoe Corporation, the largest single unit in the shoe trade, which branded its own lines and bought in from shoe manufacturers at home and abroad according to its requirements. Neither the independent general multiples nor the specialist British Shoe Corporation would offer outlets for the branded lines of a rival manufacturer. Hence the need for a direct presence in the high streets, which was acquired by building up a chain of specialized retail shoe-shops.[19] Apart from factory managers anxious to maximize through-put, tied shops could prevent the company being held to ransom, or squeezed out, by powerful retailing interests, and could hold the key to expansion in circumstances where the smaller local retailers were losing custom to larger high-street shops. A whole spectrum of commitments to retailing developed between the "arm's length" relationship with independent shops, dividing their custom as they wished and ordering as they liked, and the wholly owned shops, in conformity with this strategy. To the extent that rival manufacturers were large enough to trade under their own brands and had an incentive to move forward, apprehension about competitors' reactions reinforced the trend. In addition there was the basic motive: retailing was potentially very profitable—all manufacturers knew that the profit margins to the retailer were over 40 percent of retail prices—so why allow others to enjoy those profits? And, it might be thought, one's own shops in the high street would in themselves be major point-of-sale advertisements for the national brand in the same way that the fascia of every public house proclaimed its brewer.

The determinant in this situation was the power equilibrium between manufacturer and powerful independent retailing interests. But the footwear manufacturers discovered, as had the margarine manufacturers before them, that moving from manufacture into selling took them into waters where many cross-currents of interest disturbed the surface. Most obviously, moves into retailing by manufacturers could be taken as unfriendly acts by the independent retailers (and retailers' associations) whose accounts sustained the firm. If they were collectively powerful enough to threaten to cut off their custom then a difficult choice arose. Hence the secrecy of Clarks' initial moves into retailing (avoiding having their name above the shop) and the subsequent care that had to be taken to reassure independent customers that the firm's own shops would not receive special terms, or preference over deliveries, new lines, and the like. Opportunities for suspicion were manifold—particularly in times of postwar shortages. Next came straightforward management problems for directors who knew about the business of shoemaking but not about retailing—very much *sui generis*, with its own brand of expertise, for which efficient managers had to emerge, it seemed, from a retailing world rather than being transferred from the central business of the firm—manufacturing. Expansion in retailing threw a great strain on this specialized sector of management expertise. Capital was not as much of a problem as might have been predicted, considering that the capital assets to be engaged in any large commitment to retailing (in town centers) would be several times the value of fixed assets in factory buildings and plant. But renting, leasing, and "sale and lease-back" arrangements could evade the massive capital injection that the ownership of shop freeholds would require, so that the costs of trading in one's own shops fell upon the current (revenue) account of the business rather than upon its capital account.[20]

The structural problems that multifunctional operations raised were not just those of not antagonizing other retailers, of finding good managers, and of acquiring capital, but of potential conflicts of interest when seeking to maximize returns on assets in both functions. Here the context within which integration occurred was all-important—the context of structure and trading conditions. In the raw material side of manufacture, a trend of relative scarcity and rising prices would create incentives for moving back to control raw material supplies—as bargaining conditions moved against the manufacturer. Equally, with a bullish retail market and widening retail margins, there was added temptation to move forward to capture these gains. Perfectly competitive raw material markets, without concentrations of power and with very narrow margins, would offer little advantage for investing capital in the ownership of capacity here, unless technical specifications were required which could not be met by available independent suppliers. All these considerations applied also to the control of transportation. In falling markets the best advantage could be obtained, not by owning facilities but by taking the best bargains that applied in the open market and exploiting the advantage which the buyer enjoyed in these conditions. Some stake might be worthwhile to guard against the dangers of being held to ransom when market conditions swung the other way. And, in wartime, or in conditions of war scarcity, control over transportation, raw material supplies, and manufacturing capacity (for shop companies) proved highly advantageous—to the extent that zoning schemes and other regulatory devices allowed them to be exploited. Hence a common desire to hedge one's bets, just in case conditions of scarcity reemerged.

Following the logic of the factories' interests and viewing the shops as tied outlets could fail to utilize their selling capacities as a whole. If the factories failed to respond quickly to changing tastes; if the ranges of products offered were not the ideal "mix" required for the shops, then turnover would be lower than optimum and profits would fall. Moreover, able managers would be deterred from staying with the shop division if this was purely a dependant variable for the factories, without scope for growth beyond their requirements or for independent initiatives in buying and pricing. If shop managers had no freedom to improve their performance by taking decisions over buying, pricing, or styling, then they could justifiably demand special treatment, as a *quid pro quo* from the factories of the group, in preference to independent accounts. Equally, if the factories could order the shops to take what lines they had to offer, at set prices, there would be no discipline of the market applied at that stage to factory managers; however much that discipline would be apparent in falling turnover in the shops. Equally, from the factories' interests, the shops were useful insofar as they helped rather than hindered total trade. Service to the company's shops would not be worth while if it prejudiced other important accounts (which, in aggregate, would be likely to exceed the turnover through the associated shops). The retailing division could not therefore look for special favors.

Where central management adopted a different policy, the centrifugal forces created in the pursuit of maximizing returns were increased. The decentralized strategy involved setting up the retailing division as a separate entity, on equal terms in the organizational structure with the manufacturing division(s), with the heads of both divisions reporting to the central board, or defending the interests of their divisions as members of the central board. With this went—to a degree—the imperative *enrichissez-vous*, with concomitant freedom and responsibilities. The test imposed upon each function was to be the rate of return earned upon assets engaged: management was to be free to follow the path which maximized that rate of return, wherever it led. The shop division maintained its initiative over pricing and buying from the group factories. If it could buy outside more advantageously, it had the factories to do so, even within directly competing ranges. It could vary the mix, and hence change the over-all style projected by the shops, by buying different ranges. (In such a decentralized strategy it was important not to have the manufacturer's national brand identifying the fascias of the shops in the retailing division; indeed its freedom might extend to projecting a separate brand image—a retailing-based brand comparable to those of the independent multiples—within which the group's products would have a subordinate place.) On their side the factories would maintain the right to sell elsewhere on the same terms as to the group's retailing division, and if they felt other customers offered a more advantageous service they could capitalize upon that asset.

Where the same logic was applied to the functions controlled within a vertically integrated group behind the manufacturing division, those making final products had to accept an even more paradoxical and uncomfortable result. In the shoemaking industry C. and J. Clark (since 1945, the largest manufacturers in the United Kingdom) had pursued a policy of backward integration more completely than other firms in the trade, encouraged by their relative isolation in the west of England from the main centers of manufacture in the East Midlands. They even owned a tannery. The concentration of the industry in the Northhampton and Leicester regions during the nineteenth century had encouraged the development of ancillary industries with separate firms supplying specialized inputs to the shoemakers through a progressive specialization of function—components, lasts, shoemaking machinery, and the like. Clarks had for long made their own leatherboard (processing scrap-leather waste from the shoe factory) and components. They then set up their own capacity for making knives[21] and lasts, which implied considerable engineering capacity, and developed a shoe machinery department after 1950 to produce C.E.M.A. machines, and their later progeny—the technology which revolutionized shoemaking—by making and attaching soles to uppers by a rapid vulcanizing process rather than by welting and stitching.

Economies of scale in leatherboard making had long meant that the board mill supplied customers other than Clarks' shoemakers. But when all the "inputs" to shoemaking were made into a separate division and told to make 20 percent per annum on their assets employed, a much more dramatic change took place. Making knives and particularly lasts (where the real secrets of the trade and the essence of styling reside) for the trade as a whole meant selling the expertise which the manufacturing division regarded as their major competitive asset in the industry. In the engineering section, where the latest shoe machinery was made, the story was the same. Clarks shoe factories could not hope to take enough machines to keep the shoe machinery plant operating at an economic level. Yet vigorously selling the expertise which had previously been their alone to the trade as a whole was initially resented as sowing dragon's teeth abroad since the machines which were being developed primarily at Clarks in the 1950s were the most sophisticated in the industry throughout the world (the United States included). This technology, if kept confidential, might have been the means of keeping Clarks ahead of the game for a few years. This policy aim created delicate problems of confidentiality, if other shoemakers were to get their lasts made by a subsidiary of a prime rival in the trade without knowledge getting back to the Clark shoe factories. But beyond the confidentiality over specific designs, one of the main arguments for selling components, knives, lasts, and machinery competitively to shoemakers across the world was exactly that this would keep the Clark subsidiaries in these trades at the frontiers of technology, with important feedbacks for the Clark shoe factories. One of the problems of creating "tied" input capacity, like the problem of having a retail division selling only tied products—a general condition of slave relationships—was precisely that initiative would be lost; that key designers and engineers would tend to lose touch with the rest of the trade; that their horizons would become limited to Clarks' needs and Clarks' opportunities; that they would lose the opportunities of expansion by successful sales to the shoe industry as a whole, as well as the responsibility created from having to sell competitively to factory managers in Clarks. For the shoe factories of the group maintained their own freedom to purchase all their inputs from outside suppliers if price or quality suited them better than the alternatives available from within the group.

The blend of freedom and responsibility created a series of carrots and sticks for all divisions as competitive relationships were established between all the main functions contained within the integrated enterprise. Competition was internalized and maximization pursued as an end for each function, rather than in an aggregative concept for the group as a whole. The organizational structure containing these multiprofit centers, with each main function institutionalized in a separate company or series of companies, forming a quasi-independent division, was run to follow where profit beckoned rather than to maintain functional cohesion within the whole. The assumption was that all would profit collectively as each constituent part pursued its own interests—not simply through maximizing the profits of each, but from the various feedbacks to the organization as a whole. Each section faced out toward its own world of expertise, and profited from the incentives which had been internalized in all sections of the organization. Clearly, the central board was approximating the role of an investment trust, or at least a "conglomerate." Tight financial controls were maintained on all divisions: all surpluses were centralized, never staying with the divisions that made them; all major investment decisions had to be approved by the central board; no major commitment was undertaken beyond the shoemaking industry; all major decisions passed through the central board; the central board monitored the management efficiency (and selected the top management) for the whole concern; and in each main division one or more senior directors was a member of the family, which buttressed the formal chain of command more intimately. Although the enterprise was very large for the shoemaking industry, it was small by comparison with the "superfirms," and this gave greater coherence to the whole. The fact remained that the essential criteria upon which the central board acted were the tests of judging each division according to its success in making a return upon its assets, and its creator, Bancroft Clark, certainly had the courage of his convictions.

Potential centrifugal forces were built into the system. The path of maximization for different divisions could lead away from maintaining a tight functional relationship with the rest of the group; so that (from the shoemakers' point of view) the time might come when the tail wagged the dog, if it did not become quite disconnected from the dog. The logic of specialization in leatherboard manufacture, for example, might well lead in the future toward making this function tributary to the paper industry, fitting more economically into the pattern of output and markets of firms based quite outside shoemaking. With technology growing more massive, demanding higher output and longer production runs to produce at competitive prices, in the 1980s or 1990s a board mill might have only a very small percentage of its output taken by the shoe industry as a whole; while the demands that boardmaking made on investment resources, to keep up with the advance of technology, could easily make it too expensive on capital account as a function to be maintained within an enterprise centering on the shoe industry. The same might be true of the path of future evolution of the machinery division. Shoemaking machinery may become dependent on some other branch of the engineering or chemical industry, with very large firms moving in with resources which could not be matched by any organization not astride an industry far removed from shoemaking. The choice would then be posed: either to accept a major commitment outside the base industry of the group, with all the attendant requirements of capital and management expertise, or to reduce the frontiers of the group. Conceivably, a similar choice could face the retailing division if there were a structural change in shopping habits from the use of specialist shoe shops to the large department-store multiples; or if most shoe-buying became a matter of joint-purchase with clothes (and hence a dependent variable of branches of retailing dominated by very powerful retailing interests). When commitments outside the base function of manufacturing led along paths which forfeited coherence for the group as a whole, and where the scale of resources needed if these activities were to be pursued on at all an efficient scale threatened the viability of the rest of the enterprise, then the centrifugal forces built into the group by such a strategy of growth through integration had to be acknowledged. Beyond that point lies the logic of the conglomerate rather than that of an integrated enterprise—the mirror-image of the logic of integration.

This conclusion was seen in a previous example of unconstrained vertical integration. Thomas Lipton set up one of the first, and most successful, multiple provision and grocery chains, the foundation of his trade being the mass demand by working-class families in dense urban concentrations for a handful of basic commodities—ham and bacon, tea, sugar, butter (subsequently margarine also), lard, cheese, and flour.[22] From this firm base of rapidly expanding trade across the counters of his own shops he threw out new enterprise at every point in the business where he thought profit could be made (or profits paid to others eliminated): the hotel and contract trade; printing; tin box and carton making; ham and bacon factories; subsequently jam factories and processing plants for an extended number of lines such as jellies, pickles, sauces, biscuits and cakes, cocoa, chocolate, and a host of others. He bought supply depots in Ireland; railway provision trucks, meat-packing plants in Chicago and South Omaha, Nebraska; refrigerated rail cars, tea plantations in Ceylon, and a world-wide network of agencies to develop the tea trade. Each new function was to become a profit center and seek trade where it could be found, rather than just to be tributary to the Lipton shops in the United Kingdom.

Such undisciplined integration and expansion quickly outran the possibilities of effective supervision or efficient management. Many conflicts of interest were built into the situation, including the fact that Lipton developed a world-wide tea trade, selling a branded article through agencies to independent retailers, while in the United Kingdom the presence of the Lipton shops precluded a national branded product being accepted by independent retailers. The American Tea Company, in particular, turned its back on the parent organization and passed into separate ownership. Some of the factories suffered the opposite fate. Nationally branded products developed by food manufacturing companies, kept before the public eye by extensive advertising, increasingly found their way onto the shelves of Lipton shops in response to public demand. These competing brand names cut into the market for Lipton's own factories, which were also excluded by the branding logic from gaining national sales to the trade as a whole. In such circumstances the advantage of owning high-cost factories was quickly called into question. Factories making products where "branding" had a low premium (on sausages, bacon, etc., unlike biscuits or chocolate) could be more successfully integrated.

These few examples of the changing boundaries of integrated enterprise have been used to illustrate the opportunities and problems which an increase in the scale of business invokes when it becomes associated with differentiation of function. The variables which collectively make up the balance of forces determining the frontiers of a business are not easily formulated in terms which have predictive value, or even much regularity of incidence. The determination of a man or a committee can push out the frontiers of a business, where the context gives room for manoeuver—and great fluidity clearly exists across a wide spectrum of business. Examples of both successful and unsuccessful vertically integrated and non-integrated businesses are widespread in the same industries. But the context itself can exert powerful conditioning influences. This, coming partly in response to technology, affects the logic of various combinations and groupings of processes, which can change as technology changes. The context is also much affected by the logic of power relationships between firms in different, related industries; between centers of power in retailing and manufacturing. What is the underlying logic to explain the integration of the oil industry, as far as its main international firms are concerned, down to retailing, while other equally powerful industrial interest groups, such as automobiles or chemicals, do not manifest such powerful forward drives into retailing? Can the explanations which lie behind these individual instances be construed into a general theory or explanatory schema?

Theory offers few guides through these largely uncharted waters. Industries group and regroup; the appropriate frontiers of firms change with these changing contours of coherence if the organization is to be maintained in any functional relationship (apart from finance and undifferentiated management expertise) and profitability maximized. Power as well as profit and efficiency determine choices; and power relationships in business have proved more resistant to theoretical analysis than profit orientations. The dynamics of integration, and the deterrents to growth by integration do, however, reveal some of the forces which have shaped the business corporation the most influential institution of the last two centuries, and which help to determine, in what is now a justifiably famous phrase, its strategy and structure.

NOTES

1. For authorities see: H. W. Macrosty, *The Trust Movement in British Industry* (London: 1907); P. Fitzgerald, *Industrial Combination in England* (London: 1927); W. J. Asley, ed., *British Business* (London, 1903); A. Plummer, *International Combines in Modern Industry* (London, 1934); M. A. Utten, "Some Features of Early Merger Movements in British Manufacturing Industry," *Business History*, vol. 14 (1972).

2. W. J. Ashley, ed., *British Business* (London, 1903), pp. 223–26.

3. *Ibid.*, p. 222.

4. H. C. Edey and P. Panitpakdi, "British Company Accounting and the Law, 1844–1880"; H. Pollins, "Aspects of Railway Accounting Before 1868," in A. C. Littleton and B. S. Yamey, *Studies in the History of Accounting* (London, 1956).

5. P. Mathias, *The Brewing Industry in England, 1700–1830* (Cambridge, 1959), ch. 7.

6. E. Garke and J. M. Fells, *Factory Accounts* (London, 1887).

7. *Ibid.*, pp. 472–74.

8. J. Slater Lewis, *The Commercial Organisation of Factories* (London, 1896). The author was general manager of a firm of engineers and rolling mills at Manchester.

9. His judgment on the stationery is significant: "The style adopted by Government Departments, railway companies and banks may be regarded as the one which commends itself to the favour of men of business" (*ibid.*, p. 116).

10. J. Mann and H. G. Judd, *Colliery Accounts* (London, 1909), p. 15.

11. F. G. Burton, *Engineers' and Shipbuilders' Accounts; Commercial Management of Engineering Works* (London, 1905); W. Moss, *Cotton Spinners' Accounts* (London, 1906); J. Hazelip, *Multiple Shop Accounts* (London, 1908). There are 51 volumes in this particular series.

12. F. W. Taylor, *Shop Management* (New York and London, 1911), p. 62.

13. *Ibid.*, p. 63.

14. F. W. Taylor, *The Principles of Scientific Management* (New York and London, 1911). He was, of course, very forward-looking in his "high productivity" orientation, for equating the interests of employers and employees by equating high wages with low labor costs through scientific management.

15. N. A. H. Stacey, *English Accounting* (London, 1954); *History of the Institute of Chartered Accounts in England and Wales, 1870–1965* (London, 1966).

16. C. and J. Clark Ltd., of Streit, Somerset, England, the largest shoemaking firm in the U.K. and one of the largest in the world. Founded in 1825 and still a private company, it is the most completely integrated large firm in the U.K. shoe industry. The records of the firm have been made available to the author.

17. P. Mathias, *Retailing Revolution* (London, 1967), pp. 195–258; Charles Wilson, *The History of Unilever* (London, 1954), 2: 252–63.

18. P. Mathias, *The Brewing Industry in England*; J. E. Vaizey, *The Brewing Industry, 1880–1950* (London, 1960).

19. Peter Lord Ltd. and various other small multiples trading under their own names.

20. In the case of C. and J. Clark Ltd. this point was important. As a private, family-controlled company the extra capital required would almost certainly have involved a public flotation, changing the nature of the entire business.

21. The steel cutters in the shape of the various pieces of leather which made up the uppers and soles of shoes.

22. P. Mathias, *Retailing Revolution.*

Comment

Barry Supple

Before commenting directly on Professor Mathias's paper, I think it might be in order if I tried to give you a few words on British business history in general, and on the problems of applying Professor Chandler's extremely fruitful concepts of structure and strategy to business history.

As Professor Mathias himself has just said, in terms of scholarship, whether the scholarship of the technical press or that of the historian, the problem in Britain is that we are relatively underdeveloped in our knowledge of various aspects of the development of business administration. In many ways we are still very much at the handicraft stage. That is to say, much of the minute historic knowledge of these subjects derives from the work of a few individuals examining mostly very specific business enterprises rather than attempting the sort of comparative studies which we all know to be the only way in which we can move forward.

Further, although there has been much work done by individuals in accumulating general data about the evolution of business, very few of us have asked the sort of questions about strategy and structure and managerial development which are relevant today. This is partly because, although it is fully fifteen years since Professor Wilson published his study of Unilever, we are still in the early days of investment in the pursuit of knowledge, systematic and academic, of British business history. And it is partly because, if you imagine American businessmen have been coy about the release of the records of the recent past, British businessmen, until extremely recently, have been positively neurotic about it! But the situation is changing and I suppose one of the tasks of this part of the discussion is to see how much we know and how much more we *can* know.

Two relevant problems in regard to British business history, to which Professor Mathias's paper is addressed, relate to the actual growth of large-scale enterprise in Britain and the adaptation of management and organization to that growth. The actual growth of British big business pales into relative insignificance, of course, in comparison with its history in this country, certainly at critical periods in history, and most notably in the late nineteenth century. The first fumbling attempts at British mergers, as described in the first part of Professor Mathias's paper, took place at that time. But it was not until the early twentieth century that there was a more decisive emergence of multifirm, multiproduct international enterprises, with ICI, Unilever, and Shell dominant, as mentioned by Professor Mathias.

Also, in a field with which I have had some acquaintance, the insurance industry, in this period (the late nineteenth or more particularly the early twentieth century) there began to emerge very large-scale insurance companies, operating internationally and in many instances drawing more than half of their revenue from overseas. Secondly, the adaptation, or the failure of British management organization to adapt to large-scale operations, must obviously figure as an important strand in our discussions. The twin concepts of strategy and structure have been proffered to us, on the basis of Professor Chandler's pioneering work, as possible themes for discussion.

On this score Professor Chandler taught us, in his own words, that structure follows strategy—that the short-term disposition of resources and efforts matches the reappraisals of the long-term conception of the needs and allocations of the resources of the firm. Now, this is obviously an extremely useful distinction. But it is made on the assumption that there was and is a linear relationship between the two concepts: that businessmen set strategy and then determine structure.

Although this seems to be an extremely valuable tool of analysis it also seems to be right to indicate slightly different ways of looking at the problem. In this respect I should like to emphasize two points. First, growth in the scale of enterprise, which we think of as the consequence of strategy in a sense, may not be the outcome of conscious policy. It may in fact "just happen." Scale may be an adaptation to problems which are not clearly thought out, the end product of an evolution which is not an explicit reflection of a strategy, the aim of which is growth, but, rather, of a policy of a much more diversified, diffused and disparate kind. To some small extent, of course, this is exemplified in the examples that Professor Mathias gave of the extremely loose merger movement of the late nineteenth century.

Second, and more important, there is the point, amply exemplified in Professor Mathias's paper, that there is a symbiotic relationship between strategy and structure. In other words it need not be a one-way process. Strategy may in fact follow structure rather than the other way round. Thus Professor Mathias deals with problems of management organization—problems which were perhaps exposed by unwitting, unexpected, or unplanned growth. And these problems of structure themselves produce the need for strategic changes.

More explicitly, the goals of the institution, of the business, may have to be adapted to the organization, rather than the organization of the business always having to be adapted to the goals. At the micro level, of course, this is exemplified in the paper under discussion, where the problems of retailing outlets, of forward integration, did lead to a redefinition of long-term strategies.

Now if I may turn to an examination of Professor Mathias's paper, I think we can see some implications of what I have been trying to say. And I would like to consider his two principal examples—which are those of lateral and vertical integration. When we deal with lateral concentration in Britain in the late nineteenth century, we are largely concerned with fairly loose groupings and associations, analogous in most ways, I suppose, to the early cartel or trade association phase of the rise of American big business. In Britain—in the chemical, textile and other industries—a large number of firms came together as amorphous groups, with no very specific thought as to the way in which they could be organized.

Now the apparently striking feature of this, which comes out in Professor Mathias's paper, was the failure to restructure management or to adapt management techniques to the new forms, that is to the new scale of operations. And this was a failure of structure to follow strategy. As Professor Mathias points out, this presumably arose because the main objective of the "mergers" was the mitigation of price competition, the protection of the inefficient, the exercise of power by the firms who came together for self-preservation, and not the deployment of competitive or profit-oriented techniques for the enterprise considered as a new sort of unit. It was, in fact, a multifirm rather than a multifunctional organization of a fairly loose sort. The absence of a coherent strategy on the part of this sort of organization exposes various problems which Professor Mathias's paper underlines—for example, the problem of accumulating and assessing information through internal accounting systems. He sees this as an independent variable: that is to say, the absence of effective cost accounting is seen as an inhibition on the perfection of the mergers. On this score, however, I find it difficult to understand why this was so, since on the evidence of the paper the demand for improvement in accounting—that is to say the demand for improvement in the techniques which would have enabled businesses to have been run efficiently—was apparently there. It was the response which was very poor. In this respect too, perhaps, we have not yet laid the ghost of Britain's supposedly poor entrepreneurial performance at this period of its history.

A second problem worth discussing is why, in Professor Mathias's words, size and market share were no guarantee of success with multifirm lateral mergers. I assume that it was not simply because accountancy and internal management techniques had not developed, but rather because the strategy which would have been appropriate to provide some sort of guarantee of success had not yet evolved. And this failure of the appropriate strategy to evolve prevented the appropriate functional differentiation, which would have made sense of potentially large accumulations of capital and enterprise. Growth at this level occurred as an immediate consequence of defensive moves. Presumably some of these defensive moves made considerable profit for those whom we would now stigmatize, and perhaps were then stigmatized, as speculators—those people who actually brought the merger about. Other potential profit recipients simply staggered along conservatively with less than perfect mergers.

So we again encounter one of the main issues with which we would have to be concerned if we explored this particular topic at greater length —namely the quality of British entrepreneurship, and the question of why, if there was such an important challenge to it and if the cost of failure was so high, it failed to respond.

The second and more obviously interesting type of example, from our present viewpoint, is that of vertical integration, where the motives are those outlined by Professor Mathias: to seek profit and security, to maintain turnover. As he rightly points out, vertical integration almost necessarily involves the restructuring of organizations, which in the main took the form of decentralization and devolution of decision-making responsibility because of two pressures.

First, the competitive pressure for integration of retailing led to competition between the firm's outlets and other outlets for similar sorts of commodities. This is often most effectively handled by allowing the retailing or sales division to have a greater degree of autonomy. Second, devolution derived from the pressure toward the maximization of returns on the assets involved in a particular function (in this case the retailing function, or in the other example which Professor Mathias gives, the input function to the shoe manufacturing firm). But the main burden of his argument, which I think is an extremely interesting one, is that decentralization is not in itself a solution because it may bring new sorts of problems to the firm through the independence of the drive for profits on the part of the division. There is a danger, in Professor Mathias's words, not merely of the tail wagging the dog, but of becoming disconnected from it.

This, too, is an example of the process to which I referred earlier. Strategy, scale, and integration led to a structure (namely, decentralization) which in turn obliged the enterprise to reshape its strategy into new forms in order to encompass and try to harmonize the conflicts which necessarily flowed from its first efforts. The examples given in Professor Mathias's paper are those of forward integration to retailing and backward integration to the inputs and capital goods needed for the manufacture of shoes. And I took Professor Mathias's partial conclusion to be that it was rather difficult (given the explanatory models at our command) to explain in any theoretical, systematic way, the sorts of problems that emerged at different levels with regard to this conflict of interest. At the same time, however, I would argue that we can usefully distinguish between the problems of explaining the differential impacts of the trend to integration—why some firms integrated and others did not—and the problems of explaining the varying success (in terms of intrafirm conflicts) of the structures which resulted from the new strategy. At the end of his paper Professor Mathias hypothesizes that the differential impact of power, as much as profit, may have been at the root of this situation: that power, as well as profit and efficiency, determines choices, and that power relationships in business have proved more resistant to theoretical analysis than have profit orientations. Granting and accepting all of this, I wonder if it may not be possible, in fact, to make some sense of the systematic differences between industries in terms of their responses to the problems of functional differentiation. Thus, if we take Professor Mathias's example, forward integration to grocery stores immediately raises two problems. First, an enterprise can rarely sell as limited a range of goods as it manufactures, so that forward integration for the manufacturer of margarine means that he has to sell other commodities as well. Second, as far as the consumer is concerned, the differentiation of the actual product involved makes it extremely difficult for the store to confine itself to its own line of a particular product. It is therefore in the economic interest of the retailing division in this situation to do things which may well be interpreted as conflicting with the interests of the manufacturing division.

Presumably the reason for this, which Professor Mathias touched upon in his summary, is that the structure of retailing is not, in regard to these products, homogeneous. Put another way, the structure of retailing in these instances prevents the parent firm from capturing the externalities of concentrating on the retailing function. The efficiency which it can bring to this is diffused, not merely to the consumer but to *other* manufacturing entrepreneurs who are able to sell differentiated products through the retailing division outlets.

In this regard it is important to bear in mind the comments that Professor Chandler made in the earlier discussion about the consequences of the fact that motor cars are now homogeneous products: that this could lead to a degree of centralization which before was very difficult. The homogeneity, whether real or artificial (that is to say, whether inherent in the nature of the product, or merely the consequence of very effective advertising), is very pertinent indeed. Homogeneity or heterogeneity of product can obviously make an enormous difference to the degree of centralization or decentralization which it is possible to have, and to the nature of the problems which flow from these structures. Therefore (and this is not a particularly novel idea) it seems to me that retailing competition in multiproduct, highly differentiated markets is very likely to produce exactly the sort of problem that Professor Mathias touched on.

I suppose a similar example of this argument can be applied to the second theme that I wanted to isolate from the paper, namely backward integration in shoe manufacturing. As Professor Mathias pointed out, a conflict arose here from the fact that the input divisions (the manufacture of the knives, lasts, and machinery) had to make profits, and therefore had to sell to competitors. This conflict is an example of the fact that the indivisibilities of this aspect of the operation led to economies of scale which forced divisions of the enterprise to utilize bigger markets than were available within the organization itself. In other words, once again the firm could not itself retain the externalities which were created by its specialization, and some of those externalities had to be shared with other firms or enterprises which were competitive with the parent division of company.

I think this last argument also comes into focus when we take two other examples touched on in Professor Mathias's paper, namely those of the brewing and the oil companies which integrated forward with much less of a problem of internal conflict. This was presumably because they were dealing with products which were much more homogeneous in terms of the consumers' regard for them. Breweries acquired public houses with no real danger that this would produce a conflict, that the outlet would begin to sell the products of competitors or that it would have to sell other sorts of products than beer. To a similar extent I think, this is true in the case of oil companies which are integrated forward through control of gas stations. On the other hand, I am not entirely persuaded of the validity of the two other sorts of reasons for lack of conflict that Professor Mathias gave, namely the use of licensing (i.e. monopoly) and the need for large capital investment. After all, the licensing of public houses was merely one form of institutional constraint on competition, while the capital intensity of beer or gas retailing does not in itself explain why retailers turned to the parent institution for the capital rather than to other investors.

Finally, I should like to turn to another set of examples of the relationship between structure and strategy. This is derived from my own research into the history of British insurance. British insurance companies up to the late nineteenth century tended to be specialized, on a fairly large scale, by types of insurance: life, accident (casualty, as it is called in the United States), fire insurance, and so forth. This was as much a specialization in function as in product or type of service offered. Now, in the late nineteenth century two sorts of things began to happen. On the one hand there was much fiercer competition, partly from foreign companies (primarily American) in the British market. The response to this competition was to scale up the level of operations of British life firms, to begin to offer cheaper and much more varied policies, and above all to seek lower unit costs by enormous increases in sales. Second, and much more significantly, the nature of competition and the nature of consumer demand in Britain led to an integration of functions. Firms ceased to be single-line insurance companies. Instead, they increasingly combined the four main branches of life, casualty, fire, and marine insurance. The age of the composite insurance company came to Britain. This led to a substantial diversification for individual companies, and an enormous degree of concentration as far as the industry was concerned. At the same time it was associated with a massive and successful counterinvasion of world markets, and particularly the American market, for fire and casualty insurance.

Now this led to structural problems of a very high order, because where previously most important insurance companies had confined their activities (and organization) to a single function or product (e.g. life insurance), now companies combined a variety of products and functions. And when a group of multiproduct insurance companies emerged, each of them had to sell a variety of products, each of them had to organize its branches, and each of them had to face up to the intrafirm conflicts that arose between functional departments (which wished to control their own sales outlet and policies) and between branches and home offices. The inevitable result was a trend toward centralization within the firm. This was the era of the general manager, a figure in insurance who had hardly existed before 1900, and who was needed in order to force the fire, life, casualty, and marine branches to operate as one firm. It was also the era of the agency manager, who was needed in order to co-ordinate the sales activities of all branches, and all types of insurance selling agencies within the firm. In other words, it proved impossible to attain all the economies of scale without breaking the independence which had up to then been preserved by the individual functional divisions and branch units. Later on, in the interwar period, as the merger movement continued and insurance firms became huge, the sheer problems of scale obliged companies to begin the process made familiar to us by Professor Chandler's work: the creation of divisions, essentially miniature regional companies, to sell the whole array of insurance products and insurance services. They did this because the problems of scale had now reached a critical threshold. In many ways I think this provides an interesting set of parallels—lagged and refracted, if parallels can be refracted—as between Britain and the United States.

My final point, which is a rather general one, although it has been implicit in much of what I have had to say, is that the imperfect state of our knowledge obviously prevents us from making the sort of attempt at systematic generalization about the British experience which Professor

Chandler made about the American. Moreover, we can hardly piece together some of the vital elements in the British story in order to begin to see the degree to which there might be parallels or divergences.

Perhaps the real problem is one that is touched upon in a variety of ways, by different people, including of course Professor Galbraith in his opening address, and by Professor Mathias—as well as by most historians who have ever discussed British economic performance. That is the problem of how can one distinguish between "market forces" and what one might label individual, social, and psychological forces when discussing economic growth and business development. In this context it is worth emphasizing that much historical ground still has to be covered and that it is perhaps too easy to be pessimistic and negative about the "non-economic" characteristics of British businessmen. It is one of the many merits of Professor Chandler's approach that it obliges us to consider much more realistically whether a simple sociopsychological explanation of entrepreneurial performance is satisfactory. Certainly, with regard to the British case, we should find out a lot more about the real market structures and organizational pressures in the late nineteenth and early twentieth century before condemning our forefathers.

4. Landed and Moneyed Princes:
The Harvest of Tradition and Conflict
in German Business and Politics

HANS A. SCHMITT

In Germany before and after the onset of the industrial age, business and
banking depended for propulsion on the resources of princes and aristocrats. An unusual number of the most affluent and powerful among these
combined estate ownership with territorial sovereignty: 7 electors, 75
princes, 98 counts and 350 knights of the empire engaged in something
more than mere exploitation of agrarian resources. Centuries ago the
most eminent and powerful had ópted or been forced to opt for the priority of statecraft. Their bureaucracy had separated into an administration of the state and an administration of the family domain.[1]

Political and economic leadership, therefore, as well as concomitant
social eminence, were often concentrated in the same hands. The dictum,
"In the beginning was the dynastic and territorial state," must introduce
every synthesis of any major aspect of German economic or business
history. The many large studies of industrialization in Prussia confirm it.[2]
Thanks to Wolfgang Zorn we can test it in the more divergent Bavarian
climate,[3] while we are indebted to Wolfram Fischer for full investigations
of the early partnership of public and private enterprise in Baden.[4] Helen
P. Liebel recently concluded that "the . . . administrative civil servant in
the German petty state" constituted the primary entrepreneurial type for
the initial periods of industrialization.[5]

Yet not every pioneering concentration of capital bore this statist
stamp. The summary and often arbitrary reforms of Napoleon Bonaparte
roughly divided the ruling houses of Germany into a relatively small
corps of some thirty families who retained their crowns, and a vastly
larger number which was "mediatized," or subjected to the governance of
local rather than imperial authority. A new upper nobility emerged, equal
socially and often economically to the sovereigns of Europe—with whom
they continue to intermarry freely to this day—retaining freedom of movement and exemption from military service, acquiring hereditary seats in
the upper house of every German state in which they owned property,
preserving even certain patrimonial rights over local schools, courts, and
churches, but surrendering the basic attribute of sovereign independence.

These *Standesherren* were to make their own striking contribution to
Germany's industrial development. To begin with they salvaged from the
wars of the French revolution properties covering many more acres than

such small states of confederate and imperial Germany as Lippe, Reuss, and Schwarzburg.[6] As late as 1900, the estates of the Princes of Thurn and Taxis, licensees of the hereditary postal monopoly under the Holy Roman Empire, made up an aggregate of 308,000 acres, scattered across Central Europe from Poznan to Croatia. These dethroned princes of the Holy Roman Empire possessed to an unusual degree the leisure and ambition to invest. What Thurn and Taxis was to lose in 1918 in Poland or Yugoslavia seems to have been more than regained in Brazilian ore mines, and large—often controlling—interests in a variety of industrial and banking enterprises. When Bavaria decided to build a new university in Ratisbon some years ago, it purchased the land from the current head of the clan for a reputed 36 million Deutsche marks.[7]

Location of *standesherrliche* estates turned out to be as important as their size or fertility. The Dukes of Arenberg own land under which Providence placed some of the most productive coal mines of western Europe. The Wolf-Metternich zu Gracht branch of another famous princely family has likewise watched its countryside change into a moonscape of mine-shaft entrances and slag heaps at what one may assume to be exceedingly profitable and steady rentals.[8] Finally, this particular elite has not camouflaged its interest in profit and enterprise behind a false front of seignorial indolence. Gustav Mevissen, the redoubtable Cologne banker and railroad tycoon, who rubbed elbows with the mediatized nobility in the Prussian house of lords from 1866 to 1891, had discovered as early as 1847 that they understood the economic aspirations of burgeoning national liberalism even in restoration Germany. As producers of agricultural surpluses they took a natural interest in railroad building, but like their bourgeois partners, they quickly scattered their eggs among many baskets and supplemented this monetary participation with personal appearances on growing numbers of supervisory and directoral boards.[9] Cut loose from the moorings of monarchic isolation the *Standesherren* nimbly rolled with the punches of each successive upheaval. Investment banking, railroad investment, mining, steel, textiles, food processing, and ultimately lobbying, including the plunge into parliamentary politics, have challenged their energies. Since 1949 a Fugger, a Sayn-Wittgenstein and a Löwenstein have communicated the warmth of their aristocratic bodies to the plebeian seat of a *Bundestag* bench, while Castells, Öttingen-Wallersteins, and others have lent to the German banking world in particular the aura of a small-scale restoration of the imperial diet of Ratisbon.[10]

This aristocratic facet of German business and industrial history puts us at once on the scent of a development frequently observed and discussed: there was an industrial revolution, but all it seems to have changed were the means of production. The powers of the agrarian age seem to have preserved their preponderance under the industrial age that followed.

That is of course an exaggeration. Survive they did, and prosper they did, but no longer in the exclusive solitude of feudal and absolutist times. The nineteenth and twentieth centuries furnished them with new competition and new partners. Unlike the society which is somewhat slanderously said to have chiefly danced at Vienna and which also included their crowned cousins and their inferior baronial acquaintances, the elite which today dances, wheels and deals at Bonn and on those playgrounds of western Europe which German wealth comes close to dominating, confronts a Bismarck with a Siemens, a *Standesherr* with the bourgeois board chairman of a large steel concern (*vieux riche* and *nouveau riche*) on terms of equality.[11] Recent German history, too, has been marked by a steadily and impressively "rising middle class."

But whence did it rise? A recently published social profile of the Rhineland entrepreneur during the first great take-off period between 1834 and 1879, identifies no Horatio Algers and narrates no epic rise from poverty to affluence. Sons of physicians (such as Röchling of the Saar), sons of teachers (Fritz Henkel), sons of clergymen (David Hansemann)—especially sons of clergymen—broke out of their environments of genteel and respectable stagnation to find material and spiritual satisfaction in building a new prosperity on industry. Sons of teachers and clergymen were of course simultaneously sons of civil servants. In a word, bourgeois leadership came from the *middle* levels of professional life and state service.[12] In a few instances, as we shall see later, a father who managed state enterprises would even be succeeded by a tycoon-son who followed in his footsteps, but in the private sector.

The industrial revolution in Germany, therefore, did not break the conservative mold of state and society. Thrones had no cause to tremble, most of all because the old wealth and the new were not enemies. Prussia provides a most telling example. The entrepreneur there faced a state entirely sympathetic to his needs. The constitutional conflict between the new minister-president Otto von Bismarck and the liberal majority in the lower house, often supported by the new managerial and entrepreneurial elite, did nothing to diminish the Hohenzollern kingdom as the haven of German laissez-faire. Some of the liberal businessmen assumed that a victory of king and army at parliament's expense would damage their interests. But they quickly learned their mistake. After the new army bested the Danes, Prussia's acquisition of Kiel spoke the unequivocal language of commercial expansion. Two years later the annexation of Hanover eased the shipment of coal to the Hanseatic ports, and—needless to say—inaugurated an era of unprecedented expansion in the annexed areas themselves. It is no coincidence that much of the leadership of post-1871 German national liberalism came from the old English exclave on the continent.[13]

The balance sheet of 1871 in liberal terms—national unity, laissez-faire, constitutional government—was a liberal triumph. Liberalism did not sell out, it got what it wanted. Germany has been created, laissez-faire was institutionalized in much of its constitution, notably the articles guaranteeing freedom of movement and progressive economic unification. The strengthening of representative government would no doubt gain substance and meaning with time. A free economy would strengthen a free polity.

Events took a different turn, as we all know. If the expectations of political liberty turned to ashes, could it have been because the assumption of German laissez-faire rested on illusions? One might look at the history of the German railroads for an example, for here was a new business attracting venturesome capital in spectacular quantities throughout Europe. Who built them in Germany and how? In Baden the private sector never entered railroading, in Württemberg the state began laying tracks in the late 1830s after private promoters had failed to raise sufficient capital. In Bavaria the first lines, including Germany's oldest from Nuremberg to Fürth, were privately built and managed, but within ten years the government dominated, as builder and as rescuer of shaky private lines. Before long, German governments found it necessary to integrate private and public networks under their jurisdiction with those of their neighbors, both within and beyond the confederation. Even in Prussia, where large spaces provided an extensive testing ground for both private and public approaches, the merger of parallel networks within the kingdom and with its neighbors quickly introduced the state as a permanent, albeit reluctant, partner.[14] Although railroad laissez-faire survived here longer than elsewhere, it did not become the wave of the future. In 1873, two-thirds of Prussian rail transport still functioned under private control, but by 1900, thirty-three thousand out of thirty-five thousand kilometers in operation had either been constructed or purchased by the state.[15] During this period, interestingly enough, German liberals themselves were of two minds about who should run the railroad. By 1873, scandals in the granting and exploitation of concessions aroused vigorous criticism in the Reichstag, where the national-liberal spokesman Eduard Lasker became an early advocate of "greater public control and more public ownership."[16]

If liberals after 1871 called upon the state to preserve the young national mystique from fiscal and political corruption, they should not be taxed with inconsistency. For centuries German commerce had suffered from the absence of political protection by a vigorous and organized state; at least that point of view is generally accepted to this day, whenever both laymen and historians discuss such questions as the decline of the Hanseatic league, or the economic state of Germany after the Thirty Years' War. Accordingly, the truly enterprising among German entrepreneurs supported German unification and most commonly under Prussian leadership. Men such as H. H. Meier of the North German Lloyd in Bremen and his Hamburg counterpart Adolph Woermann quite reasonably expected to flourish more spectacularly under a German flag than under the banner of their ancient but powerless city states. The Egestorffs in Hanover, ever hamstrung by a government whose royal master disapproved of factories and would allow none in his capital, greeted with enthusiasm and relief their kingdom's annexation to a more progressive Prussia.[17] This community of interest between a conservative state and liberal capitalism nurtured and preserved a dilemma from which neither was to find an exit. The unification of 1871 created a commonwealth with an economy more and more resembling Britain's and a government whose typological counterparts could be found on some imaginary middle ground between Austria and Russia.[18] Thorstein Veblen, the shrewdest contemporary judge of Wilhelmine Germany, observed that industrialization "has hitherto had but a slight effect in the way of inducing new habits of thought on institutional matters among the German population."[19]

Pursuing this notion beyond the empire through the upheavals of the twentieth century, one is tempted to rephrase it and affirm that the departure of Wilhelm II was succeeded by many changes of government, but no change of heart. As in France, basic laws and administrative procedures were exchanged with alacrity. The maligned revolution of 1918 displayed no timidity on that score, either at the federal or the state level. Almost every succeeding decade since then has added yet another "new" Germany to our catalogue of political novelties. Yet one enters the present with Veblen's perturbing observation still essentially beyond challenge in the sense that a succession of new constitutions has left other large areas of German life remarkably unaffected.

A consideration of business structures in this context must therefore ask: What distinctive features characterize the beginning of large industrial enterprise and which of them have persisted to the present?

The preceding observations have already drawn a clear line between the German entrepreneur and political militancy. From the outset the entrepreneur was boxed in between respect for and dependence on the state, and respect for and dependence on traditional society. Thus the "story of the structure of enterprise" in Germany is not "the adaptation of law, politics, and opinion to economic needs," as David Landes has defined it, but rather the pursuit of economic goals within a confined radius of legal, political, and moral traditions.[20] This produces a high degree of caution. One does not proceed alone, but in conjunction with others similarly interested, and after careful financial and technological preparations. Growing enterprises develop an early dependence on banks and on technical expertise, both of which—thanks to Germany's decentralized development—are available, either in the nearby princely residence or in the nearby state university. These alliances of enterprise, capital, and skill, frequently directed by a driving individual ambition, produce the basic corporate trinity. Its patterns mark German business life from the outset, its thrust produces the aforementioned fear of corruption and, one must now add, of domination, which then calls into being a desire for public control.

Yet the expected confrontation between public and private interest, between business and government never occurred. In 1873, Eduard Lasker's call for governmental supervision of the despoilers of the national dream coincided with what turned out to be a long depression, a crisis which tested the mettle of libertarian dogma, to find that it exercised a feeble hold on the community of German capitalism. Historians are now discovering that economic liberalism counted more supporters among civil servants than businessmen. Guild capitalism had scarcely subsided during the transition from commerce to industry. As markets shrank, it expanded, assuming new structural guises and rendering new and important services. Now of course it came to be called cartel, not guild.

In the course of the new crisis, association surged first as an attempt to bolster prices and apportion shares of the market. Shortly it appeared that neither purpose could be accomplished without control of production. For full effectiveness, finally, the cartel merged these three separate control operations under the roof of a *Syndikat* "in which the entire production . . . of a branch of business [was] consigned for disposal to a joint sales office." By the end of the century both coking and soft coal, potash and crude iron became syndicated. By the time of the Russo-Japanese war, cement and textiles had traveled the same road.[21] This kind of organization, dedicated to "extensive reduction of the production, administration, and sales overhead, elimination of ruinous competition and attainment of maximum profit,"[22] was but one of two major approaches to these obvious goals. The other was a combination of raw material sources and manufacturing facilities under one management. Alfred Krupp began acquiring mines and blast furnaces at such a rate in the 1860s ("Krupp buys anything" insisted many envious contemporaries) that the German government in 1874 had to bail out its premier cannonsmith with a loan. Krupp paid his debts promptly and went on buying more selectively in both directions: mines and shipyards.[23] A variety of iron smelters pursued the same quest for control of sources of raw material. When the *Gutehoffnungshütte* of the Haniel family was converted from a family enterprise into a joint stock company in 1873, it produced in its own mines 202,000 tons of the 215,000 tons of iron ore consumed annually by its rolling mills, manufacturing and shipbuilding enterprises.[24]

Cartels practiced a self-regulation that was in the nature of the inherently regulatory institution. Occasional demands for governmental supervision notwithstanding, there was no systematic predisposition on the part of government to encroach on these activities. But the reduction of the number of enterprises and of competition among them to the vanishing point obviously created conditions under which the public powers could assume control any time they chose.

Attempts before 1914 to nationalize electric utilities illustrate both the ease with which state could replace private management and the extent to which bureaucratic rivalries sometimes tended to protect private enterprise from public annexation. It was recognized at an early stage of electrification that the nature of the product ruled out any system under which a consumer could haggle with competing suppliers. Monopoly at some level appeared inevitable. By 1913, furthermore, it became clear that although some four thousand power plants operated in Germany, half of them were so small as to account for a mere 13 percent of consumption, while less than two hundred, owned either by the German General Electric Company (AEG) or the Siemens-Schuckert combine, provided almost 40 percent of Germany's electric supply. Even more important was the startling discovery that a mere 103 of the largest generating sites had the capacity of shutting down the remaining 3,897 and supplying all the electricity German industries and households needed. An earlier proposal by the Association of German Electrical Engineers demanding legislative enactment of a national power grid began to receive wider attention. To contain the specter of private monopoly to which—it was felt—so essential a public service could not be entrusted, the electrical industry lent its support. Walter Rathenau, son of the founder of the AEG, wrote no less than three extended memoranda in which he recommended nationalization to the Prussian government. He criticized the hitherto prevalent bureaucratic attitude which had seen electrical utilities as nothing more than a welcome object of taxation. The federal monopoly, he advised, should be introduced to the Reichstag as a device which would reduce consumer taxes as well as the price of the product. Rathenau argued that state monopolies in transport and federal monopolies in communication constituted successful precedents for his proposal. It was technologically possible to plan the supply of electric current on a national scale, it was economically necessary to provide it at minimum cost, and morally and politically essential to remove such a monopoly-prone commodity from the arbitrary interplay of private interests. Needless to say, he did not propose to place manufacture of appliances and installations under the same regimen. Chancellor and Minister-President Theobald von Bethmann-Hollweg, a country neighbor of Rathenau's estate at Schloss Freienwalde, supported him, but the craft law establishing a German Electric Authority was among the countless unsung victims of World War I. It is significant, however, that this state monopoly, supported by a large manufacturer of installations, was opposed not by business but by bureaucratic and political forces. The states refused to grant yet another regulatory jurisdiction to the Reich, and the conservatives viewed with alarm a measure which would add to the powers and competencies of a democratically elected Reichstag. Not until the promulgation on December 13, 1935, of the law regulating the electrical sector did a German government centralize the industry, but even then only as supervisor of rates, prices, construction, and investment priorities, not as owner or manager.[25]

Obviously the specter of state monopoly did not cause German business to mount the barricades on behalf of free enterprise. There seemed to be considerable predisposition to accept any monopoly if it benefited the interest concerned and if it promised to ameliorate public morale. If one asks whether this particular example reflects a general absence of conflict between government and business as well as a certain submissiveness on the part of the latter, the answer should probably be affirmative. Not that powerful German businessmen paraded as paragons of civic altruism. In a far more clear-cut confrontation of private purse and national policy during World War I, we see in 1915 the head of the Krupp combine rather unenthusiastically and hesitantly embracing the Pan-German annexation program, although its implementation guaranteed him a safe supply of French ore, ascendancy over the French competition, and access to the magnificent nickel deposits of French Caledonia. He was not sure, however, that the program was politically sound, and thence was also bound to ask whether it really was good business. The line between greed and true patriotism was hard to draw. At this level both seemed to depend on each other for sustenance, especially in the case of a firm which had dealt almost exclusively with governments since its founding and which was now producing for just one governmental customer.[26]

One is thus left with the paradox of a vigorous, growing industrial complex, well nourished by the proximity of natural resources, a rapidly growing labor supply, sufficient capital, an impressive reservoir of professional skill, but with a curious proclivity to avoid the risks of an open market and a marked readiness to nestle in the protective lap of a patriarchal government whose structure and spirit antedated the industrial age by several centuries. In view of this it is not surprising that the German Commercial Code of 1897, one of the large legislative blessings of national union, established a uniform corporate structure for the entire country. Under its provisions the general assembly of shareholders was the nominal dominant of a jointly owned enterprise. Continuous supervision on its behalf was exercised by the supervisory council (*Aufsichtsrat*). This council decided the distribution of dividends, and it appointed and dismissed the directors. All of its acts had to be ratified and validated by the general assembly. The German business leader, in other words, was—under the law at least—the docile subject of both government and shareholders.[27]

Yet Germany's captains of industry come through the haze of history as strong men, both in theory and practice. The top executive of a German corporate enterprise, the chairman of its board of directors (*Vorstand*), uniformly believed in the legitimacy of his position "on the basis of what are essentially ultimate values, viz., calling and private property." His self-portrait was shaped by a society whose political ideal had always been embodied in the sovereign rule of monarchs. Accordingly the corporate chief, like his king, was born to his job.[28] Business leadership was his destiny, the exercise of a species of Lutheran "freedom of the Christian man," free to do his duty, free to give full reign to his dynamic capacities.[29] These characteristics and attitudes separated him from even the highest levels of managerial employment. Whatever a manager's task and responsibility, he stood below the leader, of which each enterprise could only have one. This chosen one, marked by fate, occupied also a romantic and charismatic position. At the highest level he began, under Wilhelm II, at any rate, to mingle with court society, on a fairly regular basis if he were a Christian, although the example of the Rathenaus, a Ballin, and a Dernburg indicates that the religious barrier was far from inflexible.[30]

"Born to rule" encompassed more varieties in business than in politics. It could be literally true, as in the case of the Krupps, where Friedrich the founder was succeeded by Alfred the son, and Alfred the son in turn gave way to Friedrich Alfred the grandson. As in the case of a political succession, the rule of daughters created problems. When Bertha succeeded Friedrich Alfred, Friedrich Krupp became Friedrich Krupp Inc., even though all of its shares remained in the hands of the family. This led to a curious application of the commercial code of 1897. The directors ran the business with due deference to the supervisory council, whose decisions in turn must be approved by the shareholders, who consisted of daughter Bertha, her mother, and other members of the family, all of whom for good measure elected a delegate who chaired the supervisory council.[31] The kingpin in this clannish version of a shareholder's democracy became Gustav von Bohlen und Halbach (1870–1950), the young diplomat who married Bertha in 1906 and who was to guide the enterprise through the remainder of Kaiser Wilhelm II's reign, and the Weimar and Nazi eras.

Succession by ability and the capacity to make strategic marriages could propel a man of humble birth into the highest economic spheres of national life. On September 29, 1883, the Friedrich Bayer Chemical Works in Elberfeld hired a young graduate chemist named Carl Duisberg (1861–1935). Twenty-nine years later this son of a small farmer and part-time dyer had become director-general of the enterprise, after moving it to larger quarters and reorganizing it as the Farbenfabrik Leverkusen, and after marrying Friedrich Bayer's niece Johanna. Impressed by the organization of American trusts and challenged by the impending loss of the German dye monopoly in the wake of the First World War, Duisberg planned ceaselessly for an amalgamation in the dye industry which was realized with the founding of the I. G. Farbenindustrie, AG in 1925. Duisberg led this industrial giant until his death ten years later. By that time he had also presided over the Reich Association of German Industry and launched two of his associates into positions of political prominence: Paul Moldenhauer was German minister of finance from 1928 to 1931, Hermann Warmbold served as minister of economic affairs in the last three cabinets of the Weimar Republic.[32]

A third prototype was Paul Reusch (1868–1958), a hybrid between a Krupp and a Duisberg. Thanks to the depression of the 1870s the enterprise which he developed into a variegated agglomerate of mining and manufacturing had made the transition from the family firm founded by Franz and Gerhard Haniel to a joint stock company (Gutehoffnungshütte, Actienverein für Bergbau und Hüttenbetrieb) long before he joined it. Reusch, whose ancestors had all been civil service entrepreneurs—his father administered the state-owned iron foundries of Wasseralfingen and Königsborn in Württemberg—followed their example in the private sector. (In 1921 Gutehoffnungshütte bought his father's old bailiwick.) He joined GHH in the waning years of the nineteenth century to rise to the eminence of major-domo of the Haniel domain whose expansion he supervised until World War II. Unlike von Bohlen and Duisberg he did not marry into the ruling family. Strictly speaking he was only a "manager," a term invariably pronounced with a sneer by the people whose equal Reusch nevertheless became during his unique career. He was GHH's master during the two decades between the wars. After the defeat of 1918, Reusch, like Duisberg, developed his original strategy of survival, in this instance concentration on the export of finished products and the concomitant acquisition of a 51 percent interest in any enterprise promising to strengthen GHH's productive capacities in that sector. He infiltrated existing sales organizations in neutral countries, notably Holland. By this detour he gained access to foreign markets, European and colonial, which in the early 1920s would otherwise remain closed to German firms. Reusch, however, did not die in the saddle. Forced out of his position by the Nazi government, he left his Oberhausen office in 1943 and retired to his native Swabia. Although he survived the war by more than a decade he kept his vow never to return to the Ruhr.[33]

At the very outset this paper emphasized the aristocratic origins of German industrial capitalism. In the changing scene of constant political innovation set in motion by Bismarck, lesser barons followed the example of great magnates and joined ambitious bourgeois on the road to the bank. A recent East German study of the Alvensleben family, after being stripped of its obfuscating polemic language, provides an interesting case study in which a baronial estate owner augments his fortunes by building bridges between the agrarian and industrial spheres. On their estates near Magdeburg the Alvenslebens, an old but not spectacularly wealthy clan, engaged in a succession of food processing ventures from the construction of a sugar refinery in 1846 to a cannery in 1944. Drawn to court by Wilhelm II and raised to the rank of count in 1901, Werner Ludwig Alvo von Alvensleben (1840–1928) and his two sons Hans Bodo and Werner Ulrich eventually parlayed their increasing social luster, together with their limited industrial experience, into leading positions in the food processing, insurance, and real estate sectors of the economy.[34]

Otto von Bismarck, however, remains the most striking example of a lesser noble who transformed political and social success into a vast fortune. His rise from country gentleman to grandee constituted almost as epic an advance as Carl Duisberg's elevation from chemist to dye king. The heir of a nearly bankrupt, modest estate, Bismarck left his descendants what is now "the thirteenth largest property in the *Bundesrepublik*." On the estate itself distilleries, brick kilns, and lumber mills represented industrial supplements to agrarian wealth, whose growth in this case was accelerated by the Iron Chancellor's ability and unfailing willingness to use his office for private gain.[35]

Aristocrats at lower levels also gladly accepted the financial opportunities offered by the industrial age. Their pursuit of profit, their membership in a society of bankers, industrialists, and other giants of the world of finance redounded to the glamour and charisma of business leadership. This relationship introduced the goals and values of aristocratic society, the standards of discipline and order of a government and administration dominated by aristocrats, into the systems on which business and industry based their operations.

The year 1918 and the fall of the monarchy destroyed this identity of goals and methods which had drawn together kaiser and Ruhr magnates. Germany became a democratic republic, but German business remained caught between the theory of the commercial code of 1897 and the practice of autocratic management. The social reforms promised by the National Assembly and embodied in the constitution, notably Article 156 which "subjected private property to the social will,"[36] remained a dead letter. Business leaders continued to live in a world of monarchic values and were bound to view a different political system with feelings ranging from suspicion to antagonism. They stood humbly before a kaiser, but a social democratic president like Friedrich Ebert, who had been a saddler, or a champion of fulfillment of Versailles like Stresemann, son of a brewer and with a Jewish wife, struck them as a cruel travesty of government.

The very real and plausible immediate alienation of the business leader from this new order found a parallel in the equally distressing confusion into which the events of November 1918 plunged the churches, whose role and purpose likewise depended for temporal execution on the workings of the defunct monarchic order.[37] This divergence of values between major operational sectors of society, viz., politics, business, and religion, raises the questions which we must answer before we can pronounce on the nature and life expectancy of revolutions. As far as German history is concerned any exposition of these conflicts should lay to rest a host of simplistic theses which ascribe the fall of the Weimar Republic to such monolithic causes as the peace treaty, the neutrality of the army in times of crisis, economic depression, and/or the questionable loyalty of this or that sector of the civil service.

Nor does the adjustment problem, entrepreneurial autocracy vs. democratic state, once more realistically reduced in accordance with the modest purposes and proportions of this essay, provide the kind of easy answer which even partially explains the fall of the Weimar Republic by big business financing of the Nazi party. The work of Henry A. Turner[38] has called into question the premise that "big business" betrayed German democracy to Hitler. Alfred Hugenberg, whose newspapers, magazines, newsreels and films continually nurtured national paranoia, became in the final analysis just another ineffective rival of the Nazi leader. Heavy industry viewed Weimar, Germany's reduced international role, and disarmament with predictable distaste.[39] The chemical industry took a far more neutral position. (Carl Duisberg was the major fund raiser for Hindenburg's election campaign in 1932.) Politically, above all, big business in Germany spent considerable amounts of money with very little effect.[40] The German People's Party, Gustav Stresemann's successor to the national liberals, an uneasy and intermittent member of the Weimar coalition, became the chief recipient of its largesse. It never grew into a mass party. Severe internal factionalism led to its virtual collapse after Stresemann's death in 1929. The episode confirms one's doubt concerning the ability of the wealthy to manipulate public opinion with money alone.[41] By 1930 big campaign contributors began to give money to various causes, the National Socialists included. Some of their books have now been examined and they fail to establish any clear cause and effect relation between donations from large industrial enterprises and Hitler's rise.

Structurally the crisis of the fourteen-year interregnum between kaiser and führer merely tightened the bolts of the existing corporate system. The growing rigors of survival expanded existing horizontal and vertical concentrations, illustrated by the aforementioned examples of IG and GHH. The territorial losses to France interrupted a production cycle by which Ruhr coal fueled the blast furnaces of Lorraine and half-finished products from the latter in turn fed the finishing industry of the Ruhr. Greater vulnerability of the survivors resulted from the need to acquire new sources of raw materials and the construction or acquisition of more blast furnaces. Since the resulting capital outlay came at a time of crisis or at best uncertainty, tighter organization of the industrial complex became inevitable.[42]

The anticapitalist orientation of some national socialists and their protracted rhetorical excesses against "grabbing capital" and "interest slavery" constituted more serious threats to the corporate status quo than did the Weimar constitution. The new autocratic government which continued to pay lip service to these slogans soon wielded more political power than any of its precursors, and its belligerent foreign policy plunged the economy into a confusion of recovery and crisis. National socialism and expansionism conflicted. The first strove to reconvert corporations into personal partnerships. The needs of the second rendered corporations indispensable. Hovering over both was the rigid commitment of the Third Reich to the so-called leadership principle.

The new corporate law of 1937 brought no clear victory to either side. It abolished control of the shareholders over management, but management remained the collective body it had been under the code of 1897. In the long run the results of the move might have constituted a prelude to nationalization. During the eight intervening years before the second German collapse in 1945, developments never reached that stage. Management presented a balance sheet to an assembly of stockholders stripped of their veto. On the other hand, the corporate leadership assumed certain fixed obligations to make voluntary social contributions. (Without these management could receive no bonus.) Since these payments went to such organizations as the Labor Front, they were in reality another form of taxation. Surveillance of the shareholders and their supervisory council was exchanged for the tacit partnership of the state. Keeping up with public policy became management's first concern. Declaring dividends took on a distinctly secondary significance.[43]

A recent comparison of "West European and American management" concludes that European business leadership depends "excessively" on charisma rather than skill.[44] This applies with a vengeance to Germany. Today German management in general once again exercises effective authority which is subject to no serious challenge from lower echelons. It functions within a structure essentially retrieved from the ruins of the old imperial commercial code except insofar as this code was modified by a new shareholder's law (*Aktiengesetz*) of 1967, according to which all directors are equally accountable. No one among them can either act on his own or be held individually responsible for a specific act or policy. The supervisory council and the general assembly, either abolished or neutralized by Nazi legislation, officiate once again as the titular sovereigns of this extended corporate democracy.[45]

In the Bonn Republic, as under the empire, the structure described in the laws remains at odds with reality. A recent analysis of the relationship between leadership and labor force in industry concluded that workers believe in the legality and the legitimacy of directional authority. This faith is confirmed by a management which partakes of glamour and authority, and which knows how to manipulate and, if necessary, intimidate its constituency. The question whether an industrial organization of this type can coexist with a democratic order is coldly wiped off the blackboard as irrelevant: "Democracy is a political concept which makes no sense in the economy where only expertise prevails."[46]

Leaders of enterprises still profess a calling, they constitute an estate which dwells at the top of the social pyramid and whose work produces achievement of a high moral and creative order. They exemplify "the best in efficiency, proficiency, intention and knowledge." From this follows that, like kings, they are born not made. Business leaders, in the opinion of most Germans connected with the world of affairs, cannot be graduated from business schools.[47] This view is abetted by the greater social heterogeneity which today characterizes the origins of this elite. As indicated earlier it continues to include descendants of princes of the Holy Roman Empire, as well as glorious Prussian names.[48] A Krupp and Siemens also continue to rank high among them, and one of their most conspicuous members is the patriarch of the Klöckner concern, Günther Henle, who, a generation after Gustav von Bohlen und Halbach entered Germany's diplomatic service, married Peter Klöckner's daughter, moved into the industrial sphere as crown-prince by marriage, succeeded to the crown of industrial leadership, and—like von Bohlen und Halbach—has worn it for three decades with great success.[49] But West Germany now also has its Horatio Algers, the electronics magnate Max Grundig, the mail order tycoon Josef Neckermann, and that almost mythical waiter in Munich whose *Wienerwald* restaurants are becoming as familiar to New Yorkers as they have been for years to the eating public of Frankfurt and Hamburg.

As in America the German public derives a distinct lift from the knowledge that one of their numbers has risen to wealth and prominence. In addition, one suddenly realizes that fifty years after the fall of the monarchy, the liberating effect of that revolution is having a delayed action effect on the business world. The relationship between government and business turns out to be permanently determined not by attitudes but by operational realities. No banker and no tycoon ever could be as close a companion to kaiser and chancellor as bankers like Herman Abs and Robert Pferdmenges have been to Konrad Adenauer. And speaking of Adenauer in the dynastic context, no Bismarck married into banking, but *der Alte* did, and so did his favorite daughter Lisbeth. Clearly the rich can today move closer to the seats of power than under the monarchy.[50] Hence only few have gone into politics, even though the Bundestag of today is not the "talk shop" of old, but an unqualified center of might. A man like Günther Henle decided after one term that membership was simply too time-consuming.[51] Some large enterprises like to keep their finger on the pulse by delegating a top manager to the lower house.[52] As a whole the economically powerful simply pursue other avenues of pressure. Trade organizations, notably the Federation of German Industry, can do the job of lobbying full time, while the leaders of the member enterprises tend their growing factories and estates.[53]

The managers of the economic miracle have witnessed great triumphs, and in the economic rather than the military sphere for a change. Life has been better for them than their fathers and grandfathers whom fate seemed to offer only the dismal choice between war and depression. Their happiness has merely been diluted by the fact that the Bonn government, too, likes to keep an eye on them, that a distrustful public does ascribe a good share of Germany's past misfortunes to their machinations and that prosperity elicits a widespread desire for its more extensive distribution.

The Bonn Parliament became the first in German history to pass legislation against cartels, accepting Ludwig Erhard's dictum "that interference with the free working of competition . . . is no less deplorable and harmful when it is exercised on the part of the entrepreneurs than when it is exercised by the state."[54] The law prohibited cartels except among public utilities, financial institutions and in agriculture, which were already regulated. It also exempted coal and steel, subject to the rules laid down by articles 65 and 66 of the treaty establishing the European Coal and Steel Community. The administration of the law and the licensing of agreements which it covered were entrusted to a Federal Cartel Authority.

Equally novel and unprecedented was the codetermination law which the Bundestag passed on January 25, 1952. It applied to all enterprises engaged in mining and in manufacture of iron and steel. On their eleven-man supervisory boards five representatives of labor and five representatives of capital were to be joined by a representative of the public interest.

The board of directors was to include a labor director nominated by the trade unions in consultation with management and labor of the company concerned. Despite his special tasks and his unique appointment process this individual has since 1967 shared the collective responsibilities assigned to all directors by the new shareholders' law. The labor management act of 1952 provided in addition that supervisory boards of all enterprises employing more than five hundred would draw one-third of their membership from the ranks of labor. Four years later codetermination was extended to all holding companies "whose properties included substantial production in coal, iron and steel."[55] Experience has taught those who feared these laws that their apprehensions were groundless. Those who supported them have generally been disappointed. Labor has nowhere played a significant part in running an enterprise.

The cartel law has also been widely damned as ineffective. Critics contend that the tempo of concentration has not slowed and the thrust of consolidation not diminished. Volkswagen/Auto Union purchased NSU, Wankel rotary motor and all, and a competitor disappeared at the very moment it was getting ready to compete. The reconstituted August Thyssen Hütte's pipe manufacture merged with the other giant in the field, Mannesmann. The Ruhrkohle AG is viewed as the restoration of the coal syndicate of the 1890s. Many of the objectors to this purportedly toothless cartel legislation concentrate on the political implications of its weakness. The name of their chief nightmare is Axel Springer, the press tycoon who owns 86 percent of all German tabloids and 27 percent of *all* newspapers. He exemplifies a particularly clear and present danger to freedom of expression, now posed not by the state but by an unhealthy concentration of private economic power.[56]

Despite certain legislative innovations since World War II, then, managerial autocracy and growing concentration of economic power in cartelistic and monopolistic structures have remained constant or increased, unaffected by the genuine representative tendencies of political life, perhaps—in fact—even aided and abetted by them. Thus the unchanging corporate world would appear to be out of step with the changing political universe in the same manner in which an unchanging social structure, according to Ralf Dahrendorf, has failed to keep pace with the democratic experiments of two German republics.

Dahrendorf ascribes this dichotomy largely to the primacy of foreign policy. ("The German question of reunification seems more important than the German question of educational opportunity.")[57] Other students of German institutions feel that it reflects things as they are and should be. They often assert that as far back as 1897, laws governing business

structures reflected political ideologies completely irrelevant to the purpose of such legislation.[58] This point of view insists that collective responsibility as decreed by the shareholders' law of 1967 remains impractical.
Responsibility must be shouldered in the final analysis by one man at the
top, or it can be divided on technical grounds (most simply between
engineering and sales, for instance), in which latter case specific duties
again become associated with specific individuals. It therefore makes no
sense to them to hold the sales manager responsible for actions of the
engineering division. This point of view either leads to the conclusion
cited above, that political democracy simply provides no answer to the
tasks and challenges facing corporations, or it opts for a kind of American
presidential system which is to tackle the work in a collegiate fashion, but
assign ultimate responsibility to one chief executive.

This view obviously rejects codetermination in any form by labor as
well as by the public, insisting that people do not think, and therefore
cannot lead, in groups.[59] Faced, however, by a law, no matter how unrealistic, and a world in which government regulation of business will
continue, the analysis must find a way out of this dilemma between legislative theory and corporate practice. This turns out to be a difficult if not
hopeless task. Some seek refuge in an application of presidential democracy, striving to combine "the advantages of a libertarian, democratic
basic structure with the advantages of elements of authoritarian leadership" claiming thus to separate powers without eroding them. In practice
such a solution advocates that the components of a concern be related
to each other by a holding company whose head makes general policy
while delegating specific tasks and responsibilities to a series of market-
and product-oriented enterprises which pursue their objectives autono-
mously.[60] Others conclude first that the tried representative systems have
not proved themselves. Thus committees of shareholders have failed to
demonstrate a willingness, on the part of the small investor in particular,
to accept the burdens of participation. Representation of the public interest remains to them a theoretical ideal simply because the public interest
has no clearly identifiable representative or exponent.[61] Yet the present
society seems to demand a taming of private economic interests by the
public interest. One answer offered is an institution in which enterprise,
labor, and public interest meet on equal terms, suggesting as an example
a close look at the French *Conseil économique et social*.[62]

At this juncture the defenders of a corporate status quo impervious to
democratization touch base with those who advocate stronger measures
against conglomerations of economic power. In a recent position paper
this latter school of thought unequivocally assigns to the state the task of

aligning "economic concentrations with optimal exploitation of material and technological resources and the preservation of a competitive economy."[63]

At the end of the tour, therefore, salvation from increasingly powerful monarchically conditioned corporate institutions, with their imperviousness to the persistent representative thrust of German politics, is offered by a public interest whose equally absolute guardian remains the state. Either choice presents a walled city.

Such a conclusion requires a coda. This paper reviews the problems of the business structures of one nation. But many of the enterprises which engaged our attention have long jumped the border. The GHH affiliate MAN sells French trucks in Germany and through its French partner markets German trucks in France. Farbwerke Hoechst, one of the three giants surviving the postwar deconcentration of I. G. Farben AG, has bought into a large French chemical enterprise, each firm sending two members to the board meetings of the other. And to those haunted by the specter of national monopoly, one may point to the 1964 merger of the two European giants in the photo industry, AGFA and Gevaert. The problem of controlling combinations in restraint of trade has likewise become international. Accordingly the coordination of development in various sectors of a national culture will soon be complicated by a replay of this dilemma in the international sphere.

International corporations face a number of rather specific difficulties. Language barriers must not be underrated, for interpreters are not welcome at board meetings. Painful memories of the past intrude even where international mergers offer profits. Conceptual, hierarchic, and methodological differences of doing business intrude everywhere as part of the amorphous complex of cultural differences, but have not been meaningfully analyzed, still less resolved.[64]

After we have identified the present identity crisis of the autocratic German corporate system in a democratic state, therefore, we must not fail to recognize that an adjustment in the national sphere is but one task the system faces. At the same time it must increasingly adjust its methods and its governance to an ongoing operational partnership with the corporate structures of other nations.

NOTES

1. That this separation was more theoretical than practical and did not prevent conflicts between the spheres, nor protect princely property from public claims can be documented in a host of ways. Two derived from this twilight zone between great powers and nonentities may suffice: W. Renner, "Das Familien Fideikommiss des

kurfürstlich-hessischen Hauses . . . ," *Zeitschrift des Vereins für hessische Geschichte und Landeskunde*, n.s. 23 (1905), pp. 94–109; Walter Müller, *Die Geschichte des Domänenstreites im Herzogtum Nassau (1806–1866)* (Frankfurt am Main, 1929), esp. pp. 99–160.

2. E.g. W. O. Henderson, *The State and the Industrial Revolution in Prussia* (Liverpool, 1958); Ulrich Peter Ritter, *Die Rolle des Staates in den Frühstadien der Industrialisierung: die Preussische Industrieförderung in der ersten Hälfte des 19. Jahrhunderts*, Volkswirtschaftliche Schriften, vol. 60 (Berlin, 1961); Wolfgang Zorn, "Preussischer Staat und Rheinische Wirtschaft," in *Landschaft und Geschichte, Festschrift für Franz Petri zu seinem 65. Geburtstag* . . . (Bonn, 1970), pp. 552–60; Ernst Klein, "Der Staat als Unternehmer im Saarländischen Steinkohlenbergbau 1750–1850," *Vierteljahrsschrift für Sozial- und Wirt-schaftsgeschichte*, 57 (1970), pp. 323–49.

3. Through a rather cursory tour d'horizon in *Kleine Wirtschaftsund Sozialgeschichte Bayerns 1800–1933*, Bayerische Heimatforschung, heft 14 (München-Pasing, 1962), and through a detailed study of a part of the whole in *Handels- und Industriegeschichte Bayerisch-Schwabens 1648–1870* . . . , Veröffentlichungen der Schwäbischen Forschungsgemeinschaft bei der Kommission für Bayerische Landesgeschichte, reihe 1, band 6 (Augsburg, 1961).

4. Wolfram Fischer, *Der Staat und die Anfänge der Industrialisierung in Baden 1800–1850*, vol. 1 (Berlin, 1962) and "Ansätze zur Industrialisierung in Baden," *Vierteljahrsschrift für Sozial- und Wirtschaftsgeschicte*, 47 (1960), pp. 186–231.

5. Helen P. Liebel, "Der Beamte als Unternehmertypus in den Anfangsstadien der Industrialisierung . . ." in *Entstehung und Wandel der modernen Gesellschaft, Festschrift für Hans Rosenberg zum 65. Geburtstag* (Berlin, 1970), esp. pp. 221–25.

6. The Princes of Liechtenstein embody an unusual combination of both worlds. On the one hand they have retained a sovereign position, on the other hand their landholdings in pre-Czechoslovak Bohemia were 17 times as large as their principality.

7. Cf. Heinz Gollwitzer, *Die Standesherren. Die politische und gesellschaftliche Stellung der Mediatisierten, 1815–1918* . . . , 2d. ed. (Göttingen, 1964), pp. 254–55; Fred Lübbecke, *Das Palais Thurn und Taxis zu Frankfurt am Main* (Frankfurt am Main, 1955), pp. 413–54; Bernt Angelmann, *Die Macht am Rhein*, vol. 1 (Munich, 1968), pp. 28–61.

8. Cf. Eberhard Czichon, *Der Bankier und die Macht* (Cologne, 1970), pp. 40–50.

9. Gollwitzer, *Die Standesherren*, pp. 256–57.

10. Engelmann, *Die Macht am Rhein*, pp. 61–85.

11. Peter Brügge, *Die Reichen in Deutschland* (Frankfurt am Main, 1966), pp. 96–107.

12. Friedrich Zunkel, *Der Rheinisch-Westfälische Unternehmer 1834–1879. Ein Beitrag zur Geschichte des Deutschen Bürgertums* . . . , Dortmunder Schriften zur Sozialforschung, vol. 19 (Cologne, 1962), pp. 28–29. For a suggestive comparison with France consult J. Lambert-Dansette, "Le patronat du Nord. Sa période triomphante (1830–1880)," *Bulletin de la Société d'Histoire Moderne*, vol. 14, no. 18 (1971), pp. 2–13.

13. Zunkel, *Der Rheinisch-Westfählische Unternehmer*, pp. 218–29; Helmuth Boehme, *Deutschlands Weg zur Grossmacht* . . . (Cologne, 1966), pp. 116–229.

14. Donald S. Hoffman, "Railways and Railway Politics in South Germany: Defensive Particularism at the State Level, 1835–1870" (Ph.D. diss., University of Delaware, 1969).

15. Karl Stieler, *Die deutschen Eisenbahnen unter der alten und der neuen Reichsverfassung*, Tübinger Abhandlungen zum öffentlichen Recht, vol. 1 (Stuttgart, 1924), pp. 9–10.

16. Gordon R. Morck, "The Prussian Railway Scandal of 1873: Economics and Politics in the German Empire," *European Studies Review*, vol. 1 (1971), p. 43.

17. Wolfgang Zorn, "Wirtschafts- und Sozialgeschichtliche Zusammenhänge der Deutschen Reichsgründungszeit (1850–1879)," *Historische Zeitschrift*, vol. 197, (1963), pp. 331–32; on 1866 as a grand departure in the social and economic history of Hanover, see Ernst Pitz, "Deutschland und Hannover im Jahre 1866," *Niedersächsisches Jahrbuch für Landesgeschichte*, vol. 38 (1966), pp. 85–158.

18. Boehme, *Deutschlands Weg zur Grossmacht*, p. 9.

19. As quoted approvingly in Ralf Dahrendorf, *Society and Democracy in Germany*, paperback ed. (New York, 1969), p. 33.

20. "The Structure of Enterprise in the Nineteenth Century: The Case of Britain and Germany," in *The Rise of Capitalism* (New York, 1966), pp. 99–111; also Wolfram Fischer, "Das Verhältnis von Staat und Wirtschaft in Deutschland am Beginn der Industrialisierung," *Kyklos*, vol. 14 (1961), pp. 337–63.

21. Erich Maschke, *Grundzüge der Deutschen Kartellgeschichte bis 1914*, Vortragsreihe der Gesellschaft für Westfälische Wirtschaftsgeschichte e.V. Dortmund, heft 10, (Dortmund, 1964), pp. 19–29.

22. *Ibid.*, p. 33.

23. Willi A. Boelcke, ed., *Krupp und die Hohenzollern in Dokumenten . . .* (Frankurt am Main, 1970), pp. 59, 101–103.

24. Erich Maschke, *Es entsteht ein Konzern. Paul Reusch und die GHH (Tübingen,* 1969), pp. 23–36.

25. Helga Nussbaum, "Versuche zur reichsgesetzlichen Regelung der Deutschen Elektrizitätswirtschaft und zu ihrer Überführung in Reichseigentum, 1909 bis 1914," *Jahrbuch für Wirtschaftsgeschichte* (1968), vol. 2, pp. 117–204.

26. Boelcke, *Krupp und die Hohenzollern*, pp. 232–35. For the document embodying his views, see pp. 249–53. But note the dissent of one of Krupp's directors Wilhelm Mühlon who not only left Krupp but Germany for a temporary exile in Switzerland. Cf., Martin Vogt's review of Boelcke's book in *Historische Zeitschrift*, vol. 213 (1971), p. 441.

27. Horst Steinmann, *Das Grossunternehmen im Interessenkonflikt . . .* (Stuttgart, 1969), pp. 15–24.

28. H. van der Haas, *The Enterprise in Transition. An Analysis of European and American Practice* (London, 1967), p. 83.

29. Cf., David Granick, *The European Executive* (New York, 1962), pp. 61–62.

30. Lamar Cecil, *Albert Ballin, Business and Politics in Imperial Germany, 1888–1918* (Princeton, 1967), pp. 98–99.

31. Boelcke, *Krupp und die Hohenzollern*, p. 177.

32. Heike Etzold, "Carl Duisberg—vom stellungslosen Chemiker an die Spitze der I. G. Farbenindustrie AG," *Jahrbuch für Wirtschaftsgeschichte* (1966), vol. 3, pp. 196–218. See in the same issue of the *Jahrbuch* the text of "Die Duisberg Denkschrift zur Vereinigung der deutschen Farbenfabriken aus dem Jahre 1915," pp. 236–70. For the most recent West German Duisberg biography, consult Joachim Flechtner, *Carl Duisberg, vom Chemiker zum Wirtschaftsführer* (Düsseldorf, 1961).

33. Maschke, *Es entsteht ein Konzern, passim.*

34. Herbert Seiffert, "Die Entwicklung der Familie von Alvensleben zu Junkerindustriellen," *Jahrbuch für Wirtschaftsgeschichte* (1963), vol. 4, pp. 209–243.

35. Alfred Vagts, "Bismarck's fortune," *Central European History*, vol. 1 (1968), pp. 203–232.

36. Gerhard Anschütz, *Die Verfassung des Deutschen Reichs vom 11 August 1919*, 14th ed. (Berlin, 1933), pp. 725–29.

37. Claus Motschmann, *Evangelische Kirche und Preussischer Staat in den Anfängen der Weimarer Republik, Möglichkeiten und Grenzen ihrer Zusammenarbeit* (Historische Studien, heft 413) (Lübeck, 1969), *passim*.

38. Henry A. Turner, "Emil Kirdorf and the Nazi Party," *Central European History*, vol. 1 (1968), pp. 324–44, and for a careful and qualified outline of the general problem: "Big Business and the Rise of Hitler," *American Historical Review*, vol. 75 (1969), pp. 56–70.

39. But, here too, with qualifications, cf., Gerald D. Feldmann, "German Business between War and Revolution. The Origins of the Stinnes-Legien Agreement," in the *Rosenberg Festschrift*, pp. 312–41.

40. Henry A. Turner, "The *Ruhrlade*, Secret Cabinet of Heavy Industry in the Weimar Republic," *Central European History*, 3 (1970), 228.

41. Cf. the full treatment of the DVP as the political organization of "heavy industry and banking" by Lothar Döhm, *Politik und Interesse. Die Interessenstruktur der Deutschen Volkspartei*, Marburger Abhandlungen zur politischen Wissenschaft, vol. 16 (Meisenheim am Glan, 1970), esp. pp. 111–129, 424–26.

42. See a contemporary analysis in Arnold Tross, "Ursachen und Wirkungen der Zusammenschlussbewegungen in der deutschen Eisenindustrie," *Archiv für Sozialwissenschaft und Sozialpolitik*, 54 (1925), 716–34.

43. Arthur Schweitzer, *Big Business in the Third Reich* (Bloomington, 1964), pp. 256–61.

44. Ernst Dale, "West European and American Management. A Comparative Analysis," in *Betriebswirtschaftliche Forschung in internationaler Sicht. Festschrift für Erich Kosiol zum 70. Geburtstag* (Berlin, 1969), pp. 169–78.

45. Heinz Hartmann, *Authority and Organization in German Management* (Princeton, 1959), pp. 16–23.

46. Horst Bosetzky, *Grundzüge einer Soziologie der Industrieverwaltung. Möglichkeiten und Grenzen der Betrachtung des industriellen Grossbetriebs als bürokratische Organisation* (Stuttgart, 1970), pp. 276–316.

47. Hartmann, *Authority and Organization*, pp. 28–33, 166–73.

48. Engelmann, *Die Macht am Rhein*, pp. 269–83.

49. Günter Henle, *Three Spheres, a Life in Politics, Business and Music* (Chicago, 1971), esp. pp. 31–91.

50. They have made limited use of these possibilities.

51. Henle, *Three Spheres*, pp. 91–100.

52. For a list of the most conspicuous, see Englemann, *Die Macht am Rhein*, pp. 36–37.

53. Cf., Gerard Braunthal, *The Federation of German Industry in Politics* (Ithaca, N.Y., 1965), pp. 150–231.

54. Quoted in Theodore F. Marburg, "Government and Business in Germany: Public Policy toward Cartels," *Business History Review*, vol. 38 (1964), p. 90.

55. Günter Apel, *Mitbestimmung; Grundlagen, Wege, Ziele*, Sammlung Dialog, vol. 32 (Munich, 1969), p. 107.

56. Note especially the work of Helmut Arndt (ed.), *Die Konzentration in der Wirtschaft*, Schriften des Vereins für Sozialpolitik, N.F. vol. 20 (Berlin, 1960), pp. 125, 217, 223–25, 280–87, 292–300, 390–400, 1718–19 and his subsequent reflections in Dieter Grosser, ed., *Konzentration ohne Kontrolle* (Cologne, 1969), pp. 26–61.

57. Dahrendorf, *Society and Democracy in Germany*, p. 77.

58. Cf. note 46 above.

59. Friedrich Hoffmann, *Organisation der Führungsgruppe* (Betriebswirtschaftliche Studien, heft 31) (Berlin, 1969), pp. 58–72, 93–103, 113–19.

60. *Ibid.*, pp. 165–72.

61. Cf., O. von Nell-Breuning, "Von der Mitbestimmung zur Unternehmerverfassung," *Zeitschrift für betriebswissenschaftliche Forschung*, vol. 16 (1961), p. 672.

62. Steinmann, *Das Grossunternehmen im Interessenkonflikt*, pp. 298–301.

63. Grosser, *Konzentration ohne Kontrolle*, pp. 16–17.

64. For a beginning see Werner J. Feld, *Transnational Business, Collaboration among Common Market Countries. Its Implication for Political Integration*, Praeger Special Studies in International Economics and Development (New York, 1970), esp. pp. 29–30, 33–51.

Comment

Wolfram Fischer

My comments on Professor Schmitt's paper will be on three levels: (1) the content, (2) the method, and (3) the tone or style. I will also add some remarks aimed at complementing and correcting some of his statements.

1. The paper is less oriented to the evolution of management structures of big business in Germany than to the relationship of business and politics; this approach is tempting in the German case, but nevertheless somewhat outside the scope of our conference. Professor Schmitt repeats the often stated "community of interest between a conservative state and liberal capitalism" during the *Kaiserreich* and asserts that this "nurtured and preserved a dilemma from which neither was to find an exit." Thus, "the departure of Wilhelm II was succeeded by many changes of government, but no change of heart." He even observes, entering the present Germany, "that a succession of new constitutions has left other large areas of German life remarkably unaffected." I am enticed at this point to ask him poignantly which Germany he has recently entered, and whether he refers to East Germany, where, indeed, the commanding posts in politics and industry are closely interrelated.

Professor Schmitt asks, "What distinctive features characterize the beginning of large industrial enterprise and which of them have persisted to the present?" His answer is not correspondingly straightforward, but seems to go in two different directions. On the one hand, he points to the early dependence of German firms on banks and technical expertise which led to an "alliance of enterprise, capital, and skill" and produced "the basic corporate trinity" which marked "German business life from the outset." On the other hand, he stresses the authoritarian character of the "corporate chief" who, "like his king, was born to his job" and "occupied also a romantic and charismatic position." Due to its aristocratic beginnings, "the goals and values of aristocratic society, the standards of discipline and order of government and administration dominated by aristocrats" were introduced "into the system on which business and industry based their operations." Even during the Weimar Republic, "Business leaders continued to live in a world of monarchic values" which caused them to view not only the Social Democratic President Friedrich Ebert, but also the Foreign Minister Stresemann, "son of a brewer and with a Jewish wife . . . as a cruel travesty of government." Nevertheless, later he notes that Stresemann's liberal party *Deutsche Volkspartei* (and not the monarchistic *Deutschnationale Partei* or the authoritarian Nazis), "became the chief recipient of its largesse."

The same contradiction prevails as Schmitt enters postwar West Germany. He seems to concur with a recent study which asserts that European business leadership depends "excessively on charisma, rather than skill," but this does not prevent him from relying on a witness who thinks that democratic principles do not make sense in the economy "where only expertise prevails." I can only conclude from this that expertise for him is not an outcome of skill but of charisma. Still in postwar Germany business leaders, like kings, "are born, not made," but the relationship between government and business now "turns out to be not permanently determined by attitudes but by operational realities." While "managerial autocracy and growing concentration of economic power in cartelistic and monopolistic structures has remained constant or increased," the "unchanging corporate world" of today is confronted with an "identity crisis" because it is out of tune with the democratic form of government and has, at the same time, to adapt itself "to an ongoing operational partnership with the corporate structures of other nations."

2. I cannot reconcile these statements without analyzing the method Professor Schmitt applies to his essay. He seems to take a bird's eye view of 150 years of German history—but the bird, to protect himself against the sparkling of a fully illuminated object, wears selective glasses through which only some of the many beams can penetrate. Thus, he gets a selective picture which he takes for the whole. I would suggest that he should dive deeper to get closer to the subject; get rid of his glasses and carry some scientific instruments which allow him to test his suppositions. Economic history has recently developed some such instruments. One is statistics; another, closely related, is economic analysis. But even if one cannot or will not apply them, the long-established historical method of sorting out facts—to evaluate them and to estimate their relationships and impacts—would have had a sobering effect, even if it would have shown, as I believe, that the German "corporate world" is more complex and, therefore, more puzzling than the inconsistencies the author has run into unwittingly. To summarize: a more rational, argumentative approach which carefully states its assumptions and method would not have led to a simpler, clear-cut result, but could have been tested and would have shifted the remaining inconsistencies from the author's mind—where they ought not to be—to the ambiguous nature of a complex world where they rest until a scientific mind comes to unravel them through controllable, rational explanation.

3. This would also have afforded a different style and tone in the paper, less impressionistic and subjective, perhaps, though not necessarily less elegant, but more balanced and subtle. The language of scientific analysis usually is sober, but wit can be reconciled with argument, analysis with brilliance. In this paper, they are not.

4. It is impossible to correct in a short space the distortions which the paper has presented. Let me just indicate the way in which it could be done: (a) the use of statistics would have proven that big business in Germany, though growing for more than one hundred years, has not yet dominated the German economy. To an astonishing degree, middle-scale and small-scale business has remained viable, even vigorous, and government more often than not has tried to strengthen the industrial middle class against big business. Statistics also display an enormous change in the degree and nature of concentration, cartelization, and the relative weight of industrial sectors;[1] (b) macro-economic analysis would show some of the reasons for this high flexibility in German industry which probably is a major source of its continuing strength despite major political catastrophes;[2] (c) these findings then have to be reconciled with the statements of Professor Schmitt and others about the persisting features of German business leadership (like autocratic management, the influence of aristocratic and bureaucratic patterns, the cartel-orientation, etc.).[3] I do not deny that such persisting features exist, but their importance has to be evaluated as against other, equally persistent, features (employment of scientific and technological experts at top levels of management, close links to banks but also high dependence on self-financing, the endurance of family enterprises like Klöckner, Röchling, and until recently, Krupp) and those changing characteristics, which also can be observed (centralizing versus decentralizing forces, formalization of management structure, horizontal versus vertical centralization, technology-oriented versus finance-oriented business organizations). Micro-economic analysis is necessary to achieve this evaluation and assign each of these conflicting features its appropriate rank. Business history in Germany has not, it is true, made available a sufficiently detailed study of business organization and management to do this job fully, but the material on hand suggests a much greater variety of behavior and values than Professor Schmitt assumes. From the truly "autocratic" philosophy and leadership of the King of the Saar, Freiherr von Stumm-Halberg, to the equally consistent liberal-democratic leadership style of the founder of the Stuttgart-based concern for electrical and automotive appliances, Robert Bosch, a broad spectrum of management behavior is discernible[4] in which the pioneers of codetermination of the workers should not be forgotten.[5] Here, an additional methodological warning seems necessary: historians as well as

sociologists have tended to give too much weight to industrialists' opinions about themselves and have done too little research into their actual behavior. Some discrepancies can be observed. German tycoons (like, I assume, others) like to see themselves as heroes. They seldom are. Often, particularly in old age, they deceive themselves about their leadership qualities. Often they head an enterprise which is managed by a team of others. Co-operation was widely introduced while the man on the top still believed he ran a one-man show. In any case, truly autocratic leadership seldom survived the founder of an enterprise. The painstaking research of Jürgen Kocka into the management structure of the Siemens firms has revealed that even Werner Siemens, a man of undisputed capabilities, was not able to run his growing enterprise during the last twenty years of his life as he believed himself able to do.[6] And the thoroughgoing changes in organization, structure, and control under the chairmanship of his two succeeding sons show what dramatic changes toward decentralization, internal competition, and informal team management were possible even before 1914, while toward the outside world the image of a family business was kept alive. A comparison of Siemens with its main competitor, Emil Rathenau's German Edison Co. (later Allgemeine Elektrizitätsgesellschaft—AEG) reveals that even in the same branch, the leading enterprises could be run on quite different principles.[7] Similar insight could come from a comparison of the Gutehoffnunshütte with Krupp or from one between the Thyssen and Stinnes enterprises. Neither should scholars allow themselves to be deceived by the opinions top managers give today on education for management. While they seem to assert that business leadership cannot be learned at business schools—and no one would contest that a business school education alone will not suffice—statistics of the education of German top managers show that big enterprises rely more and more for their young managers on universities rather than on apprenticeship and self-made careers. A growing percentage of top managers hold degrees either in business administration, economics, law, engineering, or the sciences.

In many respects German big business management displays features which can be detected in many countries: merit and proven ability tend to replace connections (family or otherwise). The management structure becomes diversified. Many large corporations are no longer even formally headed by a *Generaldirektor* but by a group of equals who chair in turn; hierarchical structures are replaced by collegial, cooperative, or competitive organizations. The turnover of top managers is faster—a German worker today is better protected in his job than a *Generaldirektor* who can be replaced any time (though usually with a good pension). It is often true that the man at the top often still likes to see himself as the autocrat, but the next day he can be fired. (Lotz of Volkswagen, Hahnemann of

BHW and Vogelsang of Krupp are only the most recent examples.) Styles differ from branch to branch, from firm to firm, and from person to person as they always have done. Disputes in top management are more widely known nowadays than they were fifty years ago, but they have been going on as long as big business has existed. Strong men fought each other over all major questions of business organization and strategy; the winner of today could be the loser of tomorrow.

To summaraize, the German "corporate world" is not and never has been solely a haven for princes, landed or moneyed. Princes had a good share in business leadership as they had in other European countries; so had Jews (until 1933), merchants, bankers, inventors, chemists, lawyers, and civil servants. Business organization has been flexible and has adapted itself to very different conditions; it never has been—again, as in other countries—truly "democratic," nor is it likely to become so in the near future. The organizational pattern changes with the size, the branch and the style of the firm, but generally it has tended to become more diversified, formalized, and sophisticated. This is the price of economic progress; it has to be paid for as in other major industrial countries. But a stringent comparison of its elements would show, I strongly believe, relatively few characteristics which could be related to the political upheavals of the country. This is not to deny the enormity of the problems created for German business by these upheavals and catastrophes. In sharp contrast to Professor Schmitt, however, I feel that many if not most of the major features of German big business would have developed even if we had had a different political history. Their emergence came—not as a result of political factors—but in response to technological, economic, and social requirements.

NOTES

1. For a more detailed analysis, see Wolfram Fischer and Peter Czada, *Wandlungen in der Deutschen Industriestruktur im 20. Jahrhundert. Ein statistischdeskriptiver Ansatz.* In: *Entstehung und Wandel der modernen Gesellschaft.* Festschrift für Hans R. Rosenberg (Berlin, 1970), pp. 116–65.

2. Some such analysis has been conducted by W. G. Hoffman in *Das Wachstum der Deutschen Wirtschaft seit 1850* (Berlin, Heidelberg, New York, 1965) and several branch and regional analyses conducted by Hoffmann and his pupils (König, Müeller, Hesse, etc.) and mainly published in the *Seitschrift für die gesamte Stattswissenshaft* since 1960.

3. This is maintained also by H. Hartmann, *Authority and Organization in German Management* (Princeton, N.J., 1959) and in a comparison with American firms in Germany by the same author, H. Hartmann, *Amerikanische Firmen in Deutschland* (Köln n. Opladen, 1963).

4. For Stumm, see F. Hellwig, *Karl Ferdinand Frhr. von Stumm-Halberg* (Heidelberg/Saarbrücken, 1936). For Bosch, see Th. Heuss, *Robert Bosch* (Tübingen, 1955).

5. See, H. J. Teuteberg, *Geschichte der industriellen Mitbestimmung in Deutschland. Ursprung und Entwicklung ihrer Vorläuger im Dekken und in der Wirklichkeit des 19. Jahhunderts* (Tübingen, 1961).

6. J. Kocka, *Unternehmensverwaltung und Angestelltenschaft am Beispiel Siemens 1847–1914. Zum Verhältnis von Kapitalismus und Bürokratie in der deutschen Industrialisierung*, Stuttgart, 1969. An English summary of this rather lengthy book is to be found in J. Kocka, "Family and Bureaucracy in German Industrial Management, 1850–1914; Seminars in Comparative Perspective," *Business History Review*, vol. 45, no. 2 (1971), pp. 133–56.

7. There is no study of *AEG* which could be compared to Kocka, and due to the lack of sources, there very likely will never be one, but cf. E. Pinner, *Emil Rathenau und das Elektrische Zeitalter* (Leipzig, 1918) and A. Riedler, *Emil Rathenau und das Werden der Grosswirtschaft* (Berlin, 1916).

5. Managerial Structures in France

JAMES M. LAUX

Whatever else one may say about French industry in the twentieth century, it has grown quite rapidly. On a per capita basis, French industrial production expanded faster than that of Germany, Britain, or the United States from 1901 to 1913. From 1913 to 1929 its growth was exceeded by the United States, but it recorded a considerable advantage over Britain and Germany. But in the 1930s the French performance was the poorest of these four and it fell further behind during the Second World War. Since the late 1940s, when postwar recovery was achieved on the Continent, French per capita growth seems to have slightly exceeded West Germany's, considerably surpassed that of Britain and the United States, but failed to keep up with that of Italy. Those who a few years ago referred to the French economy as sick seem to have been hypnotized by the bad years from 1931 to 1945 and paid little attention to the thirty-five years of expansion ending in 1930 and then the resumption of this advance in the late 1940s. In judging the performance of French industry we should not let fifteen years of stagnation outweigh sixty years of growth.

So, for all the criticism, both domestic and foreign, directed against the French government's economic policies and against French businessmen, the over-all record suggests that they must have been doing something right. International comparisons of national labor productivity for 1960 indicate figures for France that are about the same as for Germany and Britain, but all these are below the United States figures.

A common practice among American observers of the twentieth-century French economy and French businessmen has been to compare their practices with those in the United States, find that they operate somewhat differently, and assume that French practices are quite unique, if not exotic, and that they represent a stubborn avoidance of the correct path leading to industrial growth and affluence, that is, the American one. I have the impression, however, that the operation of the French economy and the attitudes of French businessmen are not very different from the situation in the rest of western and central Europe, including Britain. Comparisons by Americans with the United States have tended to highlight what appear to be French idiosyncrasies, while comparisons with Germany, Italy, Britain, and the smaller industrial countries may indicate that these peculiarities really are rather typical of western and central Europe generally. Perhaps the other papers presented at this conference will have some relevance to this question. Nevertheless, my task, if I understand it correctly, is once again to compare France with America, or with a number of hypotheses drawn from American experience.[1]

I will examine first the present structure of French industry, using the scheme found in Professor Chandler's 1969 article in the *Business History Review*.[2] He divides American manufacturing firms in 1963 into groups according to the concentration of production in a few large companies, basing this on solid statistical information. My impressions of French industry are just that, impressions, and should be considered as hypotheses.[3] The two are compared in Table 1.

TABLE 1

PRODUCTIVITY CONCENTRATION IN THE UNITED STATES AND FRANCE

Concentration	United States	France
Significantly concentrated	Stone, clay, and glass Petroleum Chemicals Primary metals Electrical machinery Transport equipment Instruments Tobacco	Stone, clay, and glass Petroleum Chemicals Primary metals Electrical machinery Transport equipment Tobacco
Some concentration	Textiles Paper Fabricated metals Machinery Food	Textiles Paper Machinery Publishing and printing Instruments Food
Little concentration	Leather Publishing and printing Lumber and wood Furniture Apparel	Fabricated metals Leather Lumber and wood Furniture Apparel

If the French list comes close to reality, and I have the most doubt about the placement of instruments, publishing and printing, and fabricated metals, then the manufacturing industries of the two countries seem to have much in common. In France, as in the United States, the highly concentrated industries tend to be those that are technologically complex. An exception, tobacco, has been a government monopoly in France since 1811. In the French case this concentration was achieved in a somewhat different manner than in the United States. In some industries such as glass and rubber, the concentration probably came earlier. In chemicals and electrical equipment the French industries concentrated later but may have gone further than the Americans in the last few years.

One of the most striking differences is that the wave of mergers in the United States around 1900 had no close parallel in France. To explain this dissimilarity, I would suggest that two factors which were causal in the American experience did not operate strongly in France at that time. Firstly, markets for the products of technologically advanced products were not rigorously competitive. Sometimes competition was attenuated by the activity of ententes or pools that really worked, as in the iron and steel or chemical industries. Often it was affected by a disinclination to force competitors to the wall of bankruptcy. And perhaps most pervasive was a general ethos that the survival of the firm as an independent entity had a higher priority than maximizing profits, an attitude that lay behind a live and let live position. Von der Haas has called this reduced emphasis on competition in Europe a situation of negotiated rather than competitive markets. A second difference with the American experience was that French owners and managers of manufacturing firms paid less attention to marketing. Bemused by the problems of design and production, they paid less heed to the chore of marketing and left it to their less able subordinates. So, with some exceptions, we do not see French manufacturers expanding their activities and concentrating their industries by a policy of forward integration.

Chandler finds that the general scheme of growth for major firms in the United States was first to integrate and then diversify, with most of the diversification coming after the First World War.[4] In France there are some major examples of integration and diversification occurring at about the same time, and before 1914. Three might be mentioned: Schneider, Saint-Gobain, and Pechiney.

In 1836, the Schneider brothers took over an iron smelter and cannon foundry at Le Creusot that had been established in 1782 but had experienced serious financial problems after 1815. The Schneiders' strategy was to turn the enterprise's resources toward new industrial products—locomotives, steam engines for factories and ships, and, before long, small iron vessels and structural shapes. It moved easily into the manufacture of armor plate in the 1850s. Meanwhile the firm also integrated backward, acquiring more coal and iron mines and establishing a plant for refractory products. It adopted the new methods of steelmaking in the 1860s, at first for its railway equipment and steam engines. In the 1880s it began artillery manufacturing on a big scale and did even more with armor plate, where it developed special alloy steels. In the last two decades of the nineteenth century the firm made less of its own iron, moved further into fabricated products, and diversified into lines such as larger naval vessels (at Bordeaux), and especially electrical equipment. Thereafter, in the period before the First World War, Schneider expanded in these product areas, in armaments with torpedoes, shell casings, and optical instruments; in machinery with machine tools, Diesel engines, refrigeration equipment, even buses; and in electricity and a widening range of products. Quite diversified before 1914, Schneider's development parallels Krupp and Vickers much more than that of any American firm. The concern had establishments in various parts of France which sometimes were parts of the mother firm but frequently remained as legally distinct enterprises. The details of this company's diversification strategy and its structure to manage its activities have never been closely examined, to my knowledge. One might speculate that it found the national market actually and potentially too small for it to remain narrowly specialized in heavy iron and steel equipment. To keep its capital and technical staff employed, especially after the railway network approached completion, it looked for new lines of production with a high growth potential.

The Saint-Gobain glass company dates back to Louis XIV. Early in the nineteenth century it integrated backward and entered soda manufacturing so as to assure itself of a critical raw material. It already was the largest French producer of chemicals when in 1872 it moved further into this industry by merging with the second largest chemical firm so as to maintain its supply of raw materials and hedge against possible difficulties in the glass business, a move that was both integration and diversification. Saint-Gobain did not advance from its strong position into organic chemicals, however. Nor did it adopt the Solvay soda process until 1906.[5] In the late nineteenth century it dominated two important industries and tended to act as a conservative force, especially in chemicals. It did establish important subsidiaries making glass in Germany and Italy. It played a leading part in French sales pools in both glass and superphosphates.[6] In structure the company appears to have been split into two distinct divisions, glass and chemicals. I do not know how much autonomy these divisions had.

While Saint-Gobain moved from glass into chemicals, the firm that became Pechiney moved from chemicals into aluminum. Founded in 1855 to make sulphuric acid, soda, and other products, from 1860 to 1890 it also produced small amounts of aluminum by Sainte-Claire Deville's chemical process. Under A. R. Pechiney's leadership after 1877 the company expanded slowly and eschewed adventures into new fields. When Paul Héroult in 1886 offered the company his electrolytic process for refining aluminum Pechiney turned him down, as he foresaw no significant expansion of this market. Héroult thereupon licensed his patent to a

Swiss firm and then a French one. This new competition forced Pechiney out of aluminum production in 1890, but a few years later it returned, using Charles Martin Hall's process at a dam site in the French Alps and its own alumina. As the aging autocrat A. R. Pechiney phased himself out of the firm after 1902, Adrien Badin, a graduate engineer and one-time professor, took over the leadership and aggressively moved Pechiney more deeply into aluminum. Badin also organized aluminum sales in France, establishing a cartel, Aluminum Française, in 1912, which divided the market. Pechiney's management probably did not consider the return to aluminum in the late 1890s and its subsequent expansion as a major shift in policy, for it had a long tradition of making this product. It had nevertheless diversified, but continued to operate under its traditional Napoleonic structure with one man overseeing everything.[7]

It appears then, that diversification was not an unusual strategy for larger French firms before the First World War. We can see additional examples of it among medium-sized concerns such as Delaunay-Belleville, a boilermaker; Hotchkiss, an armament manufacturer, and Lorraine-Dietrich, a railway equipment company, all of which entered automobile manufacturing between 1895 and 1904. In these three cases the motive surely was an effort to keep the firm's resources fully employed by entering another metalworking business that appeared to be immensely profitable. The cautious movement of the Peugeot small tool firm into automobiles in the 1890s had been presaged by its earlier development of bicycles. But when one member of the family decided that the market was large enough to absorb cars by the thousand, his cousins disagreed and he had to establish a separate company for auto manufacturing. Sometimes it was not easy to decide if a new product could be fitted into one's current line, or if it represented a real diversification, and therefore a greater risk.

I have not seen any careful investigations of the managerial structure of the larger or medium-sized diversified companies mentioned. Most of them appear to have operated with a dominant president or general manager presiding over departments. In the Schneider group, however, some of the subsidiary or affiliated companies probably had considerable autonomy.

Concentration did occur more rapidly in France between the world wars, especially in the booming twenties. The automobile industry shows this clearly. In 1913 the three largest producers turned out 29 percent of the automobiles. By 1929 the three largest made 60 percent and, in 1938, 71 percent. This resulted from competitive pressure in the 1920s, followed by the temporary shrinking of the market in the early 1930s which eliminated many small firms. The aeronautical industry also concentrated by a different process. Government pressure for consolidation to improve efficiency was only partly effective by 1935 so it finally forced mergers by nationalizing most of the industry in 1936–37.

Most French firms in this period seem to have retained their traditional management structure. There are many discussions of this tradition, but few descriptions of actual firms to show how it worked in practice. One of the best general analyses is that of Octave Gelinier, found in the first part of his *Le Secret des Structures Compétitives*. Here he establishes a model of how management really operated in the traditional private firm, and contrasts this with (1) the operation of the French bureaucratic tradition, (2) modern management as developed especially in the United States, and (3) a transitional type frequently found in France since the Second World War as companies moved gingerly toward new methods. The traditional private firm described by Gelinier operated by customary and traditional rules but avoided written regulations which might limit the authority of top management. Desiring stability above all, it sought a protected or guaranteed market and found aggressive competition very distasteful. Top management centralized decisions in its hands and engaged in little consultation with subordinates. Those at the top expected loyalty and obedience from their subordinates even more than efficiency. The mobility of executives within or among firms was limited, changes in structure were rare, and reactions to major changes outside the firm were muted or grudging.

Traditionally, French management also shared the general European preference for problems of production and design rather than marketing. Partly this sprang from the strong desire among the top management for independence: a careful analysis of the market and adjusting production to what the market seemed to need would have meant losing one's independence. The firm and its management would have become dependent on outside factors beyond their control. Another aspect to this in the French case was the tradition of private business firms hiring the graduates of prestigious technical schools for their higher managerial positions. These men, after graduating from the Ecole Polytechnique, for example, usually entered government service for a few years and then "parachuted" into a top-ranking job in a medium- or large-size industrial firm. The companies would hire them not really because of any managerial talent they may have displayed in their government service, or even primarily because of their technical training, but because their status as former students of these schools seemed to guarantee that they were the intellectual cream of France. They were hired more for what they were—their essence—which in turn had been based on a high score in an entrance examination when they were eighteen or nineteen years old, than on what they had done thereafter. These men, in their schooling and their government work—building roads, inspecting mines, etc.—had received little exposure to questions of business competition or marketing. On the contrary, they had learned that they knew best what was good for other people. Such persons, with a strong technical interest and a nonmarketing or antimarketing approach, tended to dominate the management of larger French industrial firms, especially the older ones where members of the founding families no longer held the key positions.

These ubiquitous polytechnicians always pop up in discussions about French management but perhaps their significance has been overemphasized, because a similar bias away from marketing and toward technical and production problems seems common generally in Europe. There are always important exceptions, of course, as demonstrated by the case of André Citroën, a graduate of the Ecole Polytechnique who in his automobile company not only displayed the expected flair for ingenious technical solutions but gained even more renown for his bold and successful huckstering. There is the more recent example of Roger Martin, who has imaginatively guided the Pont à Mousson metallurgical firm into building materials.[8] It should not be forgotten that the polytechnicians have had a positive impact in promoting research by private firms, research that has begun to pay off for many of them in the last decade.

Gelinier finds that his model of the traditional private firm is most appropriate for the interwar years but does not appear to describe young firms so well. This seems to be because the young firm, especially if it is in a young industry, does not find a guaranteed place in the market; it has to carve out a home for itself. Therefore, it has to be more competitive than older ones, more responsive to market pressures. The French automobile industry from 1890 to 1939 is an example of a group of young firms, certainly more competitive than was typical of many other industries, and marked by considerable mobility of managerial personnel. Even here, however, there was a greater interest in technical virtuosity than aggressive market strategy. For example, there was a disinterest in providing service after the sale, especially in export markets.

Gelinier also offers a model of French bureaucratic structure, which has some relevance to manufacturing, because some French private firms have tended to resemble it and because in some areas of manufacturing, monopolies or government ownership have encouraged the development of bureaucratic operations. The bureaucratic structure operates according to written regulations, extremely detailed and formalized, so as to avoid any opportunity for personal favoritism to enter decision-making. It is indifferent to the market and ignores profit. As in the traditional private firm, decision-making is centralized, but it is limited in scope by the extensive regulations that restrict freedom of action. With the independence and security of all its members as its highest goal, the bureaucratic structure responds even more lethargically to the environment than the traditional private firm. This model tended to fit some governmental economic enterprises such as the tobacco monopoly. It would be fascinating to see how aptly it describes others such as the railways, arsenals, and aviation manufacturing, and postwar nationalizations such as the large banks and insurance companies. How far did it reach into private firms, especially old ones such as Saint-Gobain and some of the steel companies? Has the frequent movement of government engineers into private managerial posts tended to encourage this sort of bureaucratic structure and operation?

In the interwar years the idea that business management was a unique activity that could be studied and improved upon grew apace in France. One source of the management movement was Frederick Taylor's scientific management, promoted by Henry Le Chatelier and Charles de Fréminville.[9] More important for our purposes is the influence of Henri Fayol, who from 1888 to 1918 managed a mining and metallurgical firm. He published his major work, *General and Industrial Administration*, in 1916. Here he analyzed the functions of a business enterprise and distinguished the administrative ones from the technical, commercial, financial, security, and accounting functions. His emphasis was on how the head of the firm handles his administrative duties, which Fayol divided into planning, organizing, coordinating, commanding, and inspecting. Fayol's management was authoritarian and highly centralized, Napoleonic if you please, with no emphasis on decentralization of decision-making. His experience in a metallurgical firm, where centralized management seems to work efficiently, may explain his approach. Fayol's book found many readers and stood at the core of French thinking on general management between the wars. It reinforced the traditional stress on the head of the firm at the peak of a centralized structure.

In the post-1945 period the rapid growth of the economy has encouraged concentration, for the expanding markets seemed able to absorb larger amounts of production. The introduction of new technology, as in steelmaking, required larger production units to finance and utilize the new plant. But only in the 1960s did the rate of industrial concentration really jump upward.[10] The opening of the Common Market in 1959 had a greater impact than the earlier Coal-Steel Community in bringing rigorous competition to French industry, not only from the other market producers, but especially from branches of American firms established within the market.[11] Once the Algerian trauma ended in 1962, government officials and businessmen could turn their full attention to this matter.

Two kinds of reaction to this foreign competition appeared. Firstly, pressure to consolidate French firms to achieve sizes that would be internationally competitive, a conception based on the belief that size leads to competitiveness. This view found especial strength in the government ministries that had some concern with industrial affairs. It had much to do with the mergers that occured in the late 1960s. A second approach, urged by some businessmen and publicists, argued that competitiveness brings size. These people have examined the American competitors with some care, sometimes by studying at management institutes in the United States or Europe, or by reading Professor Chandler's *Strategy and Structure* or Alfred Sloan's history of General Motors. They strove to increase competitiveness by increasing management's concern for marketing, by urging more participation by all levels of employees in decision-making, and in some cases by preaching the merits of managerial decentralization. It is understandable that French bureaucrats did not tend to take the leadership in promoting these ideas, all of which are alien to the traditional bureaucratic approach, but it is remarkable that General de Gaulle, of all people, at the very end of his career adopted the slogan of "participation." So we see in the decade of the 1960s in French industry a surging movement of concentration, often involving diversification by the larger firms, paralleled by another but weaker campaign for managerial decentralization. To illustrate these trends it may be useful to describe recent developments in some industries and firms.

The chemical industry has been one of the most dynamic since the Second World War, with the 1960s marking the period of greatest change. In that decade its growth exceeded that in any other major west European country and in 1969 it passed Britain to become second only to West Germany. Parallel with this growth there has been considerable concentration, although less than would appear at first glance. In 1961 the seven largest chemical firms had sales of just 23 percent of the total industry. However, if the sales figures for the same firms were calculated to include subsidiaries the total would approximately double, so that the seven firms would have accounted for nearly half the industry's total sales.[12] Since then, international competition and government pressure on the industry to restructure itself to meet this compeition and to withstand foreign takeovers has led to much reorganization and concentration.

A great deal of the growth in French chemicals has been in new products and processes, especially in petrochemicals, and the firms' usual strategy for entry into new products was to form joint ventures or wholly owned subsidiaries rather than simply to create new divisions or departments in the old firms. Concerning the wholly owned subsidiaries, perhaps it was thought that this was a simpler way to establish a profit center and test the managerial skills of young executives, or to avoid upsetting the established routine of the old firm? Or was it for some arcane fiscal reason, always the first suggestion a Frenchman advances when asked to explain some corporate strategy? In any event, it probably made the staff services of the parent company less available than if the new operation had been placed in the existing structure, and made it harder for the parent to maintain control. The joint venture method turned up very frequently in the utilization of the natural gas from the Lacq field in the Pyrenees and for petrochemicals generally. This device provided more capital and skilled personnel for a new operation than one firm alone could manage easily, and so allowed the construction of plant large enough to be internationally competitive; it shared the risk; it ensured each of the founding firms a portion of the output of the new plant; and it avoided the need for a merger among them. Perhaps there was some defensiveness in the strategy—"we aren't sure about this move, but if it prospers we will not be on the outside." In the late 1950s and early 1960s there was a blizzard of joint ventures among the large chemical firms, including some with non-French companies.

This complex spider's web produced obvious difficulties. To whom was the management of the new firm responsible? How did it resolve conflicts among the parent firms? Who decided further strategy for the firm? Who financed it? The difficulty in answering these questions would bring problems in guiding and managing the joint subsidiaries. Toward the end of the decade the fashion for joint ventures in chemicals began to wane and was replaced by a wave of rationalization and reorganization. This brought considerable consolidation and clarification of the industry's structure.

If we examine some particular chemical firms we may get a more distinct picture of what has been going on.[13] The Saint-Gobain company expanded and diversified between the two world wars and afterward primarily by joint ventures. By 1959 it had participations in some seventy other French business firms—in chemicals, glass, and other products—along with many foreign participations. It had outgrown its old structure—two large divisions of glass and chemicals, each headed by a director general, in turn responsible to the president—and in about 1957 broke its operations into five divisions as shown in Figure 1.[14]

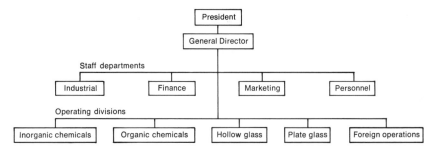

Figure 1. Saint-Gobain Structure, ca. 1957

We suspect that some crisis had occurred to cause this reorganization. But shortly thereafter, as the Common Market opened, Saint-Gobain and Pechiney decided to group most of their chemical operations in a new firm, Pechiney–Saint-Gobain, apparently to bring these activities to internationally competitive size. Pechiney–Saint-Gobain began independent operations in 1962. Late in 1968 an authentic crisis did swoop down on Saint-Gobain, a takeover bid by Boussois Souchon Neuvesel, a smaller, more technologically alert, and more profitable French glass company. With some difficulty Saint-Gobain repelled the B.S.N. boarders early in 1969, but a few months later Saint-Gobain agreed to merge with Pont à Mousson, also a smaller firm, originally in metallurgy but now diversifying into construction materials and operated by the kind of dynamic management that Saint-Gobain seemed to need. The strategy here apparently aimed to move the new creation further into construction and building materials. In the midst of these changes Rhône-Poulenc, the largest French chemical company, bought a controlling interest in Pechiney–Saint-Gobain, the chemical affiliate, and in 1971 bought all the rest of Saint-Gobain/Pont à Mousson's shares in P.S.G. So Saint-Gobain, after a century and a half, finally abandoned most of its direct interest in the chemical industry. Was the sale of its chemical operations the result of a long-planned strategy, or was it forced by the need for money to fight off the B.S.N. takeover and to invest in new glassmaking techniques? Its size now is comparable to Krupp or Robert Bosch.

While Rhône-Poulenc can trace its ancestry back to 1801, about half as far as Saint-Gobain, it became a sizable concern only in 1928, when its artificial fiber activities (Rhône) were merged with a pharmaceutical manufacturer (Poulenc). The Gillet family of Lyons has held a controlling interest in the firm from the 1920s on. In 1961 Rhône-Poulenc incorporated the fiber operations of an affiliate, Celtex, another Gillet company. In 1964 Wilfrid Baumgartner, a former minister of finance and governor of the Bank of France, became chief executive, and thereafter one sees a move into heavy chemicals and a rationalization of the tangle of affiliates and subsidiaries. In 1969 Rhône-Poulenc acquired Progil, a highly diversified chemical producer and another Gillet enterprise. Then a few months later it brought Pechiney–Saint-Gobain into its fold and merged it with Progil to form the largest heavy chemical group in France. Rhône-Poulenc's many activities (its 1970 sales of about $2 billion make it about the same size as Monsanto or Dow or the Dutch Akzo, but smaller than ICI or the three giant West German chemical firms) are grouped into three major divisions, chemicals with 49 percent of sales, fibers with 34 percent, and pharmaceuticals with 13 percent. From its international success in the latter two areas the company gained a reputation for competitiveness. Perhaps it will infuse some of its vigor into the heavy chemical branch.

Kuhlmann was another old private firm, making heavy chemicals since the early nineteenth century. In 1966 it merged with Ugine, a specialist in electrometallurgy, producing special steels and aluminum. This group in turn is now merging with Pechiney to form Pechiney Ugine Kuhlmann. Just after the First World War Pechiney merged with its leading French competitor in aluminum and thereafter has dominated French production of this metal. At the same time the company organized its activities into two departments, electrometallurgy and chemicals, and expanded both considerably during the interwar years. After 1945 Pechiney saw that aluminum production could not be indefinitely expanded due to the relatively high cost of electricity in France. Its strategy aimed to develop research to reduce the cost of production in France, to expand overseas where cheaper electricity was available, and to move vigorously into the newer areas of chemistry. Recognizing the diversification already in effect and anticipating more of it, the company adopted a decentralized structure in 1948, setting up four operating divisions, supported by central staff departments (see Figure 2). The divisions received extensive auton-

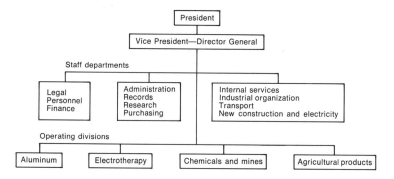

Figure 2. Pechiney as Reorganized in 1948

omy and responsibility, for marketing as well as production. The staff departments also had budgetary autonomy and offered their services to the rest of the company in competition with outside sources. Top management restricted itself to coordination and inspiration, keeping in touch with the divisions by approving their budgets and examining their results. It hoped to devote more time to the selection of higher managerial personnel and general company strategy.[15] This is the earliest example I have found of a large French firm adopting a modern decentralized management and it calls for further investigation.

A dozen years later Pechiney began to move its chemical activities into Pechiney–Saint-Gobain which Rhône-Poulenc then acquired in 1969. This suggested that Pechiney had abandoned its chemical interests. But late in 1971 Pechiney proposed (with government encouragement?) to merge with Ugine Kuhlmann, half of whose sales were chemicals. The combined sales of the two firms in 1970 were $2.7 billion, which would make the merged company the largest industrial firm in France, about the size of Fiat in Italy, and almost twice as big as Aluminum Company of America. The proposed reorganization of Pechiney Ugine Kuhlmann would comprise seven autonomous divisions: steel and titanium, aluminum, chemicals, mines and electrometallurgy, nuclear and new technology, copper fabricating, and special products. As a counterpoint to this giant combination, Le Nickel, the large French nickel producer, has recently diversified and built a second major group in nonferrous metals, acquiring a controlling interest in Penarroya (lead and zinc) in 1969, and Mokta (uranium and manganese) in 1971.

There are two other large private chemical groups in France: Air Liquide specializes in industrial gases and had sales of $447 million in 1970; and a new firm, about the same size, Centrale Roussel Nobel, a 1971 combination of several concerns, with special strength in pharmaceuticals and explosives.

The French government directly owns or controls a number of large firms associated with the chemical industry. One of these is Entreprise Minière et Chimique (1970 sales, $360 million), the name given to a 1968 merger of the government potash mining operations in Alsace and the government explosives-fertilizer company originally based on the Haber-Bosch ammonia process. This firm is diversifying from fertilizer through joint ventures with large Dutch and German as well as French chemical firms. The government-owned coal mining combine, Charbonnages de France, has moved into chemical activities as a way to utilize its coal surplus and justify its existence. In 1968, the chemical activities of the Charbonnages branches were grouped into one firm, which adopted the name CdF Chimie in 1971 (1970 sales, $235 million). It too has a fertilizer base and is diversifying into plastics, usually by joint ventures. The government wholly owns one petroleum-producing and refining company, Elf (ERAP) (1970 sales, $1,460 million), and has a controlling interest in another, Compagnie Française des Pétroles (1970 sales, $1,950 million), and both of them have intrests in petrochemicals. The two groups have established joint ventures and may ultimately merge into one very large government oil group to confront the extensive foreign-controlled oil companies operating in France.

The top of the chemical industry (excluding the oil companies) has at this point shaken out to two very large and four large concerns, all of them diversified and most or all apparently operating with some kind of decentralized management, although I should like to have discovered more evidence on this last point.

The general structure of the automobile industry has changed less than chemicals in recent years. As mentioned, a few firms came to dominate it between the wars. The strong personalities who controlled these companies operated them according to the model of the traditional private firm in France. Not until 1938 did Louis Renault organize the separate shops of his company into departments. Any sort of administrative hierarchy antagonized him, for clear-cut lines of authority and communication would restrict his power to intervene anywhere at any time in the firm. Fayol's efforts to divide and analyze the duties of management seemed to have no influence on him. At the end of the Second World War the government nationalized Renault but its only direct control has been to name the presidents, of whom there have been only two since 1945. Renault and the other auto firms have followed a strategy of developing the market and integrating backward to gain more control over raw materials and components. There has been little diversification into other lines and the managements have not experienced a strong need to decentralize. Renault and Citroën especially are noted for a highly centralized structure although they have decentralized production in the geographic sense. International competition has exerted pressure on the major firms in the industry to cooperate in research, production, or foreign marketing to gain some advantages in scale.

Since the Second World War the electrical equipment industry has moved toward a concentration of financial control in the hands of a few large companies such as the two largest, Compagnie Générale d'Electricité and Thomson Houston-Hotchkiss Brandt/CSF. Until very recently not much was done to coordinate the dozens of separate activities of these giants, so some of the benefits of size may not have been achieved. The CGE had been a large utility until 1946 when the government nationalized electricity supply and distribution. It then went into manufacturing by buying control of dozens of equipment firms. By the late 1960s it had 160 subsidiaries and gave the impression of being too much decentralized. The Thomson/CSF group has been put together more recently by Paul Richard, a former insurance man. He has gathered up, mostly since 1965, a large number of healthy and ailing firms and oriented them toward electrical equipment. A strong motive in his efforts has been to prevent foreign takeovers of some of the weaker French companies. Whether the adding together of several flabby enterprises will result in one tough and lean one remains to be seen. In 1969, these two groups agreed to coordinate their efforts so as not to compete with each other. CGE will specialize in heavier equipment while Thomson/CSF will devote itself to household appliances and light electrical and electronic articles.

Two other firms in the industry have also expanded and diversified, and have established decentralized managements. The Compagnie Electro-

Mécanique decentralized in 1956 into three groups based on the nature of their product—heavy equipment, light equipment, and household appliances. The last sector was acquired by Thomson Houston. Alsthom, founded in 1928 and until recently affiliated with Thomson Houston, has specialized in heavy electrical and mechanical equipment. In 1968 it operated through four divisions, each financially autonomous and handling its own marketing. Alsthom controls its extensive international operations through a separate international division.[16]

The government has affected strategy in the electrical industry most directly in the area of computers. The home-grown Bull company enjoyed great success until it outgrew the capacities of its management in the early 1960s. Reluctantly, the government allowed General Electric to take over Bull in 1964. Then, concerned that American firms, Bull-GE and IBM-France, would monopolize French production of computers, and that computing equipment might not always be available from abroad, the de Gaulle government in 1966 got Thomson/CSF, CGE, Schneider, and others to establish as a joint venture a national firm in this field, Compagnie Internationale pour l'Informatique, with generous support from the treasury and government orders. CII has grown slowly and recently has lived up to its name by establishing some links with British and American computer firms. In 1970 General Electric sold out control of its computer activities, including Bull, to another American firm, Honeywell.

Along with computers, steel has been an industry particularly subject to government interference, especially in the 1960s, when its structure changed considerably. It had run into trouble in this decade when demand stopped rising rapidly and it became apparent that for crude steel the future would belong to mills located on seashores where low-cost raw materials brought by cheap transportation awaited. The large expense entailed in developing these new locations and the adoption of new technologies could not be borne by the relatively fragmented French steel firms. In return for further state investment the government demanded a regrouping of companies and production facilities to increase efficiency. An agreement or *convention* was negotiated to this effect in 1966.[17]

The Schneider group after 1918 continued the prewar empire building. This policy could be interpreted as the acquisition of property for its own sake and for the power it brought, reminiscent of the activities of medieval barons. One might also see here a forerunner of the American conglomerates of the 1960s. Eugène Schneider, his five-man board of surveillance, and his general manager watched over a congeries of establishments that he owned, controlled, or participated in. All these interests tended to concentrate in four areas, metallurgy-armaments, transport, electricity, or banking. The Skoda arms firm in Czechoslovakia was among the most successful. Eugène Schneider died during the Second World War and since then there has been some effort to rationalize and concentrate the firms's interests and properties, but, like Krupp in Germany, Schneider has lost the eminence it once had.

A first-generation industrial group that has some resemblance to Schneider (or Howard Hughes) is that controlled by Marcel Dassault. Its core is an airplane design and assembly company, Avions Marcel Dassault. Other Dassault enterprises include a real estate company, an investment bank, an electronics firm, and a large women's magazine. Management of these operations is highly centralized. Some of the diversification is due to historical accident, as the magazine began as a Gaullist political organ but lost money until it found a more lucrative approach.

A much younger firm than Schneider but one with a sales total of almost equivalent size is Schlumberger Limited.[18] As Schneider had been in the late nineteenth century, Schlumberger is at the leading edge of technological innovation now. It was begun in the 1920s by two young members of a family once famous in Alsacian textiles and then in banking. Both engineers, they developed oil-prospecting techniques using electricity. The enterprise expanded rapidly after the Second World War and in the 1950s there were four legally separate Schlumberger companies operating in distinct areas of the world. In the meantime, the electrical methods used by Schlumberger led it deeply into the area of electronic measurement so that it became diversified in product as well as decentralized geographically. After the death of the surviving Schlumberger brother in 1954 a reorganization was worked out bringing all operations together under Schlumberger Limited, legally domiciled in the Netherlands Antilles and owned primarily by American and French stockholders. A managerial structure gradually evolved so as to permit a maximum of decentralization compatible with strategic planning and financial control from the center. The structure was consciously modeled on that of General Motors, as reported in Alfred Sloan's account. At the central staff level the president deals with four persons, the directors of electronics and petroleum operations, and the directors of personnel and finance. Responsible to this group are the heads of various geographic divisions who manage the production of goods and services and research activities. Presumably the central staff, organized on functional lines, can coordinate the various operations of the geographically separate divisions.

A fine example of diversification is the Beghin group. An old family firm in beet sugar refining, this company began making cardboard for its boxes of sugar in 1928. It thereafter expanded in both lines and now controls one-fifth of French sugar refining and 30 percent of the paper industry. To ensure an outlet for its newsprint production the Beghin family has extensive investments in the press. The architect of the group, Ferdinand Beghin, runs a rather centralized organization. He has strong technical interests and enjoys troubleshooting problems in his factories. Only when he retires from active management can one expect to see a new structure in the management of the Beghin companies. On the other hand, one of the best advertisements for decentralized management in France is the growth of Ciments Lafarge to become, with its subsidiaries, the largest cement company in the non-Communist world. Its head, Marcel Demonque, has a strong philosophical belief in managerial de-certralization and, as he expanded by decentralizing his plants geograph-ically, he also decentralized management, with help from a prominent American management consulting firm. The decentralization came without product diversification in this case and so is particularly noteworthy.

At this point we ask, how does the evolution of managerial structures in France compare with Chandler's analysis of the American experience? Clearly, the French, through the 1950s, paid much less attention to market demand. One finds a greater interest there in maintaining or expanding the power of the owners and/or managers and in maintaining their inde-pendence both of outside influences and of internal challenges to their authority. The centralized managerial structure did seem to respond to this interest in power and independence, and it has been more difficult to break away from it in France than in the United States. Chandler has observed, "The market was of overwhelming importance to the changing structure and strategy of American industrial enterprise."[19] In the 1960s a similar conclusion emerges for France, in dramatic fashion. The loosen-ing up of the structures of industries and of individual firms in this decade followed upon the arrival of a more competitive market, but international rather than national. An earlier example of this, the Pechiney reorganiza-tion to a multidivisional structure in 1948, occurred precisely in a firm that already engaged heavily in international competition. However, gov-ernment always plays a larger role in the French case, either in affecting the amount and nature of competition, or in forcing businesses to react to it.

Until recent years French businessmen do not seem to have been especially self-conscious about their strategy, but I am not convinced that the Americans were either. I suspect that in both countries most cases of successful diversification, upon examination, would turn out to be more fortuitous than planned. I would also suggest that diversification may have been more common among French manufacturers than Amer-ican ones in the first half of the century, for two reasons. It reflected their greater interest in technical innovation, and it served as a hedge to protect their firms from what seemed to be unpredictable market changes.

Among large firms in France, structures appear to have been either highly centralized or highly decentralized. Of the two, it may be more interesting to examine the highly decentralized type to see why and how managements permitted it to develop. One factor that might not occur to an American audience is that the threat of nationalization may have encouraged the heads of large firms at certain periods to divide their operations into legally distinct enterprises or keep them in that situation to avoid possible public takeovers. Of greater long-run significance is the problem of establishing central coordination of a decentralized enterprise. To Americans it may not seem so formidable a task as it appears to Frenchmen, because there are so many examples of it throughout American society, from federalism in the political realm and on through religious, educational, and other institutions. Americans have learned how to overcome the ambiguities and divided responsibilities and to capitalize on local initiative. Centralized authority is woven more deeply into French society, from family life through politics, public administration, religion, and education. This makes it harder for top business management to delegate responsibility, of course, but I wonder if it doesn't also make it difficult to conceive of the head of a subsidiary firm not having full control of it between the dates of the annual financial reports, difficult for him to accept responsibility for a plant's operations at the same time as accepting or engaging in coordinating activities that encroach on his authority. Finally, essential for coordination of decentralized branches is speedy and accurate financial reporting. French management may have been less confident than American that it really could develop an information system adequate to operate such a structure successfully.

Obviously, the sketchy observations made here show that more research must be done on the structure of large French business concerns. I myself have not had the resources to make a general survey of the larger firms which would identify all those with a multidivisional structure. This should be done, and from it should follow some hypotheses more valid than those made here. Investigators should be sure that a study of the morphology of these concerns does not ignore their physiology; the organizational chart alone may hide more than reveal how the company really operates. Scholars are examining the histories of some large enterprises and their findings should appear before long.[20] A study of the last century of the Schneider activities would be fascinating, and investigation of the Pechiney and Schlumberger reorganizations would be very instructive. To further test the importance of the market as affecting strategy and structure, perhaps it would be possible to scale various industries according to their competitiveness and see what effect competition has had on structures. Among particular industries, electrical equipment and chemicals stand out as needing histories, but almost any other, such as paper, publishing, or artificial textiles, is also an open field. A special problem in France is the dearth of memoirs by twentieth-century businessmen and engineers, and a parallel lack of biographies.[21] I suspect that this may change before long, stimulated by the growing sophistication of

French business journalism and by French historians' increasing interest in business history. American investigators especially should not forget that the French rate of industrial growth per capita has been quite respectable for the twentieth century as a whole, despite managerial structures that may not have optimized the talents available in the particular firms.

NOTES

1. Works I have found useful include H. von der Haas, *The Enterprise in Transition* (London, 1967); Octave Gelinier, *Le Secret des Structures Compétitives* (Paris, 1966); John McArthur and Bruce Scott, *Industrial Planning in France* (Boston, 1969); Roger Priouret, *La France et le Management* (Paris, 1968) and *Les Managers Européens* (Paris, 1970); and Michel Crozier, *The Bureaucratic Phenomenon* (Chicago, 1964). Unfortunately, files of important business magazines such as *Enterprise* and *Expansion* were not available to me.

2. "The Structure of American Industry in the Twentieth Century," *Business History Review*, vol. 43 (Autumn 1969), pp. 255–81.

3. There is some extremely helpful information in McArthur and Scott, *Industrial Planning in France*, pp. 182–221.

4. This and later references to Professor Alfred D. Chandler are to his *Strategy and Structure*, Anchor ed. (Garden City, 1966).

5. See A. Thépot, "La Fusion Saint Gobain—Perret Ollivier," *Bulletin de la Société d'Histoire Moderne*, 14th ser., no. 3 (1967), pp. 2–11.

6. See J. Choffel, *Saint-Gobain* (Paris, 1960).

7. See C. J. Gignoux, *Histoire d'une Entreprise Française* (Paris, 1955).

8. Priouret, *Les Managers Européen*, pp. 276–94.

9. See L. Urwick and E. Brech, *The Making of Scientific Management*, 1 (London, 1951), for brief sketches of these men and of Fayol; a full biography is François Le Chatelier, *Henry Le Chatelier* (Paris, 1968).

10. J. Houssiaux, "Les Motifs des Concentrations d'Entreprises en Europe depuis la Seconde Guerre Mondiale: l'Exemple de la France," *Actualité Economique* (Montreal), vol. 42 (1966), pp. 458–83, is a rather abstract analysis.

11. J. J. Servan-Schreiber, *The American Challenge* (New York, 1968), eloquently expresses French concern about this sort of American competition.

12. E. P. Learned, *European Problems in General Management* (Homewood, Ill., 1963), p. 157.

13. A useful survey can be found in the weekly *Oil, Paint and Drug Reporter*, 12 July through 23 August, 1971.

14. Choffel, *Saint-Gobain*, pp. 135–36.

15. Gignoux, *Entreprise Française*, pp. 199–201.

16. Bernard Dezert, *La Croissance Industrielle et Urbaine de la Porte d'Alsace* (Paris, 1969), pp. 150–63.

17. These developments are summarized in McArthur and Scott, *Industrial Planning*, pp. 369–76, see also pp. 198–204.

18. See Priouret, *La France et le Management*, pp. 134–51.

19. Chandler, *Strategy and Structure*, p. 474.

20. P. Fridenson on Renault to 1939; A. Thépot on Saint-Gobain; F. Caron on the Nord railway.

21. But see R. F. Kuisel, *Ernest Mercier* (Berkeley, 1967).

6. Soviet Management Structure: Stability and Change

S. A. BILLON

Coordination of human effort is an essential function in any society. Management organizations are social systems designed to attain predetermined objectives. Management systems develop in response to the need to perform certain functions which can best be accomplished through the purposeful efforts of large numbers of people. The environment has an important influence on the characteristics of the organization structure. In an open or competitive social environment, organization is structured in response to the needs or the demands of the environment as indicated in Figure 1 below.

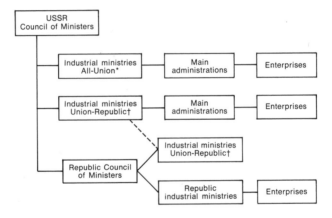

Figure 1. Industrial Management Organization Structure. All-Union ministries (*) administer branches of the economy having national importance and requiring centralized direction from Moscow. Union-Republic ministries (†) administer branches of the economy with important regional differences; direction is exercised at the republic level subject to guidance and review by the ministries' headquarters in Moscow.

The availability of resources and the value systems of decision-makers are the important factors in all situations. However, the role of values tends to be exaggerated in a closed society where the ideology plays a dominant role in setting objectives, determining the functions to be performed, and shaping the organization structure. In the closed system the controlled (internal) environment has a minor role in influencing the objectives or the organizational structure. The objectives tend to reflect the decision-makers' values rather than the interests of society in general (the environment). However, even a closed system cannot ignore the environment completely because it is part of the larger system and, to a certain extent, must perform to survive.

The purpose of this study is to examine the development of the Soviet industrial management structure. The management of Soviet industry has been called the most difficult task in the world. The task is easily the most challenging because it is the largest centrally managed industrial system, and in some ways the most complex. Its accomplishments and its malfunctions afford an unusual opportunity to gain insight into the problems of managing complex organizations. Orderly analysis of Soviet industrial management structure presents a number of problems because the rules of the system change very frequently so that it is not possible to trace all of the changes. Aside from changes in nomenclature, the essence of the system has changed little. Despite the many minor and "major" reform attempts, the system tends to return to the former patterns of operation.

THE EARLY YEARS

Lenin was instrumental in the design of the Soviet economic management structure during the early years of the system. Every Soviet article on management gives credit to Lenin for the fundamental concepts in use.

Referring to the 1965 reform one author states: "The Party's activities are controlled by Lenin's principles. Every time we ask ourselves: What did Lenin think about this?"[1]

The historic record shows that Lenin, indeed, had much to say about what should be the appropriate management system, and many of the concepts introduced by Lenin are still being used today. The direct involvement of top Soviet political leaders in structuring the management system is not unexpected. Since the government owns the means of production, it feels duty bound to determine and prescribe how economic enterprise should be managed. The actual Soviet industrial management structure at any given time is, to a large extent, a reflection of the top leader's philosophy and perception of what is needed under the environmental conditions.

Lenin, like many socialists of his day, had a highly naive conception of the nature of management. In the early days of the revolution, he went so far as to say that management was extremely simple and that anyone who could read could manage.[2] However, after a brief experience of managing the economy, Lenin changed his mind, and soon claimed that developing an effective economic management system was the most important task confronting the new regime, a task which was more difficult than staging a successful revolution.[3] Furthermore, the task was aggravated by the fact that the new regime decided not to use the prerevolution managers.[4]

The task of training a new management elite was more formidable than expected. In 1917, industry was practically at a standstill and Lenin recognized only too well that in order to survive, his regime must get industry to produce the urgently needed war material. Soon after assuming power, the regime established the Supreme Council of National Economy which was to coordinate economic effort, while similar councils were established on the district, local, and factory levels. As might be expected, the local economic organizations were organizationally weak, inexperienced, and, in most cases, incompetent.[5] As a result, industrial output declined disastrously and conditions in the factories were rather chaotic. Some workers apparently thought that now they "owned" the means of production and the need for their effort had passed. A conflict developed between Lenin, who insisted on central authority, and the "sindikalists" (headed by Tomsky), with considerable support of the industrial heirarchy at the local level, who wanted "unlimited democratism" and "anarchy."[6] In December 1918, Lenin proposed that industrial management be changed from the "collegium executive" to individual responsibility where one manager was in charge.[7]

Lenin's answer to the prevailing chaos and "irresponsibility" which prevailed in industrial management, was the principle of democratic centralism, which consisted of two major points: (1) "Centralization and unity of economic life according to a general plan elaborated by the central authorities, and (2) full and unimpeded development not only of local establishments, but also local authority, initiative, different ways and means of movement toward the common goal." But even Lenin's power was limited in those days. It was not until 1920, that the Ninth Party Congress adopted Lenin's individual responsibility of management[8] at the plant level and specifically limited committee (collegium) management to middle (glavk) and top hierarchy (union council) of the industrial authority structure.[9] Lenin stated that his reason for insisting on the individual responsibility principle in factory management was that committee management led to irresponsibility which "caused huge waste of resources."[10] It should be noted that "edinonachalie" is still the cornerstone of the line-staff organization in effect today.

The chaotic conditions which prevailed during the first few years were brought about in large part by the confused and chaotic policies followed by the regime. Lenin wrote shortly after the revolution that: "There was not and could not be a definite plan for the organization of economic life."[11] By 1921 it became apparent that unless some drastic changes were implemented, the future of the communist regime was in serious danger, not because of foreign intervention, but due to socioeconomic disorganization.

In 1921, the well-known New Economic Policy (NEP) was put in effect by Lenin. The main features were that large and particularly important industrial units would continue to be managed by the government. The rest were to be closed, or turned over to cooperatives and private interests. It is beyond the scope of this paper to analyze the reasons for NEP, but it appears that an important consideration was the regime's inability to manage the economy.[12] The early policy of nationalization and centralization of management was abandoned and the market mechanism was brought back to restore economic activity. By 1926, the economy was again functioning reasonably well, and the regime felt strong enough to set course on rapid industrialization.

Lenin and the Scientific Management Movement

Taylor's scientific management concepts had a profound influence on Lenin's management philosophy. The record shows that most of the management concepts advanced by Lenin and subsequently adopted as operating rules by the Soviet government can be attributed to Frederick Taylor, the father of scientific management, and some of his followers. Taylor's works were published in Russia as early as 1910, and Lenin became interested in this new movement years before the revolution.[13] In 1913 and 1914, Lenin wrote a series of articles, which, while criticizing some aspects of Taylor's philosophy, maintained that scientific management had many excellent ideas which should be implemented in Russian industry after the revolution.[14]

In 1918, Lenin stated: "It is necessary to study and teach Taylor's system in Russia; it must be systematically applied and adopted."[15] It was at Lenin's insistence that during the twenties the works of Taylor, Emerson, Gannt, Gilbreth, and Fayol were translated, published, and widely circulated by the state.

In the early twenties, management training and study received first priority. At Lenin's behest a Soviet scientific management movement was founded. More than ten scientific management institutes were in operation for research, study, and training in management.[16] About twenty management journals were published. Many of the top leaders took active parts in the campaign to "master" economic management.[17] According to a Soviet source: "Scientific management was promoted by all means of propaganda."[18]

In 1919, Lenin admitted that many of the mistakes in economic management were due to inexperience, but he thought that lessons could be learned from mistakes: "Just because the working class is presently in power, does not mean that it is capable of managing."[19]

At the Twelfth Party Congress, which took place in April of 1923, it was decided to "reconstruct the national management according to the scientific management framework."[20]

The decision was made to use the former management personnel even though they were considered politically unreliable.[21] Alongside the director of the enterprise, there was an experienced specialist. Shortly after NEP was adopted, the doors were opened to foreign industrial specialists. In 1921, Lenin outlined the role of the native and foreign experts as follows: "The [native] capitalists are going to be beside you, beside you will also be foreign capitalists. . . . Let them get rich and you learn from them to manage. Only then will you be able to build a communist republic. . . . There is no other way out."[22] Thousands of American and other foreign specialists were subsequently brought in to assist in the construction of new industrial plants. Many Soviet specialists traveled to the United States to learn new methods. The Ford Motor Company had a technical assistance agreement with the Soviet government which provided for the training of thousands of technicians.[23] It is little wonder, therefore, that the new giant Soviet plants were similar to American factories. "The Magnitorgorski Metallurgical, Stalingrad Tractor, Gorky Automobile, and other plants were built according to American models and with the help of American specialists."[24]

STALINIZATION OF THE SOVIET MANAGEMENT STRUCTURE

Shortly after Stalin consolidated his power, scientific management started declining and was "liquidated" in the early thirties.[25] Soviet authors give few details as to how the budding management movement came to an untimely end. A well-known Soviet economist describes this period as follows: "In the thirties, as the cult of Stalin's personality increased, scientific management was increasingly replaced with administrative measures."[26]

The Stalin period is characterized by continuing efforts to consolidate and centralize all authority at the top. Stalin viewed the plant director not as a decision-maker, but as a state employee who would faithfully carry out decisions made for him at a higher level. Apparently, in Stalin's view, the best way to manage was to send an order through channels which would specify exactly what had to be done. Very little was left to the initiative of the enterprise director except to carry out the avalanche of orders from above. Because plans were often unrealistic or ambiguous, there were many deviations from the plan. The mismanagement and non-fulfillment of plans were partially due to lack of managerial expertise because the main consideration in staffing in the thirties was political reliability.[27] The management malfunctions were attributed to treasonable activity by the "enemy of the people," which led to a wholesale purge and liquidation of a large number of managers. Not only top managers were liquidated; the arrest of the enterprise directors was generally accompanied by the arrest of their subordinates.[28] The engineering and technical staffs were also branded as "wreckers" and executed or banished to Siberian concentration camps.[29]

During 1937–38, the drive against alleged foreign and domestic "traitors" and "wreckers" reached hysterical proportions. Spies, according to the official line, were everywhere: "Experience has shown that one of the forms of wrecking by Japanese-German spies and diversionaries, who have penetrated into the food industry, was a reduction in the scale and a worsening of the quality of repairs."[30]

Many important industries (steel, pig iron) experienced declines in output, which was blamed on poor management.[31] A more likely cause was that in many cases the entire management staff was eliminated and the enterprise was entrusted to inexperienced people. Between 1938 and 1941, nearly all the staff of the *Gosplan* were eliminated.[32] The purges led to a shortage of management personnel as well as excessive turnover rates. Management became a hazardous occupation which was avoided even by ranking party members. The arbitrary methods were described by Pravda, in 1961, as follows:

> One must also take into account the pernicious consequences of the unfounded mass repressions in relation to the staffs of railways and technical personnel. As was remarked at the Twenty-Second Congress of the CPSS, Kaganovich, making use of the "theory of counter-revolutionary respect for outmoded norms" (*predel'chestva*) which he had thought up himself, organized a "mass extermination of engineering and technical cadres." Transport was deprived of many qualified specialists, their proposals to reinforce work in the technical reconstruction of transport were assessed as intending sabotage, attention to problems of reconstruction of the technical resources of transport was sharply weakened.[33]

The Stalinization process left a deep and lasting imprint on the Soviet management structure. Serious scholarly discussion of organizational problems disappeared. The golden age of Soviet scientific management movement which had flourished in the twenties came to an abrupt end.[34] Those management specialists who survived the purge had to shift their interest to administrative law, where their main duty was to interpret the administrative decisions of Stalin and his deputies.[35]

The existing climate was extremely hostile to any independent, even harmless, thought about how economic activity should be organized.

Stalin deemed this to be unnecessary since the party would tell the managerial hierarchy what to do, and any initiative on their part might endanger the complete control of the central authorities. Economists, who were criticized by Kosygin in 1965 for neglecting real problems of management, were similarly constrained. In 1952, Stalin went so far as to order economists to keep out of practical affairs: "The rational organization of production forces, economic planning, etc., are not problems of political economy, but the economic policy of the directing bodies. They are two provinces which should not be confused."[36]

A Soviet economist in evaluating the impact of Stalin on the economy stated:

> The cult of Stalin's personality had a negative effect on the economic development of the country. The fact that Stalin decided all important questions himself led to errors in plans and the lessening of the creative activity of the party, planning, and managerial organs; many questions were decided without sufficiently wide discussion among the workers, engineer-technicians, and scientists. In planning and direction of the economy over-centralization was dominant. Insufficient steps were taken to combat technological know-alls and conservatism, which infected part of the leading cadres of the party and higher management.[37]

Professor Nove points out that, while the production volume statistics were impressive, the economy was badly lagging in the quality of goods produced and in technical progress.[38]

The command-centralized structure which Stalin introduced has, after many attempts to change it, continued to this day.

THE STALIN MANAGEMENT SYSTEM

We have briefly described the emergence in the thirties of what has become known as the command economy or the Stalin model of management. We shall now turn our attention to the structure and the functioning of the major elements of the system. It must be a brief sketch and many minor changes will of necessity be omitted entirely. Our purpose will be served by a summary of the most essential features of the system.

Under state ownership of production facilities, the questions arise: whom does it serve and whose objectives should be served? Actually, the party determines what objectives shall be pursued, and the party also determines what system shall be used to implement its objectives. This explains the concern of top Soviet political leaders with management problems. Hardly a party congress or meeting goes by without a lengthy discourse on management problems.[39] The party in the Soviet system has the role of the board of directors and the controlling stockholder in the industrial management hierarchy. Supreme authority is vested in the Central Committee Politbureau of the Communist Party, which is primarily concerned with the determination of major policies, and the operation of a control system to ensure compliance in the administrative apparatus. The management structure administrative functions are performed by the Council of Ministers. The superstructure of economic management is shown in Figure 2.

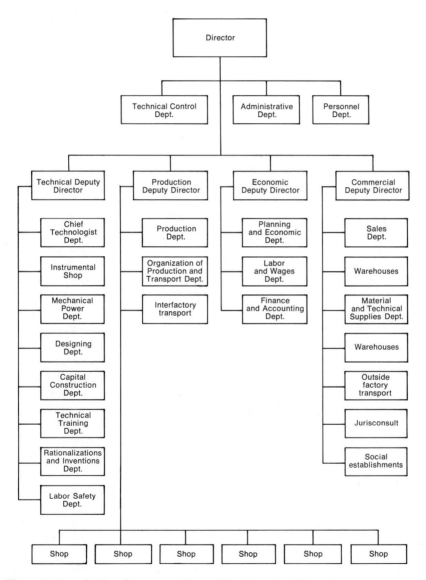

Figure 2. Organization Structure, a Large Manufacturing Enterprise

The actual management of economic activity is performed through the industrial ministries located in Moscow. The all-union industrial ministries are divided into main administrations (*glavk*) for the various branches of a particular sector. Each *glavk* manages a number of industrial enterprises. At the main administration level are also functional groups (*glavk*), such as finance, accounting, planning, supply.[40] There are also many enterprises which report to republican ministries or local government authorities, depending on the type of activity, importance, and size.

Enterprise Organization

Traditionally, as we have noted, Soviet industrial plants have been organized on a highly standardized basis. In the past, the enterprise manager was relieved of the problem of deciding how to divide the various functions and what kinds of management skills were to be assigned to each. These decisions were usually made by higher authority. Apparently, this uniform approach to organization design was an outgrowth of the centralization trends in the thirties, where the wisdom of centrally made decisions was seldom questioned. The uniformity in structure also facilitated central management functions of planning and control. Uniformity in operating practices is facilitated by parallel organization at the higher levels of the management structure. Thus, the accounting function is performed at each level in the hierarchy, and the chief plant accountant performs in accordance with standard instructions from a higher level. The standard solution was applied to extensive diversity which existed at the plant level, leading to serious rigidity and in many ways limiting the manager's authority.[41] Figure 3 shows the organization of a large plant. While some Soviet writers refer to this form as the line organization, it corresponds closely to the line and staff organization that is predominant in American industry. Division of work, staff or functional units, chain of command, unity of command, and delegation exist in both systems. Soviet industrial organization forms were established in the twenties and were patterned closely after American models of that day. While there are some important fundamental differences in the operating methods and decision-making in the two systems, there are also some basic similarities in the functions that must be performed in the production of a product.

Staff-Line Authority Conflicts

Frederick Taylor originated the concept of functional management which was widely adopted by American industry during the twenties.[42] According to Taylor, management tasks should be separated and assigned to specialists expert in specific functional areas. Only in this way could management functions be performed scientifically. The specialist would have complete authority over his functional area in the organization, and

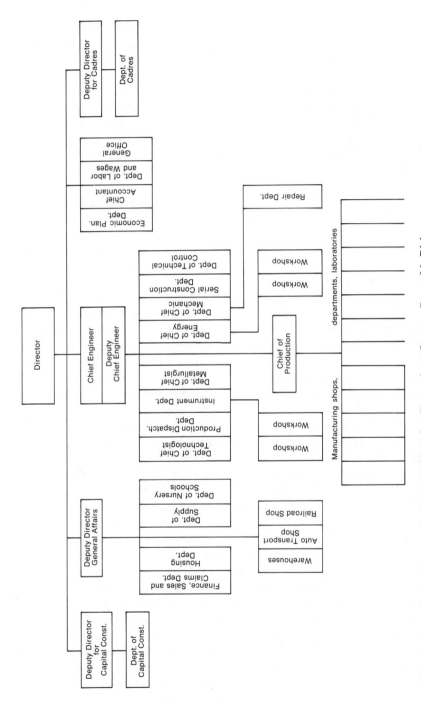

Figure 3. Organization Chart, Kharkhov Ball-Bearing Enterprise. (Source: Barry M. Richman, *Soviet Management* [Englewood Cliffs, N.J.: Prentice Hall, 1965], p. 60.)

could give direct orders to any employee in matters related to his area of specialization. Each employee under this system could have many superiors, depending on his job. The basic advantage of the functional structure is that it is possible to attain the ultimate degree of specialization and, therefore, decisions which require special skills can be made more effectively. It did not work out the way Taylor had anticipated, and the functional form was abandoned in the United States in favor of line-staff. The main flaw of the functional or pure staff structure is that it was difficult to coordinate the over-all effort and subordinates were marching to the different tunes of the many superiors. The confused lines of authority lead to severe operating problems.

The Soviet leaders adopted the functional system in the early twenties, when their own scientific management system was in full bloom, and when Taylor's theories were admired for the effect they had on American productivity. The functional system had an important advantage in a nation where managerial skills were in short supply. One specialist could supervise a great number of workers.

Functional authority dealt primarily with activities, and to that extent sacrificed unity of command for a high degree of specialization. Thus, orders would come to a department from a number of sections, such as planning, procurement, maintenance, and were in turn subject to orders from the various functional departments at a higher level. Whatever the quality of expert decision-making, the director could hardly be held responsible for something which others decided for him. If performance was not satisfactory, the enterprise director could always shift the blame onto the "functionalists" who were making all the expert decisions affecting the enterprise. Theoretically, the director of the plant was the top man with complete operative authority and responsibility; in practice, there was a functional organization which bypassed the line organization and which was organized at all levels of the industrial management structure.

In 1930, when G. K. Ordzhonikidze became chairman of the National Council of the Economy, he found a complicated and confusing industrial management system which had serious malfunctions.[43] Shortly before this, in 1929, an attempt was made to form giant production associations, patterned after large American corporations such as United States Steel and Standard Oil. The reorganization was proposed by the Holzman Commission which made a special study trip to America to get a first hand look at how giant firms are managed. As a result, large centrally managed production associations were formed in a number of industrial sectors. Thus, coal production was concentrated in "*Souzugol*," headquartered in Charkov. But the attempt to manage coalmining operations thousands of miles distant in Siberia, was a disaster, and by August of 1930, the industry giants were divided up into more manageable units.[44]

Ordzhonikidze made an attempt to break up the functional system. At that time functionalism had reached the point where officials of enterprises and trusts[45] acted like subordinates of the functional departments of the National Economic Council and the enterprise director was only nominally in charge. The functional departments in Moscow tried to bypass the director of the enterprise and gave direct orders to plant employees. Enterprise supply warehouses were under complete control of the functional departments at a higher level.[46] Functionalism led to warfare among the various specialized departments at all levels of the management hierarchy. Standards experts fought with production experts, finance with supply, and so on.

In 1934, the Seventeenth Party Congress decreed the elimination of the functional authority system throughout the various levels of industrial management. But the problem of functionalism (*funktsionalka*) persisted and was still in evidence in the postwar years, and in some forms is still encountered today. The line form of organization was adopted as the officially approved form to be used in the management of industry. Accordingly, full authority was vested in the enterprise director, who, in turn, could delegate some of this authority to department heads, and from there to foremen or section heads as the case might require. The intent was to preserve the unity command by reserving the order-giving power to the chain of command with the director at the top. Over-issuing power was specifically taken away from the functional staff. The intent was to eliminate confusion and irresponsibility which, according to Stalin, had transformed industrial management into "parliaments."

Encroachment on the managers' authority by the functional units has been a sore spot in Soviet industrial organization for some decades. But the matter is not easily resolved even in an authoritarian command system. In 1937, the party "abolished" functional authority for the second time. At the Eighteenth Party Congress, Zhdanov found it necessary to define the concept of one-man authority or unity of command:

> [The] principle of edinonachalie connotes the ability to direct, organize, select cadres, issue correct orders, demand reports of work done, and to eliminate irresponsibility and divided responsibility (remnants of the functional system). But it also implies ability to secure the support in his work of the Party organization, the activists of the factory, and its whole personnel.[47]

At that time, the functional system and the party were the major forces undermining the managers' authority. Trade unions, which were a factor in the earlier years, were squeezed out of active role in plant management. Dual subordination of the staff of the various specialized departments is a source not only of friction but of division of loyalties.[48] The main task of functional departments at the higher level is control of the formulation and execution of production plans, introduction of new technology, promotion of specialization, and cooperation with other plants. They are not independent organs of industrial management, and cannot make decisions of operational nature; they are supposed to perform predecision analysis and thereby free line executives from "the mass of minute routine matters which the functional units prepare, but, on the other hand, it is imperative to avoid the rebirth of functionalism."[49] The functional system which is routinely condemned as a barrier to efficient management does, in fact, make decisions, and since this system may operate at levels above the plant director, these decisions are transmitted through channels, not in the form of advice, which the director is free to accept or reject, but as orders which the director may not be able to ignore.

Organizational Objectives

Objectives are important to the effective functioning of any organization. Once the objectives are known, they can be translated into tasks that will have to be performed. Knowledge of the task makes it possible to design suitable organization structure to implement the basic goals.

The general goals in the Soviet system are determined by the top party leaders at the very apex of the power structure. Among the strategic decisions made at this level are the rate of growth to be achieved over some future period of time, allocation of resources to capital goods or the consumer sector, and priorities for new investments. The top leaders are not always content with specifying the major goals and letting the lower level officials specify the means. The functions of the various levels are not precisely defined and it is not unusual even today for the top leaders to become involved in the "means" problems. Control is the other important function of top leadership. Review of performance in aggregate terms also gets close attention.

Once the broad general guidelines are approved, they are transmitted to central planning for elaboration and definition of the plan as it moves down the hierarchy. The national plan is prepared by the functional group, the National Planning Committee (*Gosplan*) which reports to the Council of Ministers. There are the five-year plans and the one-year plans. The five-year plan provides a target for the economy and a projection of operations for the operating groups. The one-year plan is much more detailed and because of the shorter time span, more accurate. All levels participate in planning, including the enterprise-level planning staff, but more in terms of communicating capacity and other information which will affect plan completion capability.

Central planning (*Gosplan*) has no direct line authority over any ministry or enterprise. But the plans it prepares are approved by the Council of Ministers, and are binding on the industrial management organization. *Gosplan* makes the final decision after extensive consultation with the operating units. It is at this level that the interests (and capacity) of the operating units and national goals are weighed and priorities determined. There is considerable room for flexibility because of plan revision activities which take place almost continuously. A plan may be changed for a great number of reasons, initiated either from above or below. Frequent changes, particularly those which are initiated above, and for which the plant may not be prepared, tend to have a disruptive influence. Indeed, revisions can have a disorganizing influence to the extent of destroying the main advantage of planning. Changes initiated by the enterprise are also possible, providing they can be justified. There are suspicions voiced in the Soviet press that many of these are merely an attempt to obtain a more easily fulfilled production plan which would lead to a larger bonus.

Flexibility is also built in by the central planners in demanding more from the production units than necessary to satisfy the national plan, so that even if some plants do not come through, the results will not be serious.[50] Related to this is the issue of realism of the plan. Do central planners try to make attainable plans or inflate them beyond realistic expectations hoping that this will give an additional incentive to boost production? There is evidence that during the Stalin period, planning fluctuated from "fantastically unrealistic" during the early thirties and the Purge Era, to moderately unrealistic at other times.[51]

There is continuous interaction among the various levels in the industrial management structure. Plans are stated in broad terms at the top and are worked out in increasing detail as they move down the chain of command. The enterprise receives its plan in terms of a set of constraints on output, materials, supply, manpower, investment, wages, etc. The enterprise has a right to challenge some of the directives and limitations, and the negotiations may well lead to a more realistic plan from the enterprise point of view. The number of operating indices which were prescribed for each enterprise has varied over the years, ranging from eight at the present time to over thirty prior to the 1965 reform. There is some relation between the number of success indices which are used to plan and evaluate performance, on the one hand, and the authority of plant manager on the other. In general, the fewer the indices the more authority and independent initiative can be exerted by the director.

The Hidden Reserves

Another aspect of drawing up realistic plans is related to the existence of organizational slack at the plant level. Plant directors, intermediate management, and ministries have from time to time admitted that the central planners are not told the true capacity of the plant. This problem has existed from the beginning of central planning to this day, and has so far defied every attempt at solution. The behavior of the enterprise manager is quite rational in the sense that it allows him flexibility to beat the system. It also confirms the notion that the actual functioning of the organization structure is, as a rule, quite different from what the designers of the system had anticipated. The practice of hiding true reserves is difficult to deal with because central authorities must depend on enterprise people for information. Central decisions are ineffective not only because of the geographic distance of the central decision-making bureaucracy, but also because the complexity of the industrial system requires millions of timely decisions. So that even if, unlikely as it is, the planners somehow contrive to get the needed data, the operating system cannot delay action while awaiting directions from the top. Because it is impossible to know the situation at each enterprise, the planners "worked from some average conditions which actually did not exist in any given enterprise."[52] The ambiguity and inconsistency of the various directives from the center were unavoidable.

An economist tells of a news account that a construction project was going slowly because central authorities had forgotten to provide some equipment or instruments. How, asks the economist, can central management provide each construction project with "thousands and thousands" of various types of tools, equipment and instruments, if there are not less than one hundred thousand construction projects going on simultaneously? The economist points out that before 1965, *Gosplan* (State Planning Committee) was concerned with eighteen thousand different types of production. In addition, tens of thousands of tools, instruments and other materials were allocated by the central supply and sales organs.

> From the center, from top to bottom, approved indexes of the numerical strength of the workers of enterprises "descended" and, in a number of cases, also the size of the average wage, all the assortment of product in its entirety, by elements of the standards of fixed assets, and dozens of other indexes. But was this really economically justifiable scientific planning? Or was this merely joint attempts to observe the work of each enterprise and regulate its activities by means of small scale administrative levers? . . . It is simply impossible to control the national economy of the USSR, on its present scale and at its present rate of development, from the center and plan it by the hundreds or thousands of small and minor administrative organizational instructions and assignments.[53]

Given the constraints of the system, there has been a tendency on the part of enterprise management to understate the capacity in the expectation that this would lead to a reasonable plan. This would lead to plan fulfillment and a substantial monetary bonus.[54] Output would be allowed to go up to the bonus level, because anything beyond that would lead to a tight plan in the following year. There has been concern that even party and control personnel fail to act because they have some common interest in presenting their "area of responsibility" in a favorable light.

Party vs. Management

The Communist party organization is deeply involved in the management of industry. It parallels and overlaps the management hierarchy and must be considered part of the system.[55] It is an ambiguous role because, as we have indicated, the party is the ultimate source of authority. Despite the fact that the line organization and the unity of command principle of authority is official dogma, management officials may have a hard time maintaining their own authority.

In the past the party took a direct and heavy hand in managing industry from top to bottom of the system. Party officials made major and minor operating decisions, completely ignoring the formal industrial management structure.[56] Serious problems resulted from the party's direct participation in managing industry and the party role was changed to one of overseer or controller. But the new role did not eliminate organizational ambiguity. Although the party has no formal order-giving power to the management, the party organization is given the responsibility for the operational success of the enterprise as defined by the plan.[57] To fulfill this responsibility the party plant representative must get involved in operations. If the plant performs in accordance to the plan, the party plant representative shares in the credit and conversely if the director fails, the party man has failed to do his duty. The party man in this ambiguous role goes beyond his role of watchdog and party whip, and undermines the line organization. In doing this he must be careful not to overstep his authority because the director may have important support in the upper levels of the hierarchy. Just how far the party may interfere is not precisely clear. Gross violation of line authority is praised, in some cases, and relatively minor infractions are condemned. Apparently, the regime wants the party to make certain that the director does what he is supposed to do, and not to lose its role as a critic which would happen if the party actually took over, as it had done in some cases during World War II.

The management system is, after all, a creature of the party, to carry out the "will" of the party, so that there is no thought of raising the question of legitimacy of party interference. The line concept, therefore, is not an effective means to preserve one-man leadership and, in fact, indirect party interference is perfectly capable of destroying the concept. The real authority of the party lies in its power to force the director to change his decision, and its suggestion to introduce changes may be difficult to resist. There is no area of management responsibility which is out of bounds for the party. Interference is not constant, however; only when something is done contrary to the party goals does the director get proper "guidance." The party can also help the director by assuming an active role in mobilizing workers' support for increased output.[58] While compulsion has diminished since the Stalin era, the party has not relaxed its power.

One of the most effective means of exercising authority is through control of personnel selection for all important management positions of the enterprise. No appointment of any consequence may be made without the approval of the competent party committee. This fact certainly affects not only the behavior of the director and his subordinates, but also all those who would like to be placed on the qualifying list for important positions.

The subject of the proper role of the party in management, its interference, and "petty tutelage" has been considered periodically by the central committee meetings for several decades. The party's supervisory role in industry has been reaffirmed in 1965.[59] At the Twenty-fourth Party Congress, Brezhnev stated: "We must deal with the problem more strictly, work out and carry through a set of measures ensuring fuller use of equipment; we must place the matter under the unrelenting control of the Party committees at enterprises, and of the city and regional Party committees."[60]

Khrushchev's Reorganization

The opportunity to de-Stalinize the industrial management structure arose with the death of Stalin and the rise of Khrushchev to the top leadership position. Serious shortcomings in the economic management system were in evidence for a number of years before the 1957 reform. The economic literature was full of criticism of the mismanagement which grew out of the ministerial system then in existence. By late 1956, these defects reached a critical stage and were openly discussed at party meetings, and finally led to the lowering of the growth objectives set forth originally in the sixth five-year plan.

Faced with these problems, Khrushchev proceeded on a course of unprecedented organizational changes, which, on a smaller scale, continued until his downfall in 1964. The main impact of the changes launched on July 1, 1957 led to the abolishment of the central ministries. The management of most of industry and other enterprise was entrusted to the regional economic councils (*Sovnarkhozy*).[61] The Soviet Union was divided into 105 regions, with 70 of these in Russia and 11 in the Ukraine. The operating control passed from the ministries to the respective *Sovnarkhoz*, which in turn were subordinated to the republic council of ministers. The economic councils consisted to a large extent of former ministry bureaucrats. The central *Gosplan* took over the over-all planning functions of the abolished ministries and was given authority to coordinate the implementation of national plans.[62] The *Gosplan* of each of the national republics got the job of planning and coordination within its jurisdiction. The transfer of authority to the national republics started well before 1957. Thus, industry under republican control increased from 31 percent in 1953 to 55 percent by 1957.[63] Other actions were:

1. Prior to 1957, economic ministries were established at the republic level and some important industries were placed under republic control (coal in the Ukraine). The Chairman of the Council of Ministers of the Ukraine, Kalchenko, told the Supreme Soviet meeting in February 1957, that ten thousand enterprises in the Ukraine were transferred from central to Ukrainian control.[64]

2. Extension of the rights of the republican organs in supervision of the fulfillment of the USSR national budget (May 1956).

According to Khrushchev: "The role of the republic *Gosplan*, particularly of the Russian Federation and the Ukrainian SSR, is growing. Questions of planning and coordinating the work of the economic councils are to be decided in the first place by the republic *Gosplan*."[65]

Despite the fact that much of the economic management authority was retained at the center, the decentralization, inconceivable under Stalin, extended the national republics' authority in economic and other spheres, and represented a concession to the national republics who had always wanted some measure of sovereignty in political, cultural, and economic life. Khrushchev quoted Lenin to justify the new move: "Only great attention to the interests of the various nations removes the ground for conflicts, removes mutual distrust."[66]

Ukraine as well as the other republics undoubtedly got some measures of economic "independence," but this independence at best was severely limited by the various all-Union (central) government agencies such as the *Gosplan*. The various state committees for major industries and the party organizations were all intended to provide the required central coordination. This reform was to improve planning and control by delegating considerable initiative to the regional economic councils. The top leadership undoubtedly recognized that the complexity as well as the size of the economy had so far increased that it was quite impossible to manage it efficiently from the center.

Khrushchev's reforms resulted in some improvements, but also led to predictable difficulties which, as we shall shortly see, were, once more, the product of the system, rather than the fault of local tendencies. The improvements consisted mainly of increased local participation in plan formulation (subject, of course, to central approval), and more efficient use of available resources in the execution of the plan. Furthermore, some of the operating decisions could be made without referring to Moscow, thus reducing the cost of delay which accompanied this practice in the past. Regional development and cooperation between local enterprises were improved. The strain on the transport system due to cross-hauling under the ministerial system was reduced.

Coordination became more difficult as enterprises tended to give preference to customers within their economic region. To combat the "localist tendencies," Khrushchev set up an Economic Council of the USSR in 1962 and a Supreme Council of the Economy in 1963.[67] The 1957 reform did not live up to expectations, in part because the basic features of central management were intact, in that the decisions were now made in the various capitals of the national republics. Under the territorial system it was difficult to coordinate the activities of plants which belonged to different jurisdictions because an economic coordination mechanism was lacking and the administrative mechanism was not functioning. If this view is correct, then realistic market prices and delegation of genuine decision-making authority to the enterprise level would have provided the foundation for rational economic relationships among industrial organizations that would ultimately have led to effective coordination.

The Existing System

The Reform Debate

Discussions related to change in Soviet industrial organization are, I believe, in part due to the unfreezing of the intellectual climate during the Khrushchev years. The shortcomings in economic management were discussed relatively openly in the press. It had been reasonably obvious to Soviet leaders for some years before 1965 that mismanagement of the economy was the prime obstacle to the goals of the state. The most serious symptoms were the slow-down in the growth rate of the economy, accumulation of unsold inventories, slowdown in productivity rates of labor and capital goods, and underutilization of production capacity. Soviet authorities concluded that the problems were primarily due to two causes: the "petty tutelage," or detailed interference in enterprise level matters, and the conflict of interest between enterprise managers and central planners discussed earlier in this paper. In 1962, Professor Liberman proposed that the way to solve the complex problem of coordination and improve industry management is to upgrade the role of profit.[68] Libermanism in its original form was unacceptable on ideological grounds because it is incompatible with the Stalinist concept of management still subscribed to by the party. That concept, roughly defined, means that since the enterprise is owned by the state, it must be rigidly administered by the state.

In this scheme, there is no room for independent management of the enterprise. It cannot be managed in the enterprise's own interest.

Liberman's original proposal would probably have led to a market economy, and was in conflict with the existing ideology. After official censure, Liberman came up with a more acceptable role for profit: as a tool in enterprise performance evaluation and in distribution of bonuses.[69]

The 1965 Reform

Even though the reforms adopted in 1965 were not nearly as progressive as some of the early proposals, they promised a substantial change in the basic ground rules for industry management. The reform provisions as announced by Kosygin, and spelled out by the statute on the Socialist State Production Enterprise, contained the following major provisions:

A. Changes intended to increase enterprise authority:
1. Manpower—expansion of management rights to control wages, hiring, firing, staffing, and bonus apportionment.
2. What to produce—increase in the managers' authority to determine product-line composition, but only above the list contained in the plan. The enterprise bill of rights (statute) also gave the managers authority to do monthly and quarterly production planning.
3. Manager's control over enterprise capital derived from sale of surplus equipment and supplies and depreciation and turnover tax was to be increased substantially.
4. The enterprise manager was to be given increased authority over new capital investment. A 7.5 percent fund for this purpose was to be set up at the enterprise with the money coming from depreciation and a part of the enterprise profits.
B. The changes in the incentive system were designed to promote efficient production and make the enterprises more responsive to user needs. The size of the bonus under the new system was to be determined by indexes of sales volume and profit level. The manager was to control (according to ministerial rules and guidelines) the material encouragement fund to be used for bonus rewards to workers and managers, and the less significant social benefits (housing, etc.) fund.[70]

The reform made an attempt to remedy the weaknesses by compromise. The direct interference of central authorities in enterprise management was to be somewhat reduced but not completely eliminated. The obligatory, centrally established indicators were reduced from nearly three dozen to eight: the volume of goods to be sold; the main physical assortment of goods; the wage fund; the amount and the level of profitability; contributions to and allocations from the budget; the volume of centralized investments and the putting into operation of production capacities and fixed assets; introduction of new techniques, and indices of material and technical supply.

Major emphasis in operating objectives has shifted from volume of goods produced to volume of sales. The purpose of this measure was to make the producer more responsive to customers' needs, and thereby reduce the huge waste in terms of unwanted or poor quality products which fail to satisfy the needs of the users. The vital function of coordination in the consumer sector was to be performed, with some qualifications, by market demand. To bring managers' interests into line with those of central planners, the new incentive system was tied to sales and profits. Workers' material incentives were also to be improved.

The structural change concerned mainly, once again, the higher management bureaucracy. The territorial economic council system was eliminated and industry was again subordinated to ministries. Figure 4 shows

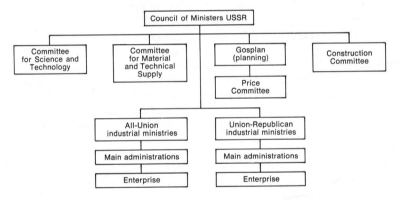

Figure 4. Partial Industrial Organization Structure, after 1965

the management superstructure after the 1965 changes. The same bureaucrats who were banished to the provinces by Khrushchev returned to Moscow to work in the industrial ministries; it would only be a matter of time before they resumed their old work habits. The 1965 reform also set up new functional groups: the State Price Committee to establish prices, the State Committee for Material-Technical Supply, an industrial supply entity, and the State Committee for Science and Technology, to push introduction of new technology.

Reform Impact

Brezhnev promised that the reforms will be carried out "efficiently and quickly," the initial goal being to have it in effect in two years.[71] But six years later implementation was still in progress. As of September 1971, 92 percent of production is under the new system and accounts for 93 percent of industrial profit.[72] The rate of conversion to the new system and the fact that the changes were implemented by the old bureaucracy led a number of western scholars to predict, correctly it turns out, that the modest changes would not lead to significant improvement.[73] The proceedings of the Twenty-fourth Party Congress leave no doubt that the party plans to continue the reforms initiated in 1965. The reformed system in its present state is a far cry from even the modest goals established in 1965. Western as well as Soviet specialists are in agreement that the impact of the 1965 reform has been slight.[74] It has failed to live up to expectations and did not solve the chronic problems of poor quality, the wrong kind of goods, poor supply system in the industrial sector, resistance to new technology, and long delays in new project completion.

Quantitative measures of performance show only modest improvement in factor efficiency. Capital productivity increased at an average annual rate of 3.4 percent during the 1966–70 period.[75] The average annual output growth for 1966–70 was 8.4 percent vs. 8.6 percent for the previous five-year period.[76]

While nearly everyone is awed by the strength, the capacity, and the size of Soviet industry, the output does not measure up to quality standards of the industrial nations. Also, with the exception of the oil industry, every industrial sector has failed to complete the plan for the 1966–70 period even though annual increases in output were substantial.[77] There is no way of knowing if the five-year plan was realistic, and therefore, it is not a definitive measure of performance.

A preliminary evaluation of reform progress by Liberman confirms that the efforts are meeting with opposition from the entrenched bureaucracy. Liberman claims that little was done to change the approach and the habits of the central planners and managers whose methods have changed little over two generations.[78] The increased autonomy of the enterprise provided by the 1965 reform has remained largely on paper. Recently, at the Twenty-fourth Party Congress, Brezhnev admitted that the new system had not solved many of the problems of industrial management.[79]

Available evidence indicates that in some sectors of industry there has been substantial improvement in over-all effectiveness. Also, as Professor Goldman points out, the situation would have been much worse if the 1965 reform had not been initiated.[80]

There are a number of reasons why the reforms have failed to deliver what was promised in 1965. In a recent study addressed to this question Professor Schroeder concludes that the bureaucratic process of the system has rendered the most promising provisions impotent. Professor Schroeder states: "By what tactics has the bureaucracy reduced the reform to impotence? Merely by doing what comes naturally to large, entrenched bureaucracies anywhere when they are threatened with change—that is, procrastinating, assimilating, complicating, and regulating."[81]

Some changes were initiated to take away the limited powers which were formerly delegated through reform. This happened in staffing. When enterprises began expanding managerial and clerical staff, the central authorities, thinking this was undesirable, issued orders to cut staff and issued standard staffing plans.[82] The reform has substantially increased the complexity of the management system and led to a 38 percent growth in the central management bureaucracy during the 1964–70 period.[83]

Perhaps the best indication of the impact of the latest reorganization of industry on management can be seen in a recent survey of 241 enterprise directors. The survey asked the directors a series of questions on the effect that the reform had on the enterprise level organization. Here are the results of the survey:[84]

1. Do you consider that the economic reform expands the independence of the enterprise and the rights of its director?

Response	% of those polled
Expands significantly	44
Expands insignificantly	56

2. Can you notice any improvement in material-technical supply of your enterprise after transfer to the new operating conditions?

Response	% of those polled
Substantially improved	2
Improved insignificantly	19
No changes occurred	79

3. What were the main difficulties which you encountered in connection with the transfer of your enterprise to the new operating conditions?

(Major) responses	% of those polled
Unsatisfactory material-technical supply	48
Insufficient size of incentive funds	43
Insufficient enterprise independence; violation by higher organizations of the Enterprise Statute	34
The persistent practice of "wilful" planning from above	26
Low selling prices	24
Instability of the plan; lack of coordination among its sections	19
Absence of help from higher organizations and of methodological, instructional materials on transfer to the new operating conditions	18

The Cultural Lag in Management

Another source of opposition to change comes from a large segment of practitioners who, after decades of "petty tutelage," are suddenly forced to assume the risks of decision-making. The simple announcement of change in management structure had no effect on the authoritarian cultural lag of the present planners and managers. They have been brought up on Stalinist methods and the change may not be an easy one even if there is a genuine preference for greater freedom of action. The managerial class is comparatively old (in their sixties); many of them survived the purges and are not innovation-minded. This may be what Premier Kosygin had in mind when he criticized conservative elements in industry who were slow in adopting the changes.[85] Many of the managers "are either unable or unwilling to think and figure for themselves; such officials are quite satisfied to let higher organizations do the thinking and make decisions for them."[86]

Birman points out that many managers are accustomed to the old system when every detail of the organization's work was directed by central authority: they "continue to work in the old way, despite the hard will of the party and government, as if there never had been a plenary meeting of the Central Committee or the 23rd Party Congress" (when reforms were approved).[87] Enterprise autonomy will require a different breed of managers. The regime had the choice of changing the existing managers' capability to operate under the new conditions, which would at a minimum require extensive training, or replacing the entire remnants of the old system. The former bureaucrats were put in charge, and training programs are still in the discussion stage six years after the reform was announced.

Producing for Customers' Needs

The breakdown of coordination between the manufacturer and consumer, a problem of long standing, is well exemplified by the recently reported washing-machine crisis. There are currently some two million washing machines, which the consumers do not want, clogging up supply channels. It is not a case of market saturation, since only about half of the households own washing machines. There are twenty plants producing five hundred thousand units of the one-drum, hand-wringer type model introduced over twenty years ago. Only one plant has merited a quality rating. Semi-automatic models comprise only about 15 percent of total output. No automatic washing machines are produced at the present time. The Moscow Electrical Equipment Trade Trust has for many years tried to induce the manufacturers to produce improved models. In 1971, for example, the Trade Trust asked for only 5,300 machines with the hand wringer, but received 300,000. The factory director responds to this situation as follows: "Do we have to fulfill the state plan? Absolutely! Just as the trade people have to meet a contract. Once machines are ordered and the factory gets its plan, you have to make the products."[88]

It is more profitable to make old products. Under the current price system, there is no sufficient incentive for the plant to develop new products which typically require investment in new facilities. Furthermore, changes in production as a rule lead to disruption of output and endanger plan fulfillment and consequently the monetary incentives. There are huge inventories of television sets, sewing machines, shoes, and women's clothing, which are being avoided by consumers. Penalties have been applied against producers of unsalable products, but the output bonus for over-fulfilling the plan more than offsets the penalty.

The impact of too much control on managerial behavior is overlooked by the authorities. The existing control apparatus is a more than sufficient party check-up "on everybody by everybody." The sheer number of agencies involved, even if control functions are separated, makes duplication unavoidable. The Leninogorsk plant is a case in point. It was checked by nineteen control commissions during the first five months of 1968. These were routine checks, the plant having overfulfilled its plan![89] The party hopes that through this complex, overlapping control system, improved performance will result. Actually, the opposite result is obtained. Excessive control discourages initiative at the enterprise level and much time, and consequently efficiency, is wasted clearing minor matters with higher authorities, and documenting every move. A manager's primary concern becomes how to avoid criticism, and this he can usually accomplish with only marginal efforts, by following a "play it safe" course. It is paradoxical that the very system of absolute control, which the party designed to guarantee that nothing stand in the way of its authority in the achievement of the major goals, should also act as an important obstacle to effective management.

Recent Trends

Reflecting the tendency to use formal organizational change as a solution to management problems, a major emphasis is being placed on a new organizational form of industrial management, the production association. The association unites a number of smaller plants producing a line of similar products. The policy favoring industrial, vertical, or horizontal concentration was adopted by the party in 1965. The cited advantages include improvements in supply, specialization, introduction of new technology, and management.[90] The association can be local, regional, or nationwide. There are two basic forms that associations can assume.

Under the unified system the enterprises which make up the association lose their independence and even their plant management structure. The plant then operates as a section of the association. The typical enterprise management line-and-staff functions are performed at the association level. This structure is used mainly in associations which unite plants in a locality. Another form of production association is used to unite enterprises which are distant from each other. Here each enterprise retains its usual autonomy, but technical, economic, and planning management functions are centralized at the main plant. The third experimental organizational form is the research-production association, which brings together these two activities and achieves shorter lead times in introducing new technology.[91] Soviet managers claim that the association form reduces the need for detailed supervision by the industries, and leads to savings in management staff. Recent data show that performance of production associations as measured by output and worker productivity is superior to the conventional or small scale enterprise.[92] The latest party congress reaffirmed its decision to accelerate concentration of industrial activity in production associations.[93] It seems that an additional advantage of larger organizational units is that they will be more susceptible to central control than a large number of small plants. The trend to larger enterprise is confirmed by the fact that while in 1955 there were two hundred thousand industrial enterprise units, by 1967 there were only forty-five thousand. In recent years the rate of decline of the small plants has increased.[94]

At the present time there is impressive experimentation with organizational arrangements. First, there is considerable variation in the number of hierarchical levels in the management structure. Along with two- to three-level systems, five- to six-level systems are frequently encountered within the same ministry.[95] One may wonder if increasing the number of levels in a bureaucracy will aggravate the problems of communication. The recognition that increasing complexity has forced the system to look for more effective alternatives, to the standardized structures used in the past, is illustrated by the fact that within twenty-two industrial ministries, a Soviet scholar has found what he considers to be 125 different systems and subsystems of industrial management.[96] Under these conditions, the author insists, it is imperative that scientific methods of determining the appropriate organization structure be used at the enterprise and higher levels.[97]

Conclusion

The present Soviet industrial management structure was developed during the Stalin era. It appears suited for achieving well-defined limited objectives. Because it demands uniformity in the organizational process, the outcomes are highly predictable. When technology and other variables are stable, the system operates within tolerable limits of distortion.

During the past two decades Soviet industry has grown rapidly, though much more slowly than in the past. The pace of technological change is slowly accelerating and the conditions are no longer as stable and predictable as they were in the past. The new complexity of organizational functions demands an adaptive organization structure which allows the manager the flexibility and authority needed to solve unprecedented problems as they develop. This is not to say that all sectors of industry need the adaptive structure. But as the economy grows and the complexity increases, it will require more sophisticated organizational forms because stable technology industries play a smaller role in the economy. The area of applicability of the command system and its advantages decline while the resulting distortions and contradictions become more costly.

Under conditions of increasing complexity, the Soviet leaders have the following alternatives. They can continue the trend toward adaptive organization structures and concomitant diffusion of authority and freedom to manage. While this option would enhance economic effectiveness, the regime is fearful that it might also jeopardize its absolute authority. Events in Czechoslovakia and other East European countries made a deep impression on Soviet leaders. There, economic liberalization spilled over into the political arena. No matter how inefficient and wasteful the centralized system, liberalization carries too much risk. The regime could also continue what is essentially a polished Stalin model, certain to slow down progress, and ensure that industry will lag in technology and efficiency.

The Soviet leaders appear to have chosen a middle course, hoping to get the best of both options: central authority with "maximum" allowable initiative and enterprise autonomy at the bottom. The central managers discovered, shortly after the new system was introduced, that local initiative led to disorganizing effects, and that was more than ample justification for the bureaucracy to increase its highly detailed direction from center.[98] Soviet organizational design experience indicates that the fundamental malfunctions of centralized authority will not disappear with the "safe" reforms which provide symptomatic relief. These problems may be expected to exert continuing pressure for needed reforms. Their effective solution will require fundamental changes which the regime at present is either unable or unwilling to risk.

NOTES

1. I. V. Panomarov, *Uchitsia upravliat* (Moscow: Ekonomica, 1967), p. 8.

2. Marshall E. Dimock, "Management in the USSR—Comparisons to the U.S.," *Public Administration Review*, Summer 1960.

3. I. Kuznezov, "Upravlenie i ego, vol v. povyshenii efektivnosti," *Voprossy ekonomiky*, no. 9 (1971), p. 94. Lenin is also quoted in Panomarov, *Uchitsia upravliat*, p. 12.

4. *Ibid.*, p. 93. According to Kuznezov, "The young Soviet state could not use industrial management which existed in prerevolutionary Russia, because they were the tools of the exploiting classes. It was necessary to create proletarian organs of economic management, to teach the workers how to manage factories."

5. E. D. Kazochkina, *Iz istorii organizacii upravelenia promyshlienostiu* (Moscow, 1964), p. 49.

6. *Ibid.*

7. *Ibid.*, p. 55. "Colleague executive" was a form of committee management. The committee consisted of plant, union, and party activities. Much of the chaos and mismanagement of the early period was attributed to these plant "councils" and their lack of clear responsibility.

8. *Edinonachalie*, or one-man leadership, means roughly that everyone in an organization should have only one superior, and was meant to fix responsibility on one individual. It is similar to the Fayol's unity of command principle which is in wide use today.

9. Kazochkina, *Iz istorii organizacii*, p. 58.

10. *Ibid.*, p. 56.

11. Alex Nove, *An Economic History of the USSR* (New York: Penguin Books, 1972), p. 45.

12. *Ibid.* A detailed discussion of the NEP period is found on pp. 83–118.

13. Panamarov, *Uchitsia upravliat*, p. 21.

14. *Ibid.*

15. *Ibid.*, p. 22.

16. A. M. Birman. *Nekotoriye problemy nauki ob upravlinii khoziastvom* (Moscow: Ekonomika, 1965), p. 14.

17. *Ibid.* In addition to Lenin, other top party officials such as Dserjinsky, Swerdlow, Kalinin, Petrowsky, and Kirov spent much time promoting scientific management.

18. A. N. Scherban, *Nauchnaia organizacia truda i upravelenia* (Moscow: Ekonomika, 1965), p. 20.

19. Panomarov, *Uchitsia upravliat*, p. 13.

20. *Ibid.*, p. 60.

21. *Ibid.*, p. 14.

22. *Ibid.*, p. 14.

23. *Ibid.*, p. 33.

24. *Ibid.*, p. 34.

25. *Ibid.*, p. 63.

26. Birman, *Nekotoriye problemy*, p. 14.

27. Harry Landreth, "Creeping Capitalism in the Soviet Union?" *Harvard Business Review*, September–October, 1967, p. 135.

28. Raymond Hutchings, *Soviet Economic Development* (New York: Barnes & Noble, 1971).

29. *Ibid.*, p. 107.

30. *Ibid.* (quoting *Pravda*, 1938), p. 71.

31. Hutchings, *Soviet Economic Development*, p. 71.

32. *Ibid.*, p. 71.

33. *Ibid.*, p. 72.

34. Panomarov, *Uchitsia upravliat*, p. 61.

35. T. A. Yampolskaya, "The Development of the Structural and Organizational Forms of Governmental Administration," *Soviet Law and Government*, no. 3 (1965), pp. 43–51.

36. Nove, *Economic History*, p. 316.

37. Lokshin, quoted in Nove, *Economic History*, p. 315.

38. Nove, *Economic History*, p. 316.

39. A recent example is a speech of Leonid Brezhnev, "Report of the CPSU Central Committee to the Twenty-Fourth Congress," *Reprints from the Soviet Press*, vol. 12 (May 14, 1971).

40. *Glavk* (*glavnye upravlenya*), or main administration, are intermediate-level units which were originally set up in 1927 to manage separate industries and were the forerunners of some of the ministries. The functions and numbers of *Glavk* were changed often over the years but their essence has not changed much. See Nove, *The Soviet Economy* (New York: Praeger, 1963).

41. The mechanistic approach to the solution of complex organization problems has led to serious malfunctions and inefficiency. Western organization theorists generally agree that the organization plan should be determined only after thorough analysis of the activities and functions which need to be performed. It is a firmly accepted principle that standardized solutions to the organization design decision are inadequate.

42. John G. Hutchinson, *Organizations: Theory and Classical Concepts* (New York: Holt, Rinehart & Winston, 1967), p. 4.

43. Panomarov, *Uchitsia upravliat*, p. 139.

44. *Ibid.*, p. 140.

45. The trust is the intermediate-level management unit usually reporting to *Glavk*.

46. The following incident took place at the all-union conference of industrial workers: Ordhonikidze: "Yesterday I heard that plant warehouses are not under the plant director's authority, but someone else's. 'There are in fact two directors.' The director at this time has been removed from supply. Let us make a decision—that the enterprise director, within the framework of his legal rights, is the only manager." From *Za Industrializaciu*, vol. 39 (February 1931).

47. Report of the Eighteenth Party Congress (Moscow, 1959), p. 218.

48. K. S. Yudelson, ed., *Pravovye voprosy organizaacii i deiatelnosti sovnarkhozov* (Moscow, 1959), pp. 108–9.

49. *Ibid.*, p. 115.

50. Robert W. Campbell, *Soviet Economic Power—Its Organization, Growth, and Challenge*, 2d. ed. (Boston: Houghton Mifflin, 1966).

51. Naum Jasny, *Essays on the Soviet Economy*, vol. 2 (New York: Praeger, 1962), p. 183. The author indicated that in 1956 the Central Committee of the party admitted the former errors and decided to break with the tradition of unrealistic planning: "The *Gosplan*, the *Gosekonomkomissiy* as well as the ministries, in working out national economic plans, do not adequately consider the real possibilities for ensuring for the scheduled performances adequate supplies of raw materials, fuel, and materials; they plan for excessive amounts of construction, and this generates extreme strains in fulfilling the targets."

52. Birman, *Nekotoriye problemy*, p. 31.

53. *Novy mir*, December 1965, p. 194.

54. For a candid account of how Soviet managers manipulate performance criteria, see Gregory Ryapalov, "I Was a Soviet Manager," *Harvard Business Review*, January–February 1966, pp. 117–25.

55. For an authoritative recent analysis of the party's role in industry, see Jerry F. Hough, *The Soviet Prefects: The Local Party Organs in Industrial Decision Making* (Cambridge: Harvard University Press, 1969).

56. Nove, *Economic History*, p. 266.

57. *Pravda*, 1 October 1965.

58. A. N. Lukyanov and V. A. Rodionov, *Partyno-qosudarstvenii kontrol promuyshienosti* (Moscow: Mysl, 1965), p. 20.

59. *Pravda*, 28 September 1965.

60. Leonid Brezhnev, "Report . . . to the Twenty-Fourth Congress."

61. Hutchings, *Soviet Economic Development*, p. 141.

62. *Ibid.*, p. 143.

63. *Pravda*, 6 February 1957.
64. *Ibid.*
65. *Izvestia*, 30 March 1957.
66. N. S. Khruschchev, *Otchetny doklad* 20, Syezd partii, p. 110.
67. Hutchings, *Soviet Economic Development*, p. 144.
68. Landreth, "Creeping Capitalism," p. 135.
69. *Ibid.*, p. 136.
70. *Pravda*, 28 September 1965, and *Ekonomicheskaia gazeta*, no. 42 (October 1965).
71. *Komunist*, no. 11 (1966), p. 43.
72. Kuznezov, "Upravlenie i ego," p. 96.
73. Gertrude E. Schroeder, "Soviet Economic Reform at an Impasse," *Problems of Communism*, July–August 1971.
74. *Ibid.*
75. M. I. Goldman, "More Heat in the Soviet Hothouse," *Harvard Business Review*, vol. 49, no. 4, p. 5.
76. Schroeder, "Soviet Economic Reform," p. 44.
77. Goldman, "More Heat," p. 5.
78. *Plannovoye khoziaistivo*, no. 1 (1968), pp. 19–28.
79. Breshnev, "Report . . . to the Twenty-Fourth Congress," p. 81.
80. Goldman, "More Heat," p. 5.
81. Schroeder, "Soviet Economic Reform," p. 37.
82. *Ibid.*, p. 44.
83. *Ibid.*, p. 37.
84. *Ekonomika i organizacia promyshlenogo proizvodstva*, no. 1 (1970), pp. 101–7.
85. *New York Times*, 4 August 1966, p. 2.
86. *Voprossy ekonomiky*, no. 11 (1963), p. 122.
87. *New York Times*, 6 March 1969, p. 9.
88. *Soviet Trade*, 8 January 1972.
89. *Pravda*, 14 June 1968.
90. *Voprossy ekonomiky*, no. 8 (1970), p. 153.
91. *Ibid.*, p. 153.
92. Kuznezov, "Upravlenie i ego," p. 97.
93. *Ibid.*
94. Hutchings, *Soviet Economic Development*, p. 95.
95. Kuznezov, "Upravlenie i ego," p. 98.
96. *Ibid.*
97. *Ibid.*
98. *New York Times*, 12 March 1972.

Comment

Vsevolod Holubnychy

Professor Billon has contributed an illuminating survey, with which I have little to quarrel. My purpose here, therefore, is to amplify some portions of his paper, and to add to it some aspects and perspectives which may or may not result in a few differences in interpretation. Because of their informal nature some of my remarks might appear disconnected and cursory, but this is unavoidable under the circumstances.

In case of the USSR, in my strong opinion, we are dealing with a unique economic system. Hence, the first questions, within the framework of this conference, are, of course, where does this unique system come from and what has determined its peculiarities. Three sources of this system seem to me especially pertinent: first, the historically inherited structure of the Russian economy before the 1917 Revolution-from-Below and the 1930 Revolution-from-Above; second, the ideology of Marx, Lenin, and Stalin plus that of other types of socialisms and of alternative systems; and third and most important, the teleology of the existing system, that is, the goals which determine the means. If we define a system as a totality, an aggregate of components unified by a common function, then the system's teleology appears, indeed, as the most important determinant of its nature and peculiarities.

Let me start with the inherited structure. From the end of the nineteenth century and until 1917, Russia was going through a capitalist industrial revolution. It had several characteristic peculiarities. First, the indigenous, native Russian capital was extremely small in all respects. Industrial revolution in the Russian Empire was being carried out predominantly by foreign capital—French, Belgian (which was quite often French, too), and to some extent German and English. When Lenin took over in 1917, there were less than three thousand incorporated firms in existence (232 of them incorporated abroad), and a myriad of small-scale proprietorships. Most of the incorporated businesses were still the *commandites sans actions* and similar types of closed partnerships; less than three hundred firms had their stocks listed on stock exchanges at home and abroad. An average public corporation had no more than forty stockholders, including managers. However, all the big businesses were organized in some 100 to 140 cartel-type associations, and there were seven huge banks (all foreign-controlled), which owned controlling stocks in almost all big firms (incorporated in Russia) and through them exercised their influence over the cartels. The imperial government was very heavily indebted to the leading west European banks and, despite domestic nationalistic pressures, could not significantly resist foreign influences over Russia's industrialization.

Since at this conference we often refer to the multinational corporations (perhaps transnational is a more exact term?), it may be worth mentioning that, along with Germany, Italy, Austria, and other countries, this type of enterprise had also first appeared on the Russian scene at the turn of the century, and was quite successful in its purposes. There were, of course, such well-known investment establishments as the Société Générale of France with its conglomerate Omnium Russe and the similar Société Générale de Belgique, which financed and controlled numerous manufacturing companies in the Ukraine and Central Russia. Most of these companies were incorporated in France and Belgium, and some were doubly incorporated in Russia also; others had their subsidiaries incorporated in Russia (Russian taxes were almost nonexistent, and, with proper connections at the court, less than 40 percent of founding capital was often enough to obtain a charter). There were also multinationals not directly founded by the investment banks. For example, the Société John Cockerill, with steel mills and shipyards at Liège and Antwerp, first joined in a half-and-half venture with the Prussian Lilpop, Rau & Löwenstein Maschinenbau AG to build a very successful enterprise, the Warsaw Steel Works, and then, together with the Prussians and some French participation, established in the Ukraine the Société Métallurgique Dniéprovienne, with its own iron ore mines and steel mills, and the coalmining and coke-manufacturing Charbonnages du Centre du Donetz à Almaznaia, closing the vertical and horizontal pyramiding with the establishment of the shipbuilding Chantiers Navals de Nicolaiev (all incorporated both in Belgium and Russia). The Dniéprovienne was so efficient and big, and, of course, influential that its comprador managers led the whole Prodamet, the omnipotent steel cartel, which controlled from the Ukraine almost all steel product markets in the empire. A similar structure arose, for example, in the Caucasus oil industry. There the local Moslem firms owned the oil fields, the Nobel brothers' Russische Naphtha-Produktionsgesellschaft and Royal-Shell produced most of the petroleum, while Rockefeller transported it by pipelines and tankers abroad. One patriotic member of the Czarist Duma suggested that the Nobel brothers should be sent to Siberia in order to lower prices and to increase supply of kerosene to the Russian peasants, but the Nobels were not Russian subjects, fortunately enough.

Having inherited and nationalized the highly centralized, monopolistic structure of Russia's industries and banks, Lenin had no choice but to organize some kind of government management of this system. He was pragmatic enough to know that big business was more efficient than small, and he therefore did not consider decentralizing the "commanding heights" of his economy. On the contrary, under his New Economic Policy (NEP) system, he preserved the organization of trusts, syndicates, and combines, which became government-owned and run by government managers. Professor Billon, of course correctly, mentions Lenin's introduction of the Taylor system of scientific management as an example of the American influence, but this system was used mainly at the plant level, to increase labor productivity. At the level of "commanding heights," however, the inherited structure of the French syndicates served as the main pattern. Moreover, through emissaries sent for this specific purpose to Germany, Lenin learned from Walter Rathenau how the government should manage the cartels. Market relations were re-established in big and heavy industries as well as in the small business and the cooperative sectors of the economy. State trusts and syndicates were to work for profit and had to adapt to consumer demand. Some competition was even permitted among and within them, but this monopolistic system still resembled the French and German organization of industries more than the American competitive system. On the other hand, needless to say, the NEP was not a "planned economy" in the modern, Stalinist sense. Lenin referred to it as state capitalism. It was similar to the modern Yugoslav system, except that Lenin did not permit workers' management of the factories.

Stalin inherited highly centralized state-run monopolies throughout the economy. In 1923, for example, there were the Yugostal Trust, which had replaced the former Prodamet but was much more centralized and unified under nationalization; the Donugol Trust, which resembled the former Produgol syndicate; the Khimugol Combine, the Ukrainian chemicals monopoly; the All-Russian Textile Syndicate—the name speaks for itself; even the Zernotrest, a state trust running the state grain farms. There were about two hundred such state monopoly enterprises, monopolizing each important industry either on a regional basis (within the constituent republics of the USSR) or, in a few instances, on a federal, all-union level. Over them all was the Supreme Council of the National Economy, with subdivisions in the republics. It fixed the basic prices of the most important products and divided the markets. The transportation and banking systems were centralized in the hands of the federal government, as was foreign trade. Controlling the whole Soviet economy was the main policy body, the Council of Labor and Defense.

This whole structure was reformed and the NEP was abolished in 1930–32, when Stalin introduced his new system of centralized planning. This leads us into both ideology and teleology. The idea of centralized government planning which uniquely characterizes the present Soviet economic system was, to begin with, an old, prerevolutionary idea. It was partly Marxist in origin, but as Stalin and his advisors conceived it, quite different from a Marxist system. First of all, it should be known that at least a dozen of the Russian bourgeois economists still advocated central government planning on the national scale at the end of the nineteenth century (I. Ozerov, P. Struve, A. Volskiy, V. Zheleznov, to mention a few), and especially strongly before and during World War I. On the other hand, there were also many socialists who opposed planning. Marx originally thought of planning—as opposed to the market—as possible and necessary only at a very high level of economic development, as a means of mass distribution of goods and allocation of resources so as to avoid overproduction and depressions. Marxist planning is not concerned with production for the maximization of growth; it is concerned more with the need to centrally distribute an abundant flow of, let us say, water to a city, so that every inhabitant gets water according to his needs. Water is not scarce; it costs more to calculate and collect its price than not to do so. Hence, "value disappears," according to Marx, but a centrally planned distribution according to some norms is still necessary to prevent disproportionate allocation, shortages, waste, and flood. This approach to planning does not appear in *Das Kapital*. It appears only in Marx's manuscripts first published between 1932 and 1939, and in German (e.g., in his *Grundrisse*, which was not translated into Russian until 1968). And these ideas have not been known in English thus far. We must not forget, by the way, that of some fifty-five volumes of the writings of Marx and Engels available today only in German and Russian, not more than a quarter were available in Lenin's day. In 1931, Stalin suppressed and prohibited all Marxology, or scientific research in Marx's archives and primary sources. The reason was that by then Stalin already had his own concept of socialism—significantly different from Marx's and even Lenin's —which he proclaimed "established" in his 1936 constitution.

With Stalin, teleology became the most important part of ideology. He abandoned the NEP because that system produced insufficient capital formation for the goal of maximally accelerated industrialization. Stalin's teleology was growth, catching up with and surpassing capitalism in productive capacity, though not in consumption. This goal was justified in ideological terms as well as in terms of *Realpolitik*. It was said, first, that superindustrialization was necessary to aid the world revolution and to build socialism "in one country." Secondly, it was said that superindustrialization was necessary for defense against foreign aggressors. After World War II especially, it was simply justified on the various grounds of pure Russian nationalism, and, since 1959, as a means of constructing Communism "first of all, in the Soviet Union." These goals were not quite new either. Lenin spoke, of course, of the need to outproduce capitalism in order for socialism to be victorious. Yet even as early as 1899, the great Russian chemist, D. Mendeleev, was the first to propose that it was both necessary and inevitable that Russia should catch up with and out-produce the United States in industrial production. This goal, as you know, is still valid today: the 1961 CPSU Program foresaw exceeding the level of U.S. industrial output by 1971, and quite recently Mr. Kosygin announced that such an event will indeed take place in 1975. Whether this was said with tongue in cheek or to exhort his listeners to more productive efforts in expectation of the better future, I cannot say. Yet, it is true that today the Soviet Union already produces more steel than does the United States.

But let us go back to Stalin and 1930. The problem was how to achieve the maximum possible growth, how to create more capital than was available under the NEP. Stalin's answer was a new economic system: a totally closed and totally centralized state monopoly, or—more precisely—a combined monopoly-monopsony, without any "freedom of entry" and, hence, without competition, normal market mechanism, or consumer sovereignty. This was his concept of socialism, his idea of central planning —as a substitute for a market economy. Stalin took these ideas mainly from the left wing opposition in his party (G. Zinoviev, E. Preobrazhenskiy) and, at least by way of analogy, from Michael Tugan-Baranovsky, the great predecessor of Keynes (unfortunately still not very well known in the West). Stalin's strategy was to achieve maximum capital formation by economizing on people's consumption through a novel price mechanism: agricultural, raw materials, and other input prices were to be depressed to a monopsonistic minimum, while prices of finished consumer goods were to be inflated to a monopolistic maximum. The resulting monopolistic profit was to be taken into the state treasury by means of sales taxes and then converted into capital investments. These investments were to be made predominantly in heavy and capital-goods-producing industries, including defense, and thus the maximum possible rate of economic growth and development was to be realized. However, to divert all possible resources from consumption to growth by this mechanism, a total centralization of the economic administration, a system of total control, including political control, was needed, since the immediate, short-run goals of this system were contrary to the wishes and demands of the masses of consumers, against consumers' sovereignty. This system of total monopolistic control over production, consumption, prices, wages, etc. is known as Stalin's concept of centralized planning.

It must be said that the term "planning" is so widely used in the world today that it is easily confused. But Stalinist planning, the present-day Soviet planning, is entirely different from the French planning, which was discussed here by Professor Laux, or from that to which Professor Galbraith referred. The planning by corporations, of course, in the view of the Russian economists, is not planning at all; it is merely forecasting and adaptation to the market. In Stalin's and the modern Russian view, planning is the opposite of the market; it is a substitute for the market. Soviet planning, in addition to long-run programming of the achievement of very specific goals, means also—and mainly—the short-run, almost day-to-day *management of the whole national economy*, of every "enterprise" unit of it, from the decision-making center.

This Soviet system of planning is sometimes called the "command economy." I do not like this term because it originates with Hitler's Germany and unnecessarily confuses Stalin's and Hitler's economic systems and policies. The term "command economy" was coined by Adolph Weber and, on a more sophisticated level, by Walter Eucken, to describe the extremely chaotic Hitlerian system. To the extent that I know this system—and Professor Fischer has concurred in my impressions—it was less well organized and less efficient than the Soviet system. It was, indeed, a pure command economy, a short-lived, war-determined system, whereas the Soviet system of total state monopoly is a rationally conceived, analytically definable model, designed to last not only in wartime but also, and mainly, under peace conditions, even though one of its major goals is the maximization of the war-making potential.

Within the Soviet system of centralized planning, another term, the "enterprise," is also a confused misnomer that inadvertently injects a Western, market-competitive meaning into it. The Soviet "enterprise" (*predpriyatie*), working on the "commercial basis" (*khozraschet*), has such an extremely limited business autonomy that it can hardly be described as an enterprising, initiative-undertaking entity. Rather, it is a plant or a factory of a firm, that firm being the state, the one and only real enterprise in the system. A Soviet "enterprise" is in an even more subordinate position than, let us say, a General Motors plant in Dearborn or Gary, in Rüsselheim or Bochum, vis-à-vis the GM Headquarters in Detroit. Certainly, it is not in the position of, let us say, the Fisher Body and AC Spark Plug companies, nor in that of the Frigidaire, or Chevrolet, or Oppel divisions, all of which are relatively antonomous vis-à-vis GM, while GM is, needless to say, independent of any government and of other automobile firms. Certainly there is nothing in the Soviet system comparable to the relationship between GM and E.I. du Pont de Nemours. Even in the American system, a plant is not an enterprise in the proper sense of the word, though a division like Chevrolet or Buick is a quasi-enterprise with a considerable degree of business autonomy, if not sovereignty. In the USSR, however, even ministries and *glavki* (divisions of the ministries), with the exception of a few insignifiant types of goods and prototypes of new products, have no authority to price their output. They, as well as their "enterprises" (plants, etc.), are *told by the plan* how much to produce of what, when and where, and for whom, and at which prices and wage rates. A Soviet "enterprise" manager has the right to spend on his own (i.e., overspend the plan), in case of extreme need, no more than 5 percent of the daily revenue, and must account for it before the State Bank on the very next day. A ministry of the central government has a similar leeway of about 10 percent, and that is as far as their "entrepreneurship" goes. Furthermore, commercial credit between "enterprises" and ministries is prohibited, while the State Bank's credit is incredibly tight, almost medieval in nature. On the other hand, the Soviet managers are free, and encouraged by bonuses, to use their ingenuity to lower operating costs if they can, although limits on ways and means are also set by both the plan and the law. To put it briefly, Soviet "enterprise" is nothing but a component of a highly centralized firm, a huge state monopoly, which is run *according to the plan* on a day-to-day basis.

Let me now briefly discuss the nature, scope, and techniques of Soviet planning, for they explain and determine the real nature of the Soviet "enterprise" as well as the nature and role of Soviet management. Here are the basic details that prevail today, after all the preceding reforms of the Soviet system. First of all, only the *annual* plans for the economy of the *nation as a whole* are today the most important *macro*economic plans, carrying the distinction of being state laws (in the legal sense). The longer-run national plans for five, ten, and twenty years are merely "control figures" and "perspectives," expressing the desires and expectations of the Kremlin leadership. The calendar and territorial subdivisions of the national annual plan are also obligatory, but somewhat less so than the annual, quarterly, and monthly plans of the "enterprises" and ministries. These latter plans include both a carrot and a stick—bonuses as well as other incentives, and the articles of the Penal Code for any deliberate underfulfillment or tampering with fulfillment reports.

The process of drawing up a national annual plan begins with the decisions of the Politbureau of the Communist party's Central Committee. These decisions are made on the basis of reports submitted to the Politbureau by various specialized departments of the Central Committee, which parallel (and supervise) the government ministries. Information submitted to the Politbureau is obviously not purely economic, but also political, international, military, and so forth, and it is prepared by the most highly qualified experts in each field. On the basis of these reports, the Politbureau decides on the so-called "leading links" of the future plan. These are the priority items around which the whole plan is to be built. Leading links include, for example, the interindustry and interregional allocations of main resources (investments, strategic raw materials, highly qualified labor, etc.) as well as output targets of from 150 to 200 basic products, such as steel, oil, chemicals, aluminum, electric power, grain, machine tools, airplanes, ships, etc. The Politbureau also decides how these basic products are to be distributed among the ministries and regions during the year. All these decisions are essentially political, economic analysis is part of them only sporadically, in cases of extreme importance affecting the whole economy. (Final decisions on price reforms—relative price levels—are also made by the Politbureau.)

The next step comes when the Politbureau sends the leading links down the channels to *Gosplan*, the central planning agency. Its task is to make sure that the leading links, the leading targets, are actually attained at the end of the year. The *Gosplan* performs, first of all, a technical economic job: it calculates the input-output balances for each of the leading links, and more. If the Politbureau's leading link calls for production of, let us say, 109,500,000 tons of steel, it is the task of the *Gosplan* to calculate how much iron ore, coke, refractories, pig iron, scrap, electric power, transport freight, labor, etc., will be needed to attain this goal. This is the input-output balance for steel. Since coke is one of the inputs, the *Gosplan* must calculate an input-output balance for it, too, which would include the targets for coking coal, which in its turn is part of the coal balance, coal being one of the leading links. The same procedure is followed in case of electric power, pig iron, and so on. In this way, all leading links are interconnected within a pyramid of the input-output balances. However, all these calculations (unlike in the French plans, for example) are made in *physical*, not value, terms. The Soviet input-output balances are calculated in the *Gosplan* on the basis of the so-called technical coefficients, prepared for it by various scientific research institutes. These coefficients tell the *Gosplan* how many pounds of coke, kilowatt-hours of power, ton-miles of freight, man-hours of labor, etc., are presently needed to produce one ton of steel. These coefficients embody the present state of technology, and they change with technology. Market demand-and-supply prices do not exist in the Soviet centrally planned industries, while the government-fixed prices enter the planning scheme only at the end of the procedure and are *superimposed* upon the physical balances largely for accounting and the *ex post facto* cost analyses.

While working on the annual plan and trying to balance it around the leading links, the *Gosplan* stands in continuous working relationship with the government ministries, local governments, and the Central Statistical Administration. The administration gives the *Gosplan* the necessary information as well as *zayavki* (requests-and-proposals) of the grass-root plants and factories concerning what they want and need, to carry out their portions of the total plan. The *Gosplan* tries to satisfy their demands, but it is not obliged to do so. Its word is final.

After the *Gosplan* has prepared a draft annual plan, it sends it upstairs to the Council of Ministers, and the latter, possibly with some corrections, submits it to the Supreme Soviet to rubber-stamp it into a law. The next task of the *Gosplan* is to see to it—virtually on a daily basis—that the plan is carried out. The actual carrying out is done by the ministries and their "enterprises" under the continuous supervision of the Statistical Administration and the State Bank, which, together with the ministries, reports to the *Gosplan*. The *Gosplan* has the prerogative of making changes in the plan, if necessary, but its supreme obligation is to carry out the plan as exactly as possible, and especially to secure the fulfillment of the leading targets even at the cost of nonfulfillment of the rest of the plan. In the final fulfillment reports we usually see that, for example, the output plan for steel was fulfilled 100 percent, or even more, but the output plan for leather shoes or housing construction was underfulfilled. It might well have been necessary to switch resources in the course of the year to fulfill the steel plan at the expense of other industries.

In addition to its obligatory nature, the multitude of very specific targets, and the day-to-day supervision of its fulfillment, the most important and unique feature of Soviet planning is that it is predominantly planning *in kind*, in physical, rather than value (price) terms. It is this feature that must be clearly understood if we want to appraise correctly the true limitations and role of the management of Soviet "enterprises." The annual plan on the federal level alone consists of some fifteen thousand input-output balances, almost all of them in physical measures. The central "depository" of these balances, or rather of goods of which they consist, is a centralized institution called the State Committee on the Material and Technical Supplies (*Gossnab*). Formally, the *Gossnab* has the same status in the government as the *Gosplan*, but its functions are more earthy. It has a large network of central warehouses and similar establishments all over the country, to which the "enterprises" deliver their output whenever they don't deliver it directly to the consuming enterprises. The major function of the *Gossnab* is to administer the distribution of goods in the course of the fulfillment of the plan. On one hand, it alone distributes the goods from its warehouses; on the other, it alone assigns the producing enterprises to the consuming enterprises for direct delivery. In other words, it is the *Gossnab* system of distribution that is the actual substitute for the market mechanism under the Soviet-type planning. It is the *Gossnab*, and the *Gossnab* alone, which decides on a day-to-day basis which factory gets what, from whom, and how much, by which dates, via which routes, and so forth. If delivery breaks down, the *Gossnab* administers the state reserves and stockpiles for such an occasion. Again, it must be emphasized that the *Gossnab* does its job in physical terms. Even though the goods are assigned government-fixed prices, which the *Gossnab* has no authority to change, it is neither obliged nor motivated to minimize costs and to make profits. Its supreme task is to assure delivery and thus secure the fulfillment of the plan.

It must be obvious now that the *Gossnab* is the most hated institution of the Soviet "enterprise" managers. It is also, probably, the most inefficient institution in the Soviet economic system from the purely economic point of view, because it is responsible for much unnecessary and unexpected costs and the misallocation of resources on the *micro*economic level, but on a *macro*economic scale. The main point here is that the Soviet plant managers have no authority and very little opportunity for illegally obtaining resources except through the *Gossnab*. The *Gossnab* allocates resources, however, only in accordance with the planned balances-in-kind (it does not sell them to the highest bidder). If the manager has made a mistake, has mismanaged his planned inputs, and his output plan as well as his neck are at stake, it is extremely difficult, if not impossible, to correct that mistake by freely obtaining the needed inputs somewhere else, for they are available only at the *Gossnab*. Similarly, if the manager sees an opportunity to make a profit by an increased production, he usually cannot do so because the *Gossnab* would not allot him the unplanned resources. This is why Soviet plant managers tend to hoard raw materials, to demand in their *zayavki* more than is needed (but they seldom get more because the *Gosplan's* technical coefficients are pretty tight and exact), or to resort to the black market, if they can get away with it.

Professor Billon is quite correct, of course, when he mentions in his report that Soviet managers as such are rather peculiar people. The earlier managers were, for the most part, civil war commanders, who knew nothing about economics or management. At a later period, especially after the Second World War, some of them were still like those earlier managers, the veterans of the war, although about 70 percent were engineers by education. In the USSR, there are no business administration schools of the American kind; the first such institute was established only in 1971, and that is for a very top level personnel only. Thus far the rule has been that the Soviet plant manager must know the technology of production of specific goods; this is why most of them are engineers. However, in my strong opinion, even a Ph.D. from the Harvard Business School could not help a manager under the Soviet planned economy. A few years ago I met a manager of a big Moscow machine-building plant, and he asked me softly: "Is it true that they teach something called 'Human Relations' in the American business schools?" When I answered affirmatively, his next question was: "And what are Human Relations?" (This was asked orally, of course; hence, there were no capital letters.)

A few other points with which I would like to amplify Professor Billon's paper are these. First of all, there is one additional problem in the Soviet system, the problem of new technology. It is of crucial significance, especially as far as the future is concerned. So far the Soviet Union has been moving ahead in technology mainly through absorption of foreign technology, which it changed and adapted to its conditions and purposes. But there is now a great problem in developing its own new technology, its own inventions. The problem lies in the egalitarian attitudes and the egalitarian nature of Soviet society. Existing rewards for the inventors are incredibly small, the patent system is peculiarly inefficient, and therefore there are insufficient incentives to invent and innovate. If the existing system is not reformed and additional incentives created, technological and scientific progress will remain very slow.

As to the administrative reforms, among the major reasons for the 1965 abolition of the 1957 territorial decentralization, the following must not be overlooked. When the *Gossnab* was abolished and the distributive powers of the federal government were greatly curtailed, a serious conflict of interest in the allocation of resources and new construction arose among the economic administrative regions, among the constituent republics, and the "enterprises" under their jurisdiction. It has been the Communist party's major policy since 1930 to give priority to the development of the eastern regions of the USSR (Siberia, above all) at the expense of the western republics and regions. Now, after 1957, the western republics and regions curtailed supply of resources for the development of Siberia and other underdeveloped areas because they had little, if anything, to gain from their development. Capital was being transferred to the east without interest and not on a loan basis; it was more productive to invest locally, i.e., in the western republics. Also the "nationalities question" was injected into this controversy, Siberia being Russian and the western republics non-Russian. It was similar to the problem of relations between Quebec and the rest of Canada, or among the republics in Yugoslavia. Hence, to secure further development of Siberia—among other reasons—the system was recentralized.

Now as to the 1966–67 reforms. In my opinion, there is considerable misunderstanding in the West about the nature and extent of these reforms. First of all, the question of "profits." The Soviet Union, it has been said, is restoring a market economy and capitalism. Such reports are written in ignorance of the fact that "profits" have always been part of the Soviet economic system, and that profitsharing, bonuses based on and derived from profits, has existed in the USSR since 1923. It is nothing new. There were periods, indeed, when profitsharing was deemphasized, but it was never abolished. In 1966–67, there was merely a renewed emphasis and a slight increase in the share of profits going to bonuses. The bonuses have increased from 8 to 12 percent on the average, compared with the past, with the managers getting a 30 percent increase and workers some 2 to 3 percent. However, it is not profitsharing as it is known in the West—whether in bonuses or as dividends. Needless to say, there are no dividends in the USSR. Profits and bonuses are not in the hands of the managers of the "enterprise" that has produced the profits; they do not belong to them. As before the reform, a rate of profit is one of the targets in the plan of the "enterprise," established for it by the higher authorities. If, and only if, that target—as well as others—is fulfilled, the management and the workers acquire the right to obtain bonuses (to supplement their wages) from a portion of the profits. The rules which allow bonus rights and which regulate the distribution of profits are established by the central government (which owns all the profits) and are known to all concerned. Each worker and each manager knows when and for what he is entitled to a bonus, and the amount. Hence, profits are not distributed at the discretion of the management, except for a very tiny portion of them—and even that is considered a collective fund of the "enterprise" and is distributed under the supervision of the local union committee. There is a motive to maximize profits, no doubt, and it has always existed, but it is not the same thing as in a free enterprise economy.

The second emphasis in the 1966–67 reform is upon sales, not merely production as before. Yet this is again an overstatement, a misleading word. Except for the collective farms' markets (bazaars), secondhand merchandise, old machines, and surplus waste materials, the goods are not "sold" in the USSR in the normal sense of the word. Rather, they are *delivered in accordance with the plan* to the preassigned recipients or warehouses at fixed (not agreed-upon) prices. The new element that the 1966–67 reform has, indeed, introduced for the first time since the NEP is the legal right of the recipient to reject the delivery in case he is dissatisfied with its quality. (Prior to the reform, they had to accept whatever was delivered.) Now this right has been granted in order to improve the quality of goods produced. If the recipient does not accept the delivery, the producer suffers a loss, his plan goes underfulfilled, he loses bonuses. At the first glance, this is a rational improvement in the existing system. However, what happens in practice is different. First of all, the *Gossnab*'s warehouses have no incentive to reject the deliveries, and they are not punished in any way for stocking bad quality goods. (In Czechoslovakia, a 2 percent tax on surplus inventories has been introduced, but not yet in the Soviet Union.) In the consumer goods field, the wholesale and retail establishments do not have much incentive to reject shoddy goods either, provided they have space for them. Although their bonuses do depend on the volume of sales and profits, they are not yet proficient in appraising and forecasting consumers' demand and tastes. Market research is still in a very nascent state in the USSR. Moreover, perennial shortages of supplies (due to the policy of the state monopoly) force consumers—whether people or "enterprises"—to take whatever is offered. Consumer demand in the Soviet economy today influences only to some extent the composition and structure of the output of consumer goods, not their aggregate, total quantity. The total quantity to be produced is decided by the Politbureau and the ministries. They decide, for example, how much leather is to be allocated in a given year to the production of civilian shoes, and the consumers cannot obtain more, whatever they demand. However, consumer demand does influence the allocation of that limited quantity of leather among the factories producing men's and women's shoes, and shoes of specific sizes, shapes, and colors. Hence, one can say that freedom of choice does exist in the Soviet economy, but there is no consumer sovereignty (if these two things can be divorced in a meaningful way).

Finally, let me say a few words about the prospects for the future. I have no doubt that new reforms are inevitable. The Soviet monopoly as it is today is too cumbersome to be efficient in the era of an accelerated technological revolution. General Motors has found it expedient to decentralize, and other giants followed suit. In the Soviet Union, I can today distinguish at least four schools of thought in this respect. There are two extremist schools, which do not have many prospects. One is the conservative Stalinist school, which wants more of the same or at least no change. The other one might be described as a liberal school, which advocates "market socialism" à la Oscar Lange or the Yugoslav model. This school is interesting, but its proposals are unrealistic. "Market Socialism" has already been tried and rejected in the USSR during the NEP. What remains are the two schools between these extremes. One advocates a degree of decentralization based on the interindustry and interregional disaggregation of the input-output balances, and appropriate, corresponding division of planning authority and sovereignty in decision-making. For example, as one of the first steps, this school advocates putting the ministerial divisions (*glavki*) and the *Gossnab* system on a commercial footing (*khozraschet*), thus making them financially responsible for their allocative decisions. Their managers' bonuses would suffer if they made irrational decisions. The next step might be a degree of decentralization in the existing pricing system. The *Gosplan* and/or the ministries would continue to fix prices of the most important goods, but the lower-level echelons would be permitted to vary these prices by a small percentage point plus or minus, so as to adapt them to local and changing conditions, at the same time maintaining the pre-fixed average price level. Another step that is advocated by this school of reformers is the establishment of voluntary but long-term contracts among supplying and consuming enterprises. Prices in these contracts would be negotiated, but still would be supervised and controlled by the central authorities. One branch of this school of thought advocates transformation of the *glavki* into smaller semiautonomous units, called *ob'yedineniya* (amalgamations).

The other moderate school is future-oriented. It visualizes a thoroughly computerized economic system, in which a pyramid of computer centers is connected by teletypes and similar automatic means of communication with grass-roots "enterprises" which report continuously to these centers about everything that they are doing or that is happening to them (current output, costs, consumer demand, etc.). The computer centers, after analysing these data, send back their instructions on what should be done. The pyramid of computer centers is assumed to be both centralized and decentralized with respect to specific decision-making powers—approximately along the same lines as the ideas of the preceding school. However, what the computer school lacks are not ideas but computers, and information to feed them with. It seems to me that these last two schools do have a future, and that they will gradually gain the upper hand.

The touchstone of all possible realistic Soviet reforms is the problem of consumer sovereignty, however. As long as the Communist party is in power—the Communist party as it is today—every reform proposal that would change the goals of the system and would orient the system towards maximization of consumption are doomed to failure. Increase in people's consumption means a slowdown in capital goods and arms industries' growth, and vice versa. This is one economic "law" that guides the Communist party. It is prepared to grant concessions to consumers under pressure; it has raised the people's welfare and living standards lately, no doubt. But still it holds these raises down to a minimum, as a total monopoly would be expected to do as long as the maximum capital accumulation remains its supreme goal.

[*Author's Note.* Within a year after this had been written, the CPSU leadership adopted, on April 3, 1973, a new managerial reform to be implemented by 1975. As was expected, this new reform takes the middle conservative-progressive road. On one hand, it foresees abolition of the administrative divisions (*glavki*) in most ministries; on the other, it summarily orders merger of many thousands of small- and medium-scale "enterprises," technological research and development and design establishments, and scientific institutes, their concentration, and complete subordination to new, rather big, industry-wide and/or regional, but centralized, "amalgamations" and "combines" (*ob'yedineniya* and *kombinaty*), which in their turn would be directly managed by the ministries, the *Gosplan*, and other government agencies, both federal and those of the republics. It is nonsensical again to call these new establishments "super-corporations" or "conglomerates," as some of our news media have done, because these latter market-economy institutions do not at all fit into the Soviet state-monopoly system, in which nothing of essence has changed after this reform. The 1973 reform does not foresee any changes in the system or in methods of centralized physical planning, pricing, or distribution. The *Gossnab* has even acquired new centralized powers over the state materials reserves, which were formerly controlled by a score of separate ministries. In a few respects, the new reform seems to return to the system of industrial management abolished in 1932–34, that is, at the end of the late NEP period, but, significantly, it does not seem to indicate a return to any kind of market competition because new "amalagamations" and "combines" are still centrally planned by the government and, moreover, are rather narrowly specialized and integrated vertically, not horizontally. Hence, if product differentiation as an element of monopolistic competition (common under the NEP) is to acquire significance as a vaguely possible future result of this new reform, it might be expected to grow from the development of *regional* "amalgamations." However, the 1973 reform, as documented so far, explicitly expresses reservations against return to the 1957–65 system of regional self-sufficiency, for reasons mentioned above. It might happen nevertheless, that with the growth of variety of output regional forces would grow naturally stronger for purely economic reasons. The new reform also places noticeable new emphasis on technological research and development, hoping that Soviet economic growth could still accelerate as a result. This would require even more intensive capital accumulation, no doubt. But the reform fails as before to foresee any new incentives to inventors, innovators, and managers. Generally speaking, as of now (May 1973), the new reform seems to portend more, rather than less, centralization in decision-making, as compared to the 1966–67 reform, even though it implies some decentralization at the top of the pyramid, at the ministerial level. But, admittedly, it is still in the state of some flux.]

7. A Compromise with Culture: The Historical Evolution of the Managerial Structure of Large Japanese Firms

KOZO YAMAMURA

The mental labor involved in the preparation of this paper reminded me of my childhood efforts to grab an eel out of a bucket.[1] One hand would grasp the head of the eel, but a split second later I would find myself holding only his tail. I would then grab the head with the other hand, again only to end with the tail. Many Japanese go through this frustrating process every summer because eel is a popular delicacy in Japan. To do justice to the subject of this paper would require four hundred pages and some training in social psychology. A mere economist with forty pages at his disposal is in the predicament of a boy trying to catch an eel.

I present this analogy not only to forewarn the readers that the subject is intractable, but also to convey that it is quite Japanese in that the process of the evolution of the Japanese managerial structure can be understood only after we have become familiar with the unique characteristics of Japanese economic growth and Japanese society. My research convinced me that my assignment in fact involves not only a description of the movements of the eel, but an effort to convince non-Japanese readers why eels, despite their unpalatable appearance, are so favored by the Japanese.

Thus I shall begin with a brief summary of what I believe to be the basic aspects of "Japaneseness," meaning the sociopsychological factors and institutions directly relevant to the formation and selection of the managerial structure, and a short description of the pattern of the Japanese economic growth. This will be followed by a few case studies and general observations on the changing managerial structure during the prewar and postwar periods.[2]

THE "JAPANESENESS"

The following four sociopsychological factors and institutions, I believe, are significant factors influencing and even determining the course of the evolution of the Japanese managerial structure.

1. Japan is a "vertical" society in which vertical human relationships —the upper-lower hierarchical order among men of unequal social standing—dominate horizontal relationships among equals. A Japanese spends

most of his daily life in situations in which he must be clearly aware of his relative ranking, or in the words of a Japanese sociologist:

> In everyday affairs a man who has no awareness of relative rank is not able to speak or even sit and eat. When speaking, he is expected always to be ready with differentiated, delicate degree of honorific expressions appropriate to the rank order between himself and the person he addresses. The expressions and the manner appropriate to a superior are never used to an inferior. Even among colleagues, it is only possible to dispense with honorifics when both parties are very intimate friends. In such contexts the English language is inadequate to supply appropriate equivalents. Behavior and language are intimately interwoven in Japan.[3]

Because of the overwhelmingly vertical nature of the society which dominates their life from childhood, Japanese function best in situations in which relative rank order is clearly established. This means that, if a Japanese finds himself in a circumstance in which rank order is not clearly established, he will take infinite pains to establish it for his psychological comfort. The need for the established rank order is such that "even a set of individuals sharing identical qualifications tends to create a difference among themselves."[4] Anyone who has ever visited Japan is familiar with numerous examples of the processes by which Japanese quickly establish at the first meeting their relative rank order, by methods ranging from exchanging name cards (which invariably carry the person's title) to discreet questioning of the other's age, occupation, and the school from which he was graduated.

Because of this strong need for rank order, even in cases in which its overt establishment is discouraged, rank order, in however subtle a form, will eventually emerge.

> Some of the new, successful postwar enterprises, such as Sony, for example, or Honda, used to pride themselves on their modern democratic management; but after they had reached a certain stage of development, when the establishment had grown larger and achieved stable success, there gradually developed within such firms this rigid seniority system as is to be found among older, larger, established enterprises. Some Japanese interpret this phenomenon as evidence that a company has "matured," for it is a general truth in Japan that the larger the size and the firmer the establishment of an institution, the greater the inclination among its personnel to develop an internal ranking order and to evolve a bureaucratic pattern. This phenomenon may be universal, but the form it takes in Japan is unique.[5]

This pervasive and strong vertical characteristic of the Japanese society produces, as its necessary consequence, a social behavior pattern which is crucial in understanding the historical development of the structures adopted by the Japanese firms. Again in the words of a Japanese sociologist who has summarized this behavior pattern most succinctly:

Whereas there is in Japan no notable horizontal group consciousness within such groups as executives, clerks, manual workers and so on, there is instead a strong departmentalism constructed along the functional vertical tie. It may group together a section head and his subordinates; in a university department, for example, the professor is closer to his lecturer and assistant . . . and to his students than he is to any of his fellow professors.[6]

This rigid vertical nature of society, a product of the past which has come to be well-entrenched in modern Japanese society, must always be kept in mind in discussing the managerial structure in Japan.

2. Another, better known, "fact of life" in Japan is that social characteristic which has been variously termed paternalism, groupism, familyism, and most recently, "Japan, Inc." This familiar aspect of Japanese society originated in the strong tradition of *ie* or the "house." Simply put, this is the Japanese sociopsychological tendency which emphasizes (in the sense of protecting, cherishing, finding needs for, or functioning best in) "us" against "them." In the context of this paper, a firm may show this characteristic by being "paternalistic" toward its employees. This can take the form of providing various welfare programs, fostering group cohesion by providing housing for employees to live as neighbors, holding daily prework sessions to recite company mottos, or conducting seminars at a Zen Buddhist temple, etc. Employees for their part place the success of *uchi* (i.e., their company, department or section) above everything.[7] Even an employee's family takes second place (in terms of time, mental energy, and emotional output) to his unit at work. What is important is that, in Japan, this can be said even of factory workers. The ultimate form of this characteristic is the well-known lifetime employment system which is still accepted as the norm in Japan. The *uchi* guarantees security in one's lifetime, and in return it demands total dedication.

This, along with its vertical quality, results in a facet of Japanese society which is important in the context of this paper. That is, the hierarchical rank order of a person is there for life, and any sign of disregarding it is not only repugnant to the harmony within an *uchi* but is also extremely costly to those who ignore it. In understanding the Japanese process of decision-making, this is of crucial importance. Though this brief observation must suffice here for this important facet of Japanese life, it should be made explicit that a purely economic explanation of this characteristic among Japanese—such as the long-run maximization of profit or income, or labor conditions—can never hope to explain it away. The importance of *uchi* is psychological as well as economic.

3. After a discussion of the vertical nature of society and the importance of the *uchi*, the institutions of lifetime employment and the seniority system—both in the Japanese sense of these terms—are easy to understand. Lifetime employment is only a socially expected form of membership in an *uchi* and seniority is the handiest and socially the least costly (least disruptive of harmony) indicator which can be used in establishing rank order. Economic explanations of these institutions can be only partially successful.[8]

Though we need not describe these two well-known institutions further, we should add that they are the major reasons for the numerous expressions of the view which might best be summarized as "men over organization." As long as the functioning of a firm is rigidly circumscribed by the lifetime employment and the seniority systems, what is most important is to hire "good" men because they will, in time, become senior enough to rise to be the decision-making officers of the firm. Latitude of selection in making promotions is severely limited in Japanese firms which, under normal circumstances, promote their employees by seniority. The advantages of a new managerial structure must be weighed carefully against the possible costs which it could incur vis-à-vis the verticalness of the society, the seniority system, and the lifetime employment system.

4. The widely used *ringi* system of decision-making is a natural one for the society which we have just described.[9] This is a system by which any change in routines, tactics, and even strategies of a firm is originated by those persons who are directly concerned with the change, and the final decision is made at the top level after an elaborate examination of the proposal which results in acceptance or rejection by consensus at every echelon of the managerial structure. The consensus-building involves at first one's immediate colleagues. If a consensus is obtained, then the proposal goes to the head of that group, and the head will circulate it among the heads of departments (or sections) which will be directly and indirectly affected by the proposed change. If a go-ahead is obtained at this level (or after a few more layers of consensus-building, if necessary to reach the top level) it will finally go to the top for sanction.

The system is ideally suited to Japanese firms because it assures harmony within an *uchi*, enables senior (but not necessarily more capable) men to occupy higher-ranking positions, and the cohesion of the group is ever strengthened because no one is to be blamed should the change end in failure. Informal consensus-building, in any event, is much more efficient in getting the best view because a committee would be dominated by a senior presiding chairman, whom they would be most reluctant to oppose. In public as well as in private, a subordinate will take the greatest care in his efforts to change the mind of his senior. The process is extremely delicate and often time-consuming. But to most Japanese, what is gained by the *ringi* system is considered more important than the slowness of the process, its unsuitability for long-range planning (strategy), and (from the western point of view) its other shortcomings.[10]

This description of the *ringi* system is by no means a caricature. The system is changing and is being complemented by other methods of decision-making, but it is still used widely by the largest firms even today.

Though the institutions of seniority and life-time employment entrenched themselves gradually, the Japanese economy grew within the society which we have described. While the oft-debated question of whether Japan succeeded because of, or despite, her Japaneseness is interesting, our concern in the remainder of this paper must be focused more narrowly on how far the structures of the largest firms were influenced by Japaneseness.

As structure is a means to realize a strategy, an equally important question is: what were the strategies behind the evolving structure? In asking this question, we must note explicitly that: Japan was a late entrant to industrialization; the government actively involved itself in achieving rapid growth by various means; the highly concentrated market structure and asset holdings were and still are pervasive characteristics of the Japanese economy; and, Japanese industrialization was achieved in a capital-short and labor-abundant condition—at least relative to the western industrial economies. (We assume, following Professor Chandler, that structure follows strategy with valid justification, as will be shown in the course of this paper.) More will be said of the characteristics of Japanese economic growth as they become relevant in the course of this paper.

THE PREWAR STRATEGY AND STRUCTURE

Because of the well-known dominance of the *zaibatsu* in the prewar economy, examples for our purpose are easy to select.[11] We shall examine Mitsui, the largest of the four "big" *zaibatsu*, and Mitsubishi, the second largest. Mitsui represents in many ways Sumitomo, which also had a long tradition beginning in the Tokugawa period, and Mitsubishi can be considered to represent the last of the four *zaibatsu*, Yasuda, which like Mitsubishi began *de novo* after the Meiji Restoration. Though these four *zaibatsu* accounted for most of the largest firms and nearly 75 percent of the total paid-in capital by the 1930s, we shall also consider Matsushita, a firm which, as we shall see, was a unique innovator in managerial structure in prewar Japan. The last subsection of our observations on prewar Japan will be on the trade associations, the role of the government, and the trading companies, each of which showed characteristically Japanese responses for increasing the effectiveness of large firms in the international markets.

The Mitsui Zaibatsu[12]

By the Meiji Restoration of 1868, the merchant house of Mitsui, the largest of the clothiers and money-exchangers, had been in existence for nearly two and a half centuries. During its long existence, a well-established and elaborate structure had evolved. Mitsui's chief executive officer was a *bantō* who, after many years of service and a slow progression up the rigidly structured ladder of promotion, rose to the position of running the day-to-day business of the house. He sought decisions from the Mitsui family only if the matters involved were of special importance. A generalization on the exact scope of freedom which a *bantō* enjoyed is not possible because, during the two and a half centuries, the ability and personality of both the *bantō* and the head of the family ranged from weak to strong.

The *bantō* for the first twenty-three years of the Meiji period was Rizaemon Nonomura, whose forte, fortunately for Mitsui, was his ability to deal with the powerful officials of the new government. It is perhaps accurate to speculate that Nonomura had no strategy as such, save his desire to exploit all and any opportunities offered Mitsui by the new regime and changing economic conditions, and especially by the high-ranking government officials who were not above exchanging their influence for tangible rewards.

Nonomura managed to get Mitsui appointed an official handler of the government revenue. This meant that Mitsui had access to government money, interest-free, in exchange for the services which the Bank of Japan was to perform, beginning with its establishment in 1882. In 1876, the Mitsui Bank was established under a newly enacted law, and Mitsui bought a trading company, founded by Kaoru Inoue, a leading political leader, who started the company on the strength of the exclusive right he was granted to market coal produced by the government-owned Miike mine. As all the new ventures were financed by the Mitsui family and run under the supervision of Nonomura as a branch of the House of Mitsui, there was little need to change the structure and no attempt was made to do so.

However, by the time of Nonomura's death in 1893, the Japanese economy, which had already begun the phase of active industrialization in the cotton textile industry and suffered through the Matsukata deflation and its aftermath, was quite different from that seen in 1868. A merchant of the old school, before his death Nonomura had been experiencing increasing difficulties in coping with the problems of an emerging industrial age with its modern banking, manufacturing industries, and waves of inflation and deflation which plagued Mitsui's trading business.

To lead Mitsui in the new age, Inoue, who had retired from politics and was now an "advisor" to the Mitsui family, brought in thirty-eight-year-old Hikojirō Nakamigawa as the new *bantō*, i.e., the *de facto* top executive.[13] For Mitsui to take in an outside man as its *bantō* was unprecedented, but so was the rapidly changing Meiji economy. Nakamigawa, who had shown his entrepreneurial talents as president of a relatively large railroad company, went to work immediately to put into effect his strategy predicated on the future of Mitsui being dependent on its involvement in industry. With the goal of allowing autonomy in decision-making to each of the Mitsui enterprises, existing as well as new ones yet to be acquired, Nakamigawa decided on a course of decentralization. The trading company and the clothing business were made independent companies under the direct control and ownership of the Mitsui family, and the Mitsui bank and the mining operation (which Mitsui had bought from the government) were also organized into independent entities under the control of a committee composed of members of the Mitsui family and top executives of the bank and the mine. A separate "Industries Department" was organized under the same committee, and the heads of the newly acquired paper, coalmining, and textile operations joined the committee as these operations were brought under Mitsui control.

However, contrary to Nakamigawa's intent, what he created was a structure which differed only in form from that of Nonomura's time, without a change in substance. The problem was the committee, consisting of the top executive of each branch of the Mitsui activities and the Mitsui family. Though its name was changed several times to conform with the requirements of the changing laws, the committee started and continued as the body which made final decisions, even on matters which Nakamigawa thought should be decided by each enterprise. Nakamigawa's efforts to limit the power of the committee by isolating the members of the Mitsui family only created an unwieldy "roof over a roof," as Morikawa aptly put it, and in earning the enmity of more traditionally minded top executives who headed various Mitsui enterprises. To exacerbate Nakamigawa's difficulties, the matters for which the committee acted as the final decision-maker included personnel affairs of executives and all senior officers; organizational changes; budgets; the settlement of accounts; the purchase, sale, construction, and modification of any fixed assets; contracting with other companies; the dispatch of directors to other firms; and nonoperating expenditures (such as contributions).

Thus, under a structure still heavily traditional Mitsui continued to buy more firms (mostly in textiles) to be added to its "Industries Department" by profits which were being earned by the bank and the trading company.

The managerial structure of each of the Mitsui-controlled enterprises was no different from those of most of the large firms in prewar Japan. This structure, which began to take a definite form by the beginning of the twentieth century and remained virtually unchanged until the end of

World War II, merits a brief digression. A typical *zaibatsu*-affiliated large firm, for which final strategic decisions were made by a *"honsha"* (the head office, or the committee in the case of the Mitsui), was headed by a president who may or may not have been a member of the *zaibatsu* family. In making nearly all decisions and especially in deciding important tactics and strategies to be recommended to the head office, the president took full advantage of the *ringi* system. He had no general staff to help him and none was considered necessary since he could in most circumstances rely on the head of a division or a section who came to him well armed with the *ringi* papers which had been carefully scrutinized at all levels. There were strong presidents who initiated strategies and fought for them at the *honsha* or in the top echelon committee to which he belonged. But such presidents were rare since "good men at all levels" could be relied on by the presidents, and thus the principal duty of most presidents was to "know good men" and only rarely to exercise veto power over *ringi* papers which had already traveled a long road of consensus. All the functions of a firm were organized on the "line" basis and a textbook written as late as 1955 commented: "In fact, most firms allocate nearly all of their employees to a line segment. In comparison, staff segments are nearly completely ignored. Rare indeed is a firm which has a general managerial staff as an independent unit."[14]

Returning to Mitsui, Nakamigawa, who made unsuccessful efforts to establish a decentralized structure, died in 1910. His place was taken by Takashi Masuda, then president of the Mitsui Bussan (trading company) which had been showing large and increasing profits. Masuda's strategy for growth was to make maximum use of Mitsui's huge (by Japanese standards) financial power, by purchasing firms already in existence, or otherwise extending controls over firms by means of partial stock purchase, interlocking directorships, or loans made through the Mitsui bank or by Mitsui Bussan. To carry out this course of growth, in 1909 Masuda reorganized Mitsui into the Mitsui Gōmei (the Mitsui holding company) under a committee (Mitsui *rijikai*) consisting again of the Mitsui family and the presidents of principal Mitsui companies (but not including the heads of firms indirectly controlled by each of the Mitsui enterprises). The change was more legal than structural. Masuda, as the builder of the Mitsui *zaibatsu*, continued to add new companies under the umbrella of the Mitsui holding company during his tenure as the leader of the Mitsui *rijikai*.

Under Masuda, the power of the *rijikai* at the head office remained extensive. Despite the increased volume of decisions which the *rijikai* had to make due to the increasing number of Mitsui-controlled firms, it was reluctant to delegate more authority to each firm. The only exception was perhaps the case of Mitsui Bussan, which was allowed to buy and sell goods at its own risk, moving away from strictly commission business. By the 1920s, we find that this trend had continued to the point of allowing Bussan to engage in forward buying and selling. We should, however, see this change not as a basic change in the attitude of the *rijikai*, but only as an *ad hoc* compromise forced upon the *rijikai* because of the nature of the trading company's activities.

In fact, despite obviously increasing problems arising out of the structure dominated by the *rijikai*, Masuda attempted no structural changes as such. Rather, as one of the strong believers in the "men over organization" view, he took care to hire the best men from the best universities. Because of Mitsui's size and reputation, and because of the strong desire of the graduates to be associated with the top-ranked Mitsui, Masuda had little difficulty in skimming the cream of graduating classes. It was about this time that the phrase "as good as men of Mitsui" was coined.[15]

Following the retirement of Masuda in 1914, his post was occupied by Takuma Dan, whose personal views and ability seemed to have had little to do with the growth of Mitsui empire. The First World War boom was enormously profitable, and even the interwar period, which consisted of the dismal years of the postwar recession and of the Great Depression, benefited the *zaibatsu*. The *zaibatsu* in these years were in a position to buy struggling firms and to invest the enormous profits which they had accumulated. The *zaibatsu* banks began to enjoy rapidly increasing deposits as a result of the collapse of many smaller banks during the period. Under the circumstances, Mitsui continued to grow within the structure which in substance remained unchanged from the time the "Industries Department" was created. Thus Dan, who was to become known as "Dan the indecisive," could say: "There is no need to even write down the organization of companies; people who can, can; those who cannot, simply cannot."[16] And, these words were eagerly repeated as they came from the man who headed the Mitsui Gomei which had just (in 1926) raised its capital to an enormous 300 million yen.

By the time Nariakira Ikeda became the top executive officer of the Mitsui *zaibatsu* in 1933, the Mitsui empire was a huge complex of nearly 150 firms. The major strategic decisions of about twenty principal Mitsui companies were still made by the *rijikai*, and those of the companies which were controlled indirectly by Mitsui's principal firms were made by the executives of the controlling Mitsui firm. Under these circumstances it is not surprising to hear complaints that 70 to 80 percent of Ikeda's total energy was spent in coordinating the activities of Mitsui companies.[17] But somehow the large empire under the *rijikai*, supported by "the good men of Mitsui," continued to prosper. By the mid-1930s, when the economy was rapidly becoming a war machine, Mitsui seemed to have little time to concern itself with a possible change in structure despite the increasing time the *rijikai* took to make decisions. Expanding opportunities for war-related activities preoccupied the Mitsui empire.

The Mitsubishi Zaibatsu[18]

As Yatarō Iwasaki established the foundation of the Mitsubishi *zaibatsu* after the restoration, the budding empire was his to rule. To enlarge his activities, this shrewd and aggressive founder followed a course which was not unlike that pursued by Nonomura at Mitsui. Iwasaki was second to none in his ability to extract what the new government had to offer. A few ministers of the new government sacrificed their political lives for the benefit of Iwasaki. The autocratic founder expanded his profitable enterprises from shipping, heavily subsidized by the government, to mining and to a variety of commercial ventures.

When Yatarō died in 1885, what he left was taken over by his younger brother, Yanosuke, who was as able and aggressive as Yatarō. Yanosuke in 1886 reorganized Yatarō's interests into the Mitsubishi Company, under which he could control the companies he was acquiring. The structure and its function were similar to Nakamigawa's "Industries Department" at Mitsui. And, within this framework, Yanosuke's Mitsubishi acquired metal and coal mines, a water supply company, and a medium-sized bank (the One Hundred and Nineteenth Bank). Yanosuke's strategy, like Nakamigawa's, was to expand into mining and manufacturing industries. Following this strategy, the number of enterprises under Mitsubishi control increased. This meant that some degree of autonomy was required by each enterprise to enable each to function smoothly. Yanosuke chose to yield his power only on an *ad hoc* basis and only to a trusted few among those who headed his enterprises. To make certain that his power would be delegated only at his pleasure, he issued, in 1888, a directive stating that "the appointment and resignation of officers and any problems pertaining to the execution of the business concerned, regardless of importance, shall be settled by the instruction, decisions, and approval of the president, and shall in no case be governed by any other officer."[19] However, because one man's reactions to a given question are easier to anticipate than those of a committee, Yanosuke's policy and the directive notwithstanding, the Mitsubishi firms seemed to have enjoyed smoother sailing than did the Mitsui firms under the *rijikai* if the growth of the Mitsubishi firms relative to that of the Mitsui firms are any guide.

Such a highly personalized structure, however, was appropriate and could remain efficient only under an exceptionally capable man. When Hisaya, the eldest son of the founder, took over from Yanosuke in 1893, the *modus operandi*, built on tacit understanding and the forceful but predictable leadership of Yanosuke, no longer functioned smoothly. Save for the establishment of the Mitsubishi Bank in 1893 (to replace the One

Hundred and Nineteenth Bank, whose charter was to expire in 1898), Mitsubishi under the ineffectual Hisaya only coasted on Yanosuke's accomplishments.

Fortunately for Mitsubishi, however, Hisaya was replaced *de facto* by Koyata, the eldest son of Yanosuke, in 1906. Though Hisaya remained the *de jure* head of the Mitsubishi Partners, Ltd. which was established in 1893 to meet the requirements of a new law, it was Koyata—"the reincarnation of the founder Yataro"—who commanded the empire. In 1908, following the death of his father, Koyata became the largest shareholder, and this further strengthened his hand. In the same year, Koyata carried out a reorganization of the Mitsubishi structure. The reorganization[20] increased the number of divisions, and the head of each enterprise was given increased autonomy, which included the freedom to make some investment decisions. Koyata's reorganization, however, did not grant each enterprise the power to make any strategic decisions. The new structure was used to carry out Koyata's "one-man rule," and his authority "on all crucial matters" was delegated only on an *ad hoc* and personal basis.[21]

In 1916, at the height of the First World War boom, Koyata became *de jure* head of the Mitsubishi Partners, Ltd. No longer was it necessary to consider Hisaya's wishes, and seeing the successful expansion of the Mitsui *zaibatsu* under its holding company system, Koyata in 1916 converted the partnership into a holding company with a newly enlarged capital of 120 million yen (from 50 million yen). Each of the Mitsubishi enterprises became a legally independent, incorporated entity with its shareholding opened to the public. Koyata's decision "to go public" was motivated by the relative weakness of Mitsubishi's own bank and Mitsubishi's limited access to capital (relative to Mitsui with its large Mitsui bank). As long as the holding company retained controlling shares, "going public" was the most efficient way to expand.

Through the First World War boom, the Mitsubishi empire grew rapidly, and in 1919, the Mitsubishi Trading Company was organized by Koyata to challenge its counterpart at Mitsui. Mitsubishi, like Mitsui, continued to grow throughout the 1920s. By 1928, the Mitsubishi holding company controlled nearly two hundred companies with approximately 900 million yen in paid-up capital, and by 1930 the total deposit of the Mitsubishi Bank nearly equalled that of the Mitsui Bank.

Matsushita: An Explorer[22]

Even in the *zaibatsu*-dominated prewar economy, scores of firms managed to grow outside of the *zaibatsu* empires. One of these firms was the Matsushita Electric Appliances Company, and it merits a special examination here because of the firm's role as an explorer of new managerial structure in prewar Japan.

In 1917, twenty-three-year-old Kōnosuke Matsushita quit his job at the Osaka Electric Company to start a new electric appliance company on the strength of his patent for an improved socket for electric bulbs. The initial going was extremely difficult for Matsushita, who had only a minuscule capital (100 yen), no experience in production or management, and only a few years of formal education. Making an extremely interesting and long story short, his company somehow managed to survive and grow, mostly thanks to a rising demand for his company's products, which soon included lamps and radios, and to his inventiveness. By 1928, the total sales exceeded 100,000 yen and the firm employed over three hundred men.

Despite this success, the company was still small compared to the *zaibatsu* subsidiaries which were its competitors. To compete, Matsushita added new lines of products, acquired established plants, and built new factories. As growth continued, an increasingly difficult problem arose: the problem of efficiently managing an expanding number of product lines and plants. To compete against larger firms, Matsushita needed a managerial structure efficient enough to compete successfully with his *zaibatsu*-backed competitors.

Thus, in 1934, Matsushita adopted a bold divisional structure. Four divisions, each producing related lines of products, were created and each division was divided into production and sales departments. Each division was made responsible for maintaining its own network of sales outlets, decisions involving production, coordination between sales and production research, advertising, and profit-making. In explaining why he adopted the structure which was to have many imitators a generation later, Matsushita wrote:

> The reason simply is that the number of product lines was increasing. As this happened, one person had to do the job of two or even three. When my company was small, I could supervise all aspects of the company. But then I could no longer do everything because of the increased product lines. . . . There were some lines of products with which I was not familiar. For example, I had never handled electric heaters before. . . . I asked a man to be in charge of producing electric heaters. Then, I thought why not make him completely responsible from production to sales and even to making profits. This way, he has the necessary authority to do the job well. So, I told this man that he could run the electric heater division as he saw fit, and he needed to come to me only when extremely important questions arose in his division.[23]

Given the strength of Matsushita's personality—which he was to prove most convincingly in postwar Japan—these words undoubtedly exaggerate the autonomy which the head of the division enjoyed. But whatever the degree of autonomy, we should make note of this innovative prewar structure, adopted nearly a generation ahead of its time.

Trading Companies in International Trade

Because of over two centuries of self-imposed seclusion by the Tokugawa shogunate, Japanese at the time of the Meiji Restoration were unprepared to cope with the complexities of international trade. For the first few decades following the Restoration, international trade was dominated by Americans, English, and Chinese.

Japanese responded characteristically to rectify the situation. The government mobilized all of its power to aid large Japanese concerns which had begun to compete with foreign firms. In the context of this paper, a case in point is the subsidies given, preferential regulations enacted, and the "ship Japanese" campaign waged by the government on behalf of Mitsubishi Shipping, which was battling against the Pacific and Orient (P & O) of England.[24]

Trade associations, which began to appear by the 1880s, provided, and continued to provide with increasing efficiency, a potent weapon for Japanese firms facing foreign competition. The most illustrative is the case of the Cotton Textile Trade Association which won favorable shipping rates and conditions and lower raw cotton prices for its members during the last decade of the nineteenth century. No single firm in the infant industry could have been effective against the powerful shipping lines and distant Indian cotton merchants.[25]

However, even a combined contribution made by the government and the trade associations could not match the contribution made by trading companies in increasing the effectiveness of the largest Japanese firms in the international scene. The largest trading companies were in the unique form of sōgō shōsha, or general trading companies, which dealt in commodities ranging from "noodles to warships." The largest among them were the Mitsui Trading Company (Mitsui Bussan) and the Mitsubishi Trading Company (Mitsubishi Shōji), the origins of both of which we have already described. The importance of these trading companies cannot be overemphasized in discussing the managerial structure and the effectiveness of large Japanese firms in the international market. One could go as far as to say that it was because of these trading companies that the largest Japanese firms achieved the success which they enjoyed without having an internal structure explicitly designed to deal with the variety of problems involved in international trading.

Led by Mitsui Bussan, by the beginning of the twentieth century these trading companies began to establish an increasingly efficient network of trading posts around the world. A trading post could be a large branch office in New York or a one-man operation in the interior of China, but all gathered information on new markets, technology, daily changes in prices, and even political conditions, as well as functioning as buyers and sellers on behalf of Japanese firms. By the time of the First World War boom, these trading posts were as numerous as Japanese embassies and consulates around the globe.

By the mid-1920s, large trading companies had grown from the commission merchants of the turn of the century into efficient "international divisions" of the prewar version of Japan, Inc. Of this transformation, Professor Noguchi wrote:

> The foundation of the Mitsui Bussan, the leader among the *zaibatsu-*connected trading companies, was securely established during the period of the Sino- and Russo-Japanese wars when Japanese industrial capitalism and monopolies were being established and also when an increasing emphasis was being placed on international markets. The importance of the general trading company accelerated because of the trade with China which followed the Sino-Japanese war and because of the Manchurian soybean trade which increased after the Russo-Japanese war. The Mitsui Bussan was not a mere international trader; it had its own shipping and shipbuilding divisions, child-companies and their subsidiaries which the Mitsui Bussan controlled. It indeed was a mammoth general trader. . . . In fact, it was a champion of Japanese capitalism in the international scene.[26]

Though the Mitsui Bussan was by far the largest, by the mid-1920s nearly a dozen large trading companies were competing in finding foreign buyers and sellers, in providing information relating to technological developments and market conditions abroad, and in lending all the assistance to Japanese firms which their area and commodity specialists possessed. For the large Japanese firms, which were increasingly involved in international markets, the services of the trading companies—most likely those of the trading company within the *zaibatsu* group to which the exporting or importing firm also belonged—all but eliminated the differences existing between domestic and international trade.

POSTWAR STRATEGY AND STRUCTURE

The end of the Pacific war brought dramatic changes to the Japanese economy. Along with numerous thorough-going "democratization" measures in political and educational institutions, the allied powers liquidated holding companies, dissolved *zaibatsu*, encouraged "a stock-holding revolution," enacted an antimonopoly act, legalized labor unions, and purged top executives who had been connected with *zaibatsu* and the war efforts. In fact, occupied Japan experienced a tidal wave of Americanization, and the managerial structure was no exception.[27] Since, I believe, there were two identifiable, though overlapping, periods in structural changes, let us examine each in turn.

The First Phase: 1947–57

During the period between 1947, when the reconstruction measures began to be adopted, and 1957–58, when the first postwar recession was experienced, the most important goal of the large Japanese firms was to increase their capacity by adopting more advanced technologies. Each large firm raced to outdo its competitors in investment and rationalization in order to increase its share of the market. The managerial structure adopted by many large firms (most of which were set free from the superstructure of *zaibatsu* holding companies for the first time) was a compromise between tradition and the supposedly superior (more "scientific" and "democratic") American managerial structure which was being introduced as a part of the massive tide of Americanization. One firm after another established a *jōmukai*—a committee of executive officers who may or may not have departmental or line responsibilities—as the top collective body of decision-making. A few firms, as early as the early 1950s, even went so far as to create a "general staff" and other staff sections which were to perform "horizontal" functions.

By 1958, two surveys showed that as many as 172 out of the largest 233 firms had a *jōmukai* or an equivalent, and a surprisingly large number, 75 out of the largest 125 firms, or 60 percent, had a group of men designated to perform general staff functions in a department most frequently called the planning department or management-control department.[28]

However, the number of firms with a *jōmukai* and/or a general staff is a misleading indicator of the postwar changes in the managerial structure of large Japanese firms. This is because a *jōmukai* or a general staff existing in form did not, in many instances, mean that they existed in substance. As in the introduction of western ways of life following the Meiji Restoration, the forms were easier to imitate than the substance. *Jōmukai* in most instances differed little from *ad hoc* or regularly scheduled consensus-building meetings called by a president in the prewar years. As in the prewar years, the hierarchy of the decision-making personnel was rigidly established by age from the president down to the junior executives.[29] Under these circumstances and reinforced by the strong vertical nature of society as a whole, it was next to impossible for the *jōmukai* to function "democratically" or as a place for the meaningful exchange of views. The "discussions" within the *jōmukai* were frequently a faithful replica of the prewar "exchange of view" carried on in order to build a consensus behind one *ringi* proposal among men most anxious not to offend their seniors.

The general staff and other staff charged with "horizontal" functions fared even less well. There must have been a few firms in which such a staff functioned well, but if we are to characterize the efficiency of these staff functions in general for the first phase, the only accurate assessment is to say that they were often no more than a clearing house of *ringi* proposals. An executive of the Nihon Sekiyu (Japan Petroleum Refining Company) which created a general staff division in 1952 was frank in observing:

> Now as the result of the creation of the general staff division, the *ringi* system is made to cover planning, programs and execution within various departments while delegating the authority pertaining to expenditures to department heads rather than at the top executive level including the president.[30]

The main reason why a general staff or a "horizontal" staff could not function as such in substance was the general unwillingness and inability to take advantage of such staff functions. Any horizontal relationships on an individual basis, even in the case in which the vertical relationship of the sections or divisions to which each belonged was established nominally, were awkward, if not unnatural, for Japanese. The expertise which a junior staff possessed could be shown to a senior man through a coating of several cumbersome layers of humility, only to remind all concerned of the efficiency of the *ringi* system. A general staff, created to minimize the weakness of the *ringi* system, thus frequently found itself making most use of the *ringi* system which is geared to vertical relationships. Not surprisingly, members of a "horizontal" division learned quickly that the shortest intrafirm distance between adjoining points is an inverted V going through the firm's *jōmukai*.

As the westernizers of Meiji Japan found that eating beef is far easier than liking its taste, by the late 1950s Japanese firms were aware that they were suffering from a case of indigestion from the hasty adoption of "democratic" and "scientific" American managerial structure. Thus it was not surprising to find, beginning about this period, a sharply increased journalistic attention to the strong or "one-man" presidents of Sony, Honda, and other companies. It was also during this period that corporate executives began in earnest to revive the *zaibatsu*-like superstructure by means of "an association of presidents" and by an increasing number of mergers, mutual stockholdings, and interlocking directors. Surely, one of the important causes of the "revival" of the *zaibatsu* must be that there were enough corporate executives who favored the traditional structure which had once given them their golden days.[31]

The Second Phase: 1955 to the Present

While what we have characterized as the first phase still continues for some firms and while superstructures similar to those of the prewar years continue to emerge, there has been a definite and significant transformation of the structure of giant firms beginning from around 1955 when Japan's postwar growth began to accelerate. These were changes in substance arising out of the necessity imposed on them in the form of rapidly increasing outputs and varieties of products, and of the gradually developing excess capacity which began to change the nature of competition, demanding long-range planning, research, and managerial coordination.[32]

As even a brief description of this phase requires far more space than can be allotted in this paper, let us first give two examples of such transformations to minimally acquaint ourselves with the nature of the second phase:

Tōyō Rayon.[33]   Established in 1916 on capital provided by the Mitsui Trading Company, Tōyō Rayon grew rapidly through the prewar years and continued to grow after the end of the war, thanks partly to its technical agreements with Du Pont in 1951 and with ICI of England in 1957. A former *zaibatsu* company, it had reorganized itself in 1949 to operate as an independent firm.

As the post-Korean War economic growth continued, the growth of Tōyō Rayon accelerated, and the firm began to experience "an increasing complexity of managerial problems." By 1955, it was necessary to overhaul its "topheavy, highly centralized structure." The structural changes introduced were far-reaching. Departments of managerial-control, production, and sales were organized under the president, and the distinction between line and staff, now strengthened, was clearly delineated. Complete departmentalization with all sales, purchase, and independent accounting functions was not adopted, despite a minority opinion advocating it, because the number of product categories was considered not large enough to warrant such a change. The *jōmukai* was made to consist of only the top executive officers who had no line responsibilities "so that they could more objectively participate in the general managerial decision-making." The scope of the *ringi* system too was narrowed to limit its use only to financial matters and to the amendment of budgets and payment schedules. In meeting an increasing need, in 1959 the company added a development division to specialize and coordinate research activities, and the general staff was strengthened to make planning and control of the firm's activities more effective.

Matsushita Electric.[34]   As we have already seen, this firm, which had adopted a departmental structure complete with independent accounting in 1934, continues to play the role of a pacesetter in the managerial structure of Japanese firms. Still led by the founder, the firm had grown by 1960 to employ nearly forty thousand in seventy plants, and its continuing growth enabled the firm to claim by the end of the 1960s the largest market share in twenty of the electric appliances markets in Japan.

Behind the rapid growth of Matsushita was a series of structural changes which were adopted after the war and especially after 1955. By the late 1950s, the major features of the managerial structure of this firm consisted of: (a) complete independent accounting within each division including costs, profit, and taxation; (b) each division pays "interest" of 10 percent for the capital it "borrows" from the head office; (c) each division is divided into two "profit centers," i.e., the production and the sales segment of each division attempt to maximize their respective profits; (d) in their efforts to maximize profits, each profit center has the right to refuse the purchase of parts from another profit center if these parts can be bought at a lower price in the market (this right has been exercised only a few times since the locational and financing arrangements which can be offered by another profit center within the firm can usually overcome the price differential) and; (e) strategic or important tactical decisions are subject to veto by the head office. Of course, the head office is responsible for interdivisional coordination, research activities, advertising and market research, acquisition of capital and borrowing, and other aspects of the firm's activities which require the direct attention of, or which can be accomplished more efficiently by, the head office.

The rapid growth of demand for consumer durables and the fact that Matsushita produces numerous lines of products partly explain why the firm came to adopt this structure. However, another and perhaps a more important part of the reason for the firm's structure is the innovative and bold founder who continues to preside over Matsushita, one of the most successful Japanese firms.

The second phase, coming as it did during the decade of rapid postwar growth, is gradually but steadily changing the managerial structure of large Japanese firms. Many are in the stage of Tōyō Rayon, and their structural changes are necessary responses to problems not unlike those faced by Tōyō Rayon. Their problems frequently are: (1) a structural weakness found in an inability to deal with the operational complexity created by rapid growth and by a proliferation of product or activity lines; (2) the absence or inadequacy of a general staff to advise and work for the top management which is finding the *ringi* system increasingly inadequate; (3) the weakness of the structure which is weighted either for efficiency in the acquisition of raw material or in the sale of products, depending on the firm; (4) unsatisfactory coordination of research activities; and (5) the tendency of the functional (line) vertical structure to dominate over increasingly necessary horizontal coordination.[35]

Given these and similar problems, many firms responded and continue to respond with their choice of structural changes. These changes, when seen across industry, are toward departmentalization with independent accounting, something akin to the profit center of Matsushita Electric, and toward strengthening the general staff and the "horizontal" coordination of activities. For the largest firms, the *ringi* system is being assigned a decreasingly important role as a tool of decision-making.[36]

These changes in substance, however, are being made within a society in which any attempt to modify the seniority and permanent employment systems by a large firm is news, and in which verticalness and groupism have the tenacity of centuries-old tradition. If Japanese found "horizontal" relationships in a *jōmukai* or between individuals difficult to accept during the 1950s, there is little reason to believe that a decade and increasing necessity make them any easier to accept now. Thus, what is being created is a uniquely Japanese offspring begotten of a marriage of the strategic necessities of large firms and Japaneseness. However closely we examine a firm's organization charts for before and after organization, the observed differences in the structure are no more informative than a photograph of a child in knowing his character.

As I have neither the space nor the ability to characterize the complex offspring, we must be content here with the following glimpse of the most recent structural changes. Toshio Dokō, who carried out a widely discussed "revolution" of the giant Toshiba Electric in 1960, described the "backbone" of his successful "revolution" in the following words:

> Any structure must be based on trust. The most important thing is that men on the top and at the lower echelons can trust each other. The men on the lower echelons should trust but not respect the top. "Respecting" sounds good, but it encourages authoritative attitudes among the men on top and discourages the men at the lower levels from speaking up. So, "respecting" gets in the way of smooth delegation of authority.[37]

To achieve his revolution, Dokō created a new general staff consisting only of executive officers without line responsibilities, gave virtual autonomy in strategic decision-making to the heads of newly created divisions, streamlined the hierarchical structure of the firm by demoting nearly one hundred less able managerial personnel, and carried out a variety of other measures. The revolution was successful enough to reverse the trend of falling profits. But, most revealingly, the crucial element—the "backbone" —of the revolution, at least in the mind of Dokō, was not these changes but his leadership in "providing an environment of mutual trust in which the delegation of authority became possible" and his ability "to get the maximum out of everyone."[38]

If we detect an echo of the prewar "men over organization" view in the words of Dokō, we are a step closer to understanding the character of the paradoxical offspring of Japan's desire for rapid industrialization and her Japaneseness. It may be well to remember that this offspring has many siblings produced out of just such a necessity during the past century of Japanese industrialization and modernization.

The Postwar Trading Companies

If one asks an executive of a large postwar Japanese corporation what structural changes his company adopted in order to operate more effectively in international markets, his answer would be either "virtually nothing because exports are increased by offering lower prices for a given quality of products" or "we have an export division and a staff who specialize in foreign markets." Both answers, however, are negative in that even the second answer could and often does mean merely an increase in the number of special staff within an unchanged structure.[39]

If no significant structural change was carried out to increase Japanese firms' efficiency in international markets, how did Japan accomplish its phenomenal increase in exports? A part of the answer of course is competitiveness in price, as has been frequently confirmed in econometric testing, and another, no less significant, lies in the trading companies which made all the necessary structural changes for the purpose of increasing efficiency in international markets.

The large trading companies were dissolved by the Allied Powers, but by 1954 the Mitsubishi Trading Company reemerged, regrouping again all of the smaller independent trading companies created by the Allied Powers. By 1959, the Mitsui Bussan too "revived" to lead other trading companies. As before the war, these two plus several other large trading companies are the key to the success of Japanese firms in the international market. In 1960, the ten largest trading companies accounted for 52.2 percent of all imports and exports, and the figure rose to 58.2 percent by 1965. If we take the percentages of exports and imports handled by trading companies for only the largest firms, the figures are much higher.[40]

The postwar trading companies are replicas of those of the prewar years, except that they are much larger and much more efficient. They are actively supported by the government through extremely lenient tax policies and special preferences in receiving low interest loans by the Bank of Japan and by government agencies. The postwar trading companies perform many functions. They finance the trading of the capital-hungry postwar Japanese firms, a function possible because of their privileged access to major banks and to government loans, and because their well-established credits are readily accepted. They are increasingly bold risk-takers who are willing to underwrite large firms' investments abroad. Many overseas investments and new ventures of all types by large firms are initially suggested by these trading companies. It goes without saying that, because of efficient networks of branch offices now established literally around the world, they perhaps are the world's best private sources for economic intelligence.

In short, trading companies function as extremely adept information-gathering divisions as well as the sales and purchasing divisions of many of the largest Japanese companies. This is the reason why an export department of a large firm is often little more than a liaison office with the Mitsui Bussan or its competitors.

To fully analyze the Japanese managerial strategy and structure, these general trading companies, which are "the objects of envy and fear" as the *Economist* of London put it,[41] yet require a thorough analysis. Here all we can do is to suggest that anyone who wishes to conduct thorough research into Japan's managerial strategy and structure must analyze the roles of these trading companies with utmost care.

AN ASSESSMENT

The managerial structure of large Japanese firms and the path of evolution which it has followed are products of the unique course of the last century of rapid Japanese industrialization and the deeply ingrained, homogeneous sociopsychological characteristics of Japan.

From the beginning of Japan's industrialization, the factors which crucially influenced and even determined the structure to be adopted differed in several significant respects from those facing firms in the West. In Japan, which began to industrialize from the lowest level of per capita income among the successful industrializers and with little accumulated capital in comparison to any western nations, there were, by the 1880s, a small number of families and individuals who commanded extremely large amounts of capital by the standards of Meiji Japan. That is, the emerging *zaibatsu* had all the advantages of the first and largest firms in an industry. Furthermore, the rich literally grew richer, especially with the large subsidies, cooperation, and encouragement provided by the government which was most eager to industrialize the nation as rapidly as possible.

The chosen few bought the government's pilot plants and mines, often at only a fraction of cost, and acquired going firms which invariably seemed to have been strapped for expansion capital. To do this by making maximum use of their large amount of capital, the structure which they had at the beginning of the industrialization seemed sufficient, whether it was a traditional *bantō*-system or a virtual autocracy by able heads of a family. As Nakamigawa was probably made painfully aware before his death, Mitsui with capital could grow, even under the command of a cumbersome committee.

The command by the *zaibatsu* over the scarcest resource in Japan became more encompassing due to the extremely profitable World War I boom and through the recession of the 1920s. Therefore, the *zaibatsu* holding companies, which continued to function as the supreme headquarters of their respective empires, were able to spread their fine webs of control. Their capital increased, thanks to the giant *zaibatsu* banks which continued to grow, to profits accruing to oligopolists favored by the government, and to high returns enjoyed by large firms which were able to extract all the benefits of economies of scale in production and marketing.

The structure seemed to matter little as long as the *zaibatsu* possessed the capital and as long as their "good men" could be counted upon to give their utmost to their lifetime employers. In the hands of their junior and middle-echelon executives, who were chosen from the best of the universities, the *ringi* system seemed to do the job. Those leading a *zaibatsu* enterprise could count on the *ringi* system to produce the best of decisions. However, even with the seemingly well-functioning *ringi* system, the highly centralized prewar structure was cumbersome. It took an increasingly longer time to make strategic decisions. The costs of cumbersomeness and the resultant delays, however, seemed unimportant to the *zaibatsu* which continued to enjoy increasing profits and growth. Many, holding the "men over organization" view, continued to believe that the costs were chargeable to human weaknesses and not to structure.

In a comparative sense, one must not overemphasize the Japaneseness of the prewar *zaibatsu* structure. As Professor Chandler's study on American firms has shown, the types of strategy and structure which we have just seen are those to be expected of large firms which have already accumulated sufficient capital for growth. Seen this way, though with Japanese variations, the *zaibatsu* followed the course which, in the main, is to be expected of such large firms. The *zaibatsu* holding companies too were multidivision operations, each of which expanded to take advantage of increasing demand. Though much more study is needed to make the comparison truly meaningful, the reason why executives in Japanese *zaibatsu* empires may have met less hindrance in their efforts to expand their activities in the allocation and uses of *zaibatsu* resources than their American counterparts in the largest firms may have been the fact that *zaibatsu* firms, because of their extremely large size relative to other firms, had more control over markets, and because of numerous government policies favoring them. The *zaibatsu*, unlike thousands of smaller and medium-sized firms in Japan, could control many of the risks by means of cartels, agreements among *zaibatsu* firms, and government policies, and by their sheer size.

In contrast, Matsushita followed more closely the structural pattern of large American firms, and for similar reasons. Here the important point to be made is that, within the Japanese context, for any man with less ability and power than possessed by Matsushita, his bold structural changes could have meant an effective loss of control over various divisions. For most Japanese executives in the mid-1930s, the managerial comfort resided in their knowledge that they had at least the nominal power to make all the decisions, even if it meant only sanctioning *ringi* proposals.

The end of the Pacific War brought about an Americanization of the managerial structure which, like many other measures of Americanization, was a hasty grafting of American "democratic and scientific" branches onto the old Japanese stump. Despite all the inducements to change and the disappearance of the holding companies, the stump proved resistant and the grafting seemed to fail. However, the rapid growth brought all the problems which Professor Chandler's four large American companies faced, and measures had to be taken to nurse the seemingly failing branches back to health.

Despite the "revival" of the *zaibatsu*, mostly due to the high dependence of rapidly growing Japanese firms on bank loans, the economy is much more competitive, and postwar firms must be able to react to the numerous tactical and strategic problems much more efficiently than did the prewar *zaibatsu* firms. The problems which the executives of large firms faced during the last few decades include: an increased rapidity of technological change; investments on a larger scale and the consequent problems of excess capacity; slowly but steadily rising imports; the increased necessity of producing and marketing "a whole line of products" under a single managerial structure rather than under an umbrella of a holding company; and many other increasingly complex problems of the postwar Japanese economy.

However, growing in Japanese soil, the fruit on the branches are more Japanese than American. The new structure has all the trappings of Du Pont or General Motors, but appearances are deceptive. The structure emerging is an exquisite compromise between necessity and Japaneseness. The necessity is expected to be felt even more deeply now because of the increasing liberalization of Japanese economy and the birth of many "multinational" companies. The Japanese characteristics, at the same time, are beginning to show signs of change—permanent employment and seniority systems are being questioned and the *ringi* system is constantly being reevaluated. But, as of now, the beginning of the 1970s, the dominant structure is a Japanese compromise. Though a careful study of the internal workings is still needed, I believe this observation would apply even to the structure adopted by Matsushita who, after all, is the best known supporter of the postwar version of "the Japanese spirit and western technology."[42]

There is little one need add concerning the postwar structural changes which large Japanese firms have adopted to increase their efficiency in the international market. As for the prewar years, their collective secret is the trading company, and a government which is dedicated to "Growth through Exports." Why the general trading companies developed and continue to be so effective are questions which I plan to investigate in the near future. However, if I may be permitted to speculate, the answer most likely lies in the importance of historical accident, in those qualities which we call Japaneseness, especially those meant by "Japan, Inc.," and in the obvious economic advantages.

To condense in the fashion of Professor Chandler, capital was the most important factor in the historical development of the Japanese managerial structure. Because of Japaneseness, and all the advantages enjoyed by the *zaibatsu* firms, the personnel problems required less explicit attention than in American firms. This is what Noda meant when he said that in Japan, "being an executive is to fulfill a status and not a function."[43] The *uchi* counted but not the individual. At a different level, the lateness of entry into industrialization and the consequent rapidity of growth, achieved in a highly concentrated market structure, were as significant in determining the Japanese managerial structure as was the government which placed high premium on rapid growth.

Many western students of Japanese managerial structure have expressed surprise and even astonishment. Its "inefficiency" and the "executives who seemed to know little" have been severely criticized. Both the surprise and the criticisms are only partially justified. When the path of the evolution of the Japanese managerial system is better appreciated and an understanding of Japaneseness is acquired, it is easier to understand why an "inefficient" structure and seemingly little-knowing executives managed to produce the third largest industrial economy in the world.

NOTES

1. I am painfully aware that this paper lacks detailed descriptions of the internal workings of decision-making within large Japanese firms and specific examples of strategic problems faced and means adopted to solve them. While I willingly admit my limited knowledge, I wish also to assign some of the blame to the limitations imposed on me (time and location; the latter is Hawaii which can boast of beaches but not books) and to the lack of studies in Japanese on the subject of this paper. This lack, I believe, is due to the unique nature of the process of the evolution of the managerial structure in Japan, which has led many economic historians to examine entrepreneurs as business leaders rather than as executive, managerial, de-

cision-makers and to perceive *zaibatsu* as "monopolistic capitalists" rather than as a structure. However, because of recent developments, managerial structure and strategy, as defined by Professor Chandler, are beginning to receive attention in Japan. Professors Hidemasa Morikawa and Kazuo Noda are leading students among a handful of men who are currently working on the subject. To Professors Morikawa and Noda, who both so kindly and generously aided me in my efforts to write this paper, I express my most sincere thanks. My appreciation also goes to several busy executives of large firms, especially Mr. Masaki Kojima, a director of Marubeni-Iida, Ltd., who gave valuable time to answer my many questions.

2. Due to the limitation of space, many points and observations made are not developed as fully as I wished. Interested readers are referred to a long bibliography contained in H. Rosovsky and K. Yamamura, "Entrepreneurial Studies in Japan: An Introduction," *Business History Review*, vol. 44, no. 1 (Spring 1970).

3. Chie Nakane, *Japanese Society* (Berkeley: University of California Press, 1970), p. 30. For anyone interested in the Japanese managerial structure, I most strongly recommend this book.

4. *Ibid.*, p. 25.

5. *Ibid.*, p. 37.

6. *Ibid.*, p. 38.

7. The word *uchi* means "house," but can be used to refer to any unit, large or small, to which the speaker belongs.

8. Among many good sources on these systems, the most recent works include: Robert E. Cole, "The Theory of Institutionalization: Permanent Employment and Tradition in Japan," *Economic Development and Cultural Change*, vol. 20, no. 1, (October 1971); Robert E. Cole, *Japanese Blue-Collar: The Changing Tradition* (Berkeley: University of California Press, 1971); and, Hiroshi Hazama, *Nihon-teki keiei no keifu* [The Genealogy of Japanese Style Management] (Tokyo: Nōritsu Kyōkai, 1963).

9. The best concise discussion of the system is found in M. Y. Yoshino, *Japan's Managerial System—Tradition and Innovation*, (Cambridge, Mass.: MIT Press, 1968), chap. 9.

10. In addition to what is described in the text, the advantages of the *ringi* system include the fact that a decision made by this system need not be "sold" to others in the firm. This means that the total time required between the inception of an idea and its execution is not necessarily longer than the time required in the West where "selling" one's plan may take considerable time.

11. In an earlier article, I defined a *zaibatsu* as having the following three characteristics: (a) semifeudal characteristics in that centralized control rests in a *zaibatsu* family which extends its power through strategically arranged marriages and other personal knight-vassel-like relationships; (b) well-knit, tightly controlled relationships among the affiliated firms by means of holding companies, interlocking directorships, and mutual stockholdings; and (c) extremely great financial power in the form of commercial bank credit, which is used as the central leverage to extend control in all industries. Kozo Yamamura, "Zaibatsu Prewar and Zaibatsu Postwar," *Journal of Asian Studies*, vol. 23, no. 4 (August 1964), pp. 539–40. This article also presents quantitative data on the absolute and relative economic power of each *zaibatsu*.

12. As there exist no sources in English which examine the structural changes of Mitsui, all the sources used are in Japanese. The most useful were: Shigeaki Yasuoka, *Zaibatsu keiseishi no kenkyū* [A Study of the History of the Formation of the Zaibatsu] (Tokyo: Minerva Shobō, 1970); Kazuo Shibagaki, *Mitsui, Mitsubishi no hyakunen* [One Hundred Years of Mitsui and Mitsubishi] (Tokyo: Chūō Kōron, 1968); and a dozen standard Japanese works on *zaibatsu* which are cited in my article

mentioned in note 11. This section also owes much to the current research of Professor Hidemasa Morikawa, who made his findings freely available to me.

13. For a further discussion on Nakamigawa, see Tsunehiko Yui, "The Personality and Career of Hikojirō Nakamigawa," *Business History Review*, vol. 44, no. 1 (Spring 1970).

14. Eiichi Furukawa, *Keieigaku* [A Study on Management] (Tokyo: Seirin Shoin, 1955), p. 140.

15. Masuda's "men over organization" view is fully described in Kazuo Noda, *Zaibatsu* (Tokyo: Chūō kōron, 1967), pp. 15–19.

16. *Ibid.*, p. 138.

17. *Ibid.*, p. 29.

18. For sources which are available only in Japanese, and for further discussion of the founding of the Mitsubishi *zaibatsu* and the changes in its managerial structure, see Kozo Yamamura, "The Founding of Mitsubishi: A Case Study in Japanese Business History," *Business History Review*, vol. 41, no. 2 (Summer 1967), and Hidemasa Morikawa, "The Organizational Structure of the Mitsubishi and Mitsui Zaibatsu, 1868–1922: A Comparative Study," *Business History Review*, vol. 44, no. 1 (Spring 1970).

19. Quoted in Kazuo Noda, *Zaibatsu* (Tokyo: Chūō kōron, 1967), p. 33.

20. For a detailed description of the reorganization, see Morikawa, "The Organizational Structure of the Mitsubishi," pp. 67–68.

21. The president of the Mitsubishi Shipbuilding Company recalled: "He really was an one-man ruler" and "no one dared to speak against him" when he proposed any new idea. Noda, *Zaibatsu*, p. 163.

22. The major sources used for this section are: Kazuo Noda, *Matsushita Konosuke: sono hito to jigyō* [Konosuke Matsushita: The Man and His Enterprise] (Tokyo: Jitsugyō no Nihon, 1968); and Shirō Ishiyama, ed., *Matsushita keiei* [The Management of Matsushita] (Tokyo: Diamond, 1967). In both the prewar and the postwar sections relating to Matsushita, I benefited greatly from generous assistance given me by Professor Kazuo Noda.

23. Noda, *Matsushita Kōnosuke*, pp. 195–96.

24. See Yamamura, "The Founding of Mitsubishi."

25. Keiichirō Nakagawa, "Organized Entrepreneurship in the Course of Industrialization of Prewar Japan," International Conference on Economic Growth, September 5–10, 1966, Tokyo, mimeogaphed.

26. Tasuku Noguchi, *Mitsui Konzern* (Tokyo: Shin-hyōron, 1968), p. 20.

27. All these postwar "democratization" measures and the Japanese policies which followed them are discussed in detail in Kozo Yamamura, *Postwar Japanese Economic Policy: Growth vs. Economic Democracy* (Berkeley: University of California Press, 1967), chaps. 1–6.

28. The results of these surveys, conducted by Keidanren (the Japanese counterpart of N.A.M.) and *Kindai Keiei* (Modern Management), an influential monthly, are fully discussed in Kazuo Noda, *Nihon no jūyaku* [Japanese Executives] (Tokyo: Diamond, 1960). The Keidanren survey, much the more detailed of the two, is appended in its entirety to the Noda study, pp. 312–77.

29. According to Noda's calculations based on the data obtained from the Keidanren, the mean ages of various levels of Japanese executives of 232 largest firms in 1958 were: board chairman (*kaichō*), 68.0; presidents (*shachō*), 64.9; vice-presidents (*fuku-shachō*), 61.0; executive directors (*semmu*), 59.5; directors (*jōmu*), 57.9; and, deputy-directors (*hiratorishimari*), 53.8. Around 30 percent of these executives served less than four years at each level, and only 6–15 percent served more than 8 years. *Ibid.*, pp. 320–21.

30. *Ibid.*, p. 129.

31. The observations in this and the preceding paragraphs are based on my interviews with several Japanese executives, and recent issues of magazines and journals on management.

32. Despite the expressed wish of Keidanren to legalize holding companies, they still remain illegal.

33. Japan Productivity Center, *Kaisha soshiki* [Company Structure], vol. 2, Japanese Management series, (Tokyo: Japan Productivity Center, 1959), pp. 143–78.

34. Ishiyama, *The Management of Matsushita*, pp. 3–24.

35. These are common denominators which I deduced from the ten case studies included in: Japan Productivity Center, *Kaisha sosiki*, and interviews with several Japanese executives.

36. Among a score of useful publications on recent structural changes, the most informative are Kuniyoshi Urabe, *Jigyōbusei no unei* [The Workings of the Departmental System] (Tokyo: Nihon Nōritsu Kyōkai, 1961); and Shin Takamiya, ed., *Shōsu-seieishugi no keiei-taisei* [Management Structure Adapted for Management by a Small Elite] (Tokyo: Diamond, 1971).

37. Masajiro Ikeda, *Tatakau Businessmen* [The Fighting Businessmen] (Tokyo: Nihon Bungeisha, 1968), pp. 67–68.

38. *Ibid.*, pp. 56–67.

39. Because of space limitations, I was not able to discuss the role of the government which also had an impact on managerial strategy as well as structure in the large postwar firms. The following observation, though I believe it overstates the importance of the government, suggests its role, especially that of the Ministry of International Trade and Industry: "The Japanese government corresponds to corporate headquarters, responsible for planning and coordination, formation of long-term policies and major investment decisions. The large corporations of Japan are akin to corporate divisions, with a good deal of operating autonomy within the overall policy framework laid down by corporate headquarters, free to compete with each other within broad limits, and charged with direct operating responsibility." James C. Abegglen, ed., *Business Strategies for Japan* (Tokyo: Sophia University, 1971), p. 71.

40. Katsutoshi Uchida, *Sōgō shōsha* [General Trading Companies] (Tokyo: Kodnasha, 1971), p. 64.

41. Quoted in Uchida, *General Trading Companies*, p. 41.

42. The prewar version was a catch phrase used by the westernizers of Meiji Japan.

43. Noda, *Japanese Executives*, p. 125.

Comment

Hugh T. Patrick

Professor Yamamura's paper is one of the more stimulating essays on Japan that I have read in some time, largely because I find myself in considerable disagreement with the author's premises concerning Japan's cultural uniqueness and the effects of these unique features on Japanese large-scale business. I think what has come out of the discussion today has been concern that there are cultural differences among societies, even within Europe, and we ought to find some way to handle them. This paper is the only one, it seems to me, to tackle that problem directly.

My uneasiness about this thesis of Japanese uniqueness expresses itself at two levels—one broad, general, probably rather superficial level, and the other somewhat more detailed and specific. So at the broad level, I sometimes have a feeling that Anglo-Americans have developed so-called rational models of behavior and organizational structure, which we claim, and to a considerable extent, have succeeded in persuading others to believe, are universal models. And then when we find that some other country—France, or Germany, or Japan, or elsewhere—has a different condition, we regard them as deviants, or perhaps we call them unique. This seems to me like cultural or intellectual imperialism.

I find a comparison between France and Japan startling and interesting because there appear to be many similarities in organizational structure, even though they have quite different attitudes about market share and competition, and different cultures and histories. I don't know why the similarity exists, but I suspect it has something to do with their reaction to the markets and to market size, and with the roles of government in each.

As I read Professor Yamamura's paper I thought first of all about a best seller in Japan called *The Japanese and the Jews*, which traces similarities and characteristics between the two ethnic groups. (I point out as an aside that the Japanese mother can be as piously self-sacrificing as the Jewish mother, although perhaps she is a little less obvious in her domineering and dominating qualities.) I next thought of *The Godfather*, which I had just been reading on a plane trip to Japan. I was much impressed with its description of the hierarchic structure based on the force of personality together with groupism, the "family" as it is called, factionalism, cooperation, and competition. All these features of a Mafia

organization Professor Yamamura also described as traditional in Japan—
what people there refer to as feudal; hence, they are by no means unique.
I suppose someone will write a book next called *The Japanese and the
Sicilians.*

At a somewhat more theoretical and concrete level, it seems to me that
there are at least two competing theories of international comparison of
organizational structures and their evolution. One of the things that has
bothered me about the conference is that we are discussing a series of
discrete cases without much attempt at cross-country comparison or development of a conceptual framework. I don't pretend to be the organization specialist to provide that, but I would like to make some comments
along those lines. One thesis, the convergence thesis, is that similar structures develop in different economies and different cultures due to similar
strategies in response to similar problems. There are two variants of this
thesis. One is that the late comers adopt the structures that they can find
in the already existing industrial economies. Japan in some sense is a
good example of this. It adopted the corporate form with great enthusiasm
in the 1870s, 1880s, and 1890s. A second variant is that each country
may develop similar structures independently because the nature of the
problems and the strategy response are such that such a structure emerges,
regardless of cultural differences. The family-owned conglomerate seems
to be an example of this.

The second thesis for international comparison, which I shall call the
culturally unique thesis, stresses that different types of structures emerge
in different cultures when trying to solve similar problems and even
though they may pursue similar strategies. And that is because there are
different value systems, different social structures, different histories. This
seems to be Professor Yamamura's position.

A third, perhaps more integrative hypothesis (I suspect it's really closer
to the first thesis than to the second) is that there evolves a similarity in
structure, but not full identity. What happens is that in every society, in
the process of responding to similar problems, in determining the structure
that develops, the people look selectively at their tradition, at their values
and historical traditions, and select those parts which will reinforce the
sort of structure that they think will also solve the problems. It is this
kind of selective adaptation or utilization of a traditional mythology or
ideology that seems to me very important in analyzing some of the specific features of different structures.

Professor Yamamura emphasizes two traditional, psychosocial characteristics: hierarchy and groupism. They are not unique to Japan, though
perhaps the way they are combined in Japan is somewhat different from
most other countries. Then he cites two features of large Japanese business organizations which derive directly from this tradition: the system of

permanent employment with seniority promotions and seniority wage increases, and the *ringi* system of decision-making.

First of all, the permanent employment system did not develop until about thirty or forty years after Japan's industrialization process begins. It was not a traditional continuity. Abegglen in his book *The Japanese Factory* was wrong; an interesting literature has developed which has proved this quite conclusively. Actually the permanent employment system was a rational response by management to what it regarded as undesirable labor market characteristics, high rates of turnover and competition for skilled labor, in attempting to get greater labor stability. The unions, particularly after World War II, when there were too many workers and they were interested in job security, later stressed relating wage payments in the early postwar chaos to needs based on family and family size, which turned out to be related to age. So we find that here was a system that developed some forty or fifty years after industrialization began, a quite reasonable response and one that had many traditional and cultural sanctions, and yet there was no continuity. This example supports my hypothesis of selective borrowing from the tradition to support particular structures.

Second, regarding the *ringi* system of decision-making, Professor Yamamura presents the received and dominant view. Indeed 90 percent of most Japanese firms (90 percent of a sample of a thousand firms in 1968 to be specific) say they still use this system of decision-making. He stresses that it is a natural consequence of a society valuing hierarchy and groupism.

I have two comments. First, I can report there is now a revisionist view in an unpublished manuscript by Professor Bernie Silberman of Duke University (a copy of which I handed Professor Yamamura five minutes before this session started, being careful of my timing). His argument is that the *ringi* system evolved in response to the specific organizational needs of large-scale complex organizations in Japan, and is characteristic of only large-scale organizations, never small ones. To demonstrate this he does a comparative study of Japanese and United States bureaucracies and finds certain common features.

Professor Yamamura says that where there are large-scale organizations and where there are high succession rates of the top people—conditions both in Japanese institutions using the *ringi* system of promotion and in the American military bureaucracy—the common features are limitations on personal executive authority, clear definition of the degree of authority, and a strong commitment to organizational values, such as hierarchical values and decision-making by so-called experts. Experts tend to be unsuccessful generalists, that is those who don't get promoted in this managerial process and don't get transferred upward from one section to another, from one division to another. They are the persons who therefore remain in a particular area and develop an expertise which, I suppose, gives them a rationalization for existing; this kind of expertise is then relied upon by the generalists for important decisions. This is a characteristic, it is argued, of the United States military and of Japanese government bureaucracy. Unfortunately Silberman's work is not on Japanese business organizations, so we don't know whether his analysis pertains. It is a persuasive argument though.

Parenthetically, the thought has occurred to me that the process of expert decision and the reliance on internal experts leads quite naturally to reliance on outside experts, à la the management consulting firm in England, where the assumption is that the staff of the management consulting firm are not failed generalists but are people of greater quality. This may be one reason why a firm goes outside, in the first place, for expert advice.

The conclusion of Professor Silberman is that the *ringi* system does not reflect primarily the persistence of traditional behavior, but is the result of the conditions of large-scale organizations; and accordingly the development of the system is not particularly tradition bound. This is only the first shot in what seems to be a new battle and all I can say is that the culturist view is challenged. We will have to see how the dust settles.

I think a more important point is that the *ringi* system is no more than a formal ratification, for the record, of decisions that have already been reached informally. I was writing a memo at Yale for some administrative matter at the time that I was also reading Professor Yamamura's paper and I thought, *ringi-sei* sounds very much like what I am doing. I will send a copy of this memo to X, Y, and Z "for the record." This analogy of sending copies "for the record" in America is not a perfect analogy because in the United States one just informs the people and hopes that they don't open their mouths.

In the case of the Japanese *ringi* system, a person puts his seal of approval or agreement to the document, which implies a greater acceptance of the decision. At any rate in Japanese firms there is a very important process of informal consultation which may parallel the way the *ringi* system operates, though not nearly so clearly. Part of the reason this is not as clear is that there are important clique formations in Japan. The cliques (*habatsu*) are hierarchically vertical in nature; much of decision-making has to take into account the operations of these cliques.

Because of this and because the *ringi* is really paperwork, just to ratify, I become somewhat skeptical of the view that senior management in Japan is stupid, incompetent, or passive. It is true that there are some such senior managers in some firms in all countries; it is surprising to find that there are dumb people at the top, but it does not seem to me to be more true in Japan than elsewhere. Nepotism is not important in Japan.

Management tries to develop objective criteria for promotion. Certainly promotion is not selective. It is like the army where every officer gets to be a lieutenant colonel. There is some process whereby a few of the lieutenant colonels get to be generals. The same thing is true in Japanese firms, so I think you have some pretty able people at the top.

The real problem is one that we all have, which is the sort of putty-clay model of human education analogous to the vintage stock theory of machines. We have learned a certain amount by the time we get out of school, and maybe we learn a bit more subsequently (the machine has been adapted). The younger persons are better trained than the older people and know more. Thus junior people in Japanese companies say that the senior management are dumb, no damned good, or that they don't do anything. They may be correct, but nonetheless the senior men are the best of their age group around.

These analogies suggest my skepticism about the views that senior executives in Japan do not make the basic decisions, or that they do not take the initiative in seeing what is a problem, that it should be studied and a decision reached. Through their *habatsu*, the clique, senior managers can get the word down to junior staff as to what they should be looking at; it comes back up through channels. Similarly I suspect, as Professor Mathias commented regarding imperial Germany, the centralized structures may hide the very effective powers of a strong personality at times; this is certainly true of Japanese corporations. Thus while Professor Yamamura stresses a compromise between Japaneseness and necessity as a trade-off between the two, I interpret them as reinforcing each other.

Let me turn to various alternative types of structures: unitary, multidivisional, and federations or free forms. Japan has had all these types of business structures. Federations are free forms, characterized in the literature by cartels or by one type of U.S. holding companies. We see very many such federations in postwar Japanese "groups," some of which are outgrowths of the prewar *zaibatsu* but are quite different from *zaibatsu*. Some Japanese firms also evolved from unitary to multidivisional structures.

I think Japan has had two particularly interesting forms of structure, which need to be analyzed more carefully: the *zaibatsu*, or family-owned conglomerate; and the general trading company. I will not describe the *zaibatsu* but we should ask why they should develop so early in historical time in Japan and so early, particularly, in the development pattern. Why did the United States lag in the development of the conglomerates? This seems an interesting question to ask.

I suggest three reasons why *zaibatsu* developed. It appears to me that, first, the size and growth of the domestic market and the foreign competition in it is very important. America has a large market economically and geographically. In Japan firms reached the size of the domestic market pretty quickly and had to think about how to grow further. It was hard to compete internationally. Therefore they diversified in domestic production. I regard this an interesting hypothesis. Moreover, a firm may be forced to diversify, in part by the very fact that it must be competitive at home because it faces foreign imports. Japan was a free-trade country until World War I; this must have imposed a great constraint, relative, say, to the protective markets of France or Germany.

Second is the ability of firms to enter foreign markets. Leader countries may do this since a firm may be able to continue its product line on a global basis rather than on a national basis. Japanese *zaibatsu* were not exporting large quantities very early in the game or even in the 1920s. Japan's exports were silk and cotton textiles, industries in which *zaibatsu* were not predominant. Rather, they diversified domestically.

Finally I suggest that we should look at the owner-entrepreneur in his idiosyncrasy of having *de facto* centralized power regardless of structure. Again I am struck by the similarity of France to Japan; it is only as family direct leadership gives way to higher top management that substantial change in the firm structure evolves.

The other interesting Japanese structural form is the general trading company. This large-scale organization seems to be unique in modern industrial society as a distribution device, at home and abroad, for a wide range of products, although it has been pointed out to me that the East India Company and the Hudson's Bay Company, and perhaps Jardine-Matheson, are good examples of industrialization in earlier phases. One of the questions that we want to ask is why did this form develop in Japan and not elsewhere? Professor Yamamura makes some interesting suggestions relating the form to markets. We need to pursue this issue much further.

Let me end with some general comments on strategy and structure. First, strategy vis-à-vis labor markets. The discussion of strategy seems to be very much focused on product markets, with a few asides about the relationship with government. This is too simple; the relationship with government is very important and underlies many matters both of strategy and structure. It has also occurred to me that there probably are strategy problems which relate to structure in terms of labor markets as well. This gets me back to cultural differences; I am thinking particularly of models of worker motivation.

We have a western, rational, bureaucratic model of organization à la Weber in which the worker is really motivated by his rational self-interest, money, and status, and he is rewarded on the basis of his performance. The rest of his life is his own, independent of the firm for which he works. This strategy of motivation and the structure it implies may have been appropriate in circumstances where labor was ample, wages were low, and workers valued material rewards highly. One might argue that this strategy becomes much less appropriate where wages are high and workers develop a strong sense of alienation. Part of this sense of alienation comes from outside the enterprise, from being in an industrial society, but part of it may come from within the enterprise. One thinks of the recent General Motors Vega plant problems which seem a reflection of the inadequacies of a "rational structure" of labor mobilization to obtain a high degree of motivation on the part of the workers.

Certainly this idea is not new. It is embodied in American organizational studies of worker motivation, considering alternatives to the rational model; for example, how workers respond when lights are made stronger, or weaker, or in pretty colors. It seems to me Japanese organizations are not based on the western rational model of impersonal human relations. In contrast, they strongly emphasize personal relationships. Firms make a deliberate attempt to obtain worker loyalty. This is not just a given factor derived from the Japanese traditional culture, by the way; Japanese firms make a deliberate effort to give employees at all levels a sense of participation and involvement in the operations of the enterprise.

It appears to be true that Japanese workers are generally much less alienated than American workers at all levels, both managerial and blue collar. What we don't know is whether this has been simply a carry-over of Japanese traditional values, or as with the permanent employment system a more recent and deliberate management response to a perceived need of how to get the most out of their workers. Nevertheless I would suggest this internal strategy by a firm towards its labor force and their motivation, in contrast to an external strategy towards product markets, and the structural responses in Japan, seems to work very well in a modern industrial society. We might end by asking whether this is a model that the United States should follow.

8. Multinationals, Management, and World Markets: A Historical View

CHARLES WILSON

Whatever meaning one may choose to attach to that many-splendored chameleon, the multinational company, the two companies chosen for study in this paper seem to qualify for the title. Both Unilever and Imperial Chemical Industries trace their origins to companies founded by men of several different nationalities—Dutch, British, German, Swedish, and Swiss (to select only an obvious few), while some of the most influential, like the Monds and the van den Berghs, were Jewish. They developed and exploited, in turn, the inventions of an even wider circle of scientists, including the ever-fertile genius of the French. They ransacked the earth for the materials they needed—whale oil from the Arctic and Antarctic, animal fats from the American Middle West, palm oil and ground nuts from West and East Africa, copra from the Solomons. They sold their manufactured products throughout western and central Europe, North and South America, and as far east as China and Japan. And in the making they also employed advisers, managers, and bankers of many nations, just as they utilized the capital and labor of thousands of Europeans, Africans, and Indians. All this world-wide activity did not have to wait for the twentieth century. It was beginning to bubble in the 1860s when Alfred Nobel was starting his restless travels in North Europe; growing in the 1870s, when two undistinguished butter merchants in the obscure and unattractive Brabant village of Oss temporarily ceased their socioreligious quarrel (Catholic against Jew) to peer along the profitable vistas opened up by an equally obscure French inventor, Mége-Mouries, who had found a cheap way of replacing butter supplies for the army of Napoleon III. Something of a climax was reached in the 1880s, when the resourceful son of a Lancashire grocer (reputedly of Dutch origin) William Hesketh Lever, was examining the products and organization of the British soap trade, and finding it sadly wanting. By the same token he also found it full of promise.

Here are a few of the tangled roots of two later world-wide multinationals. Thus far I have only emphasized their common international character. It is this which explains in large part their later growth. The ebullient capitalism of the nineteenth century was already finding its style cramped by political boundaries which had indeed expanded to comprehend larger and larger areas, but which no longer corresponded to the

193

immediate needs, much less to the aspirations, of men determined that the world itself was their market. Having said that, we must go on to admit that beyond their common sense of internationalism, neither the founders of our two businesses, nor their creations, had much else in common. Pellerin, an early margarine maker, was the first man to buy Cézannes (he owned a hundred). Lever (a Nonconformist of no known theological convictions) liked Wedgwood, Napoleonic relics and pre-Raphaelite or Greek ladies, preferably unclad. Henry van den Bergh had the best eye for Chinese porcelain of all London's best collectors. Nobel, maker of lethal explosives, relieved his conscience by founding a prize to draw mankind to the pursuit of peace. Brunners and Monds opted, without much success, for politics. And so on. In short, they were all much like the business Maecenases anywhere.

Their business creations, however, immediately, and by their very nature, took different paths. The British and Dutch businesses which were to coalesce finally in 1929 as Unilever, were from the start consumer goods industries, highly conscious of human preferences and repulsions, the importance of social changes, the changing purchasing power of the masses—in short all the social factors that went to make up and influence the markets in which they sold their product to customers (mainly housewives) by the hundred thousand, if not the million. The Brunners, Monds, Solvays, Nobels were a different breed, less salesmen than scientists, drawn onward by a curiosity that was scientific as much as economic. They supplied, for the most part, not individual consumers, but other businesses and governments. They dealt in alkali for soapmakers, bleaching powders for textile manufacturers, blasting powders for mining-contractors, explosives for armies and navies. Their relations were therefore not with the masses, or even with the thousands of shopkeepers who ministered to the masses, but with companies and ministries which were numbered by the score (or less), or at most by the hundred. And from this basic difference many other differences of outlook, method, and ethos were to spring.

Lever Brothers, the British parent of Unilever, was founded in 1885, in a characteristic piece of audacity, plumb in the middle of the Great Depression. Not least in his overseas ventures that led to the multinational company, Lever was the perfect exemplification of the eighteenth-century maxim that "the tradesman always stands at the head of the manufacturer." His observation that there was room for a good free-lathering soap which would abridge the housewife's labor was one base of his decision to stop being a grocer and become an industrialist. The other was his flair for the sociological observation from which he concluded that a vast new working-class market was taking shape. It sprang from the fall in the price of necessities, the rise in real wages, and the improving standards of working-class life in towns, combined with the growing dirt pollution of that life by industry. Simultaneously the Jurgens and van den Berghs in the Netherlands were systematically providing a cheap butter substitute for the new urban masses in Germany, where the population rose from 40 to 56 million in the last three decades of the century. As Clapham remarked: "The figures suggest a whole nation rushing to town." Provision for betterment or provision for poverty, the entrepreneur's business was to look after his opportunity, wherever it was found.

The Dutch margarine makers found their markets abroad from the start: the German cities were their obvious opportunity and Germany long remained their chief target. But it was not long before Lever, too, felt the itch to expand. Long before he had beaten into pieces the time-honored partition of Britain into spheres of influence for local soap manufacturers based on (as it were) treaties of nonintervention, he was off on his travels abroad in search of new raw materials, new markets, and new ideas. His basic tenet had always been that costs were kept low by modern technology and by automatic repetition of the same process. "Advertising," he wrote, "is as near bringing the manufacturing conditions of repetition to the *selling* side of the business as possible." Time and again in the late eighties and nineties he was prospecting in Europe, India, Australia, but above all in North America. He wrote in later years of the "enormous strength" he had got from his knowledge of selling and advertising in the United States. (It was not only commercial knowledge: his diaries reveal that he never went into an American soap factory without pinching a manufacturing gimmick or two.) "I owe much more than I can ever tell to the fact that . . . in December 1888 I began to open up overseas businesses. It reminds me of the quotation, 'What should they know of England who only England know.'" This then was the phase of overseas expansion, and the problems it encountered were met by the highly personal supervision of Lever himself, assisted by a small number of trusted subordinates, some of whom were placed in strategic posts abroad.

Raw materials were always in his mind, because their cost was the largest single influence on the soap price and thus on his competitive position and profits. His earlier U.S. venture was to purchase an oil mill at Vicksburg in the Mississippi Valley to produce cotton oil for his English factory, just as in Australia he bought an oil mill at Balmain (Sydney) to crush copra from the South Sea Islands. His first venture into raw-material growing (1901) was his company in the Solomon Islands.

But these were only a part of his expansion vision. Already in 1888, when his English works at Port Sunlight were still being built, he was in the United States, his roving eye fastening on what he deemed were the essentials of his soapmaker's situation there. These included what were to prove some of the most persistent problems facing his overseas companies through the coming years (they are still present). They were tariffs, competition, local tastes and antitastes, problems of transport (especially over vast distances), xenophobia, local laws and conditions.

Basic to all future developments was the tariff problem. In 1890, Lever's business was still an export trade in British-made soap and it was not a happy time. Tariffs were rising everywhere in the industrializing world. The Dutch margarine makers felt the draft of the Bismarck tariff of 1887 in precisely the same way, and responded as did Lever. "The question of erecting works in another country," he wrote, "is dependent upon the tariff or duty. The amount of duties we pay on soap imported into Holland and Belgium is considerable, and it only requires that these shall rise to such a point that we could afford to pay a separate staff of managers with a separate plant to make the soap to enable us to see our way to erect works in those countries. When the duty exceeds the costs . . . it will be an economy to erect works in the country so that our customers can be more cheaply supplied from them."

This was an argument Lever repeated almost daily. It was indeed necessary because of the abuse which fell upon him from those (perhaps unconscious) disciples of Hobson who alleged Lever was robbing English workmen of their livelihood. There was not a word of truth in it, he thundered to his shareholders. "Suppose . . . the World was free trade and soap could be imported with merely the question of freight . . . there would be no need to manufacture soap in Germany . . . " and so on. The local factory, that is to say, and the beginnings of the multinational, were, according to Lever, rooted in the need to jump over the tariff wall, and thus maintain that volume of trade which had previously been an export trade.

Basically this was correct at the time. As time went on, however, it was to become evident that local manufacture had many other advantages.

The first move was to survey the market situation and this he did in person in the United States (and in many other places). In the populous east he was confident he could get a foothold. But California was too far away and too thinly populated—"with only one and a half million of population we could never sell enough to pay expenses." Lever's thus remained virtually prisoners of their eastern bastion, Cambridge, Massachusetts, with only life lines to what they called the "General Territory" beyond. Nor did Americans take kindly to the major products which had been the weapons of victory in Britain—Sunlight and Lifebuoy soap. This last was a disinfectant product and it aroused great hostility. One of Lever's correspondents said he had seen a woman customer "take the sample of Lifebuoy, smell it and throw it across the store." Even Sunlight made a very bad showing. Americans thought it poor value for money. So not until the arrival of the genius of Lever's American scene, Frances

A. Countway, did the U.S. business really get under way. Countway re-organized the selling arrangements to meet the powerful competition of Procter and Gamble and the other large American manufacturers. He persuaded Lever to let him drop Sunlight—a triumph this, for it was the apple of Lever's eye—and concentrate on Lux soap flakes. These had been introduced in Britain in 1897: but they and their advertising were to become as characteristic of the U.S. scene as Coca-Cola or Spearmint.

Countway's achievement, in fact, was to turn Lever's into an American business, run on American lines. Lever, though a dictator himself by nature, never failed to respect a man who knew his job. His own adver-tising ideas owed much to U.S. influence. (One of his most famous adver-tising slogans—"Why Does a Woman Look Older than a Man?"—he bought from Frank Siddal, a Philadelphia soapmaker, in 1888 and the early records are filled with transatlantic ideas.) So he never grudged Countway his success, nor the vast advertising budget on which it rested. To critics who groused about its size, he observed: "Mr. Countway gets results and meets competition without injury to the business, which we must bear in mind." Countway was the clearest recognition (though not the only one) by Lever that some of his markets were too strange and remote to be managed from home. They demanded a local man with local knowledge and wide powers of discretion to act.

Further north, in Canada, as in Australia and South Africa, the major problems were large distances and small populations. Lever's answer was to buy up or build a considerable number of factories. By 1913, for example, he had constructed a chain of works (eight in all) stretching right across Canada from east to west. In Australia by 1914 a dozen or so factories were dotted all along the coast from Townsville in the north-east of Queensland to Freemantle in Western Australia. At the same date South Africa was served by four soap and oil works. How did this square with his theory (referred to earlier) that tariffs were the only barrier to concentration of production? Why not *one* factory only? One answer was that in all these territories there were abundant supplies of animal fats. It was therefore cheaper to make soap from local materials than to pay freight charges on materials and then again on the final product. Again, he was finding that the brand names of competitors whose businesses he bought were too valuable to kill off. Pugsley, Dingman in Canada, Kit-chens in Australia were formidable rivals before acquisition and cor-respondingly valuable assets afterwards. Hence his theory that local fac-tories were to be kept alive and compete with one another—an indirect way of solving many of the overseas problems.

Meanwhile in Continental Europe, his new factories were also facing the facts of life. The natural advantage, as in Britain, was a general tend-ency, until 1900 anyway, for wages to rise. But consumer tastes were bewildering and competition stiff. In north Europe generally, housewives still used a cheap variety of soft soap and it was not easy to persuade them to change their habits. The German adviser whom Lever appointed to investigate the promise of the German market warned him off strongly. "There was a soapery in every village." In France the market was flooded with soap which was a by-product of the vast complex of oil mills of Marseilles. Cheap and nasty it might be, but it sold.

In addition to economic problems, there were political ones. Swiss makers ganged up politically against the intruder. There was little love lost in Germany. Even the normally friendly Dutch were full of bitterness after the troubles in South Africa. Lever's answer to all these problems was to seek the best local advice he could get, conducting a sort of one-man market-research project. The answer lay in large measure in advertising his new products. In Switzerland, his local manager held a great *Fête de Blanchisseuses* on the Lake of Geneva, to which all the local laundresses were invited as competitors in a washing tournament, watched by crowds of spectators. In Holland, hoardings twelve meters long and three meters high "painted with fanciful subjects" praised the merits of Sunlight. Samples of it, together with copies of a pamphlet by Phineas Taylor Barnum, the American showman, were distributed by salesmen in brightly colored uniforms. Unfortunately, they were in some predominantly Catholic areas mistaken for members of the Salvation Army, and Lever, no less than General Booth, had his martyrs. In spite of all his efforts, however, Lever had to wait a long time before the Dutch housewife abandoned her use of soft soap and used Sunlight as a toilet product. In Belgium, Lever's gift schemes, which had from the start been a sensational part of his publicity, were successfully launched. Watches were offered in exchange for wrappers, and reproductions of Royal Academy art were showered on customers.

The appointment of managers of local nationality and experience helped to adapt products and advertising successfully to local tastes and meet local competition. It could not always cope so smoothly with local political feeling. It was, indeed, Lever's Dutch manager who could no longer keep his feelings about South Africa under control in 1902. With more passion than syntax, and with understandable ferocity, he wrote to Lever: "No more as English people will be governed by French or Germans or Dutch, no more will Dutch, French or Germans be governed by British and no treaty like England compelled the Dutch to pass in 1813 will surrender a colony from one sceptre to another like a herd of sheep. We do not consider ourselves the property of a King or diplomat."

Usually such feelings, where they existed, were dormant, only roused by some sharp event. They were always to be reckoned with, nevertheless, and as Lever steadily progressed, putting down a factory here and there as the growing volume of export trade seemed to justify it, he kept them in mind. To his representatives in the Low Countries he said in 1902: "I want you to continue your efforts (as agents) a little longer until we can put a Works down in your country and you are able to call on your customers and say to them: "This soap is made in Belgium for Belgian people," or "This soap is made in Holland for Dutch people.""

When he came to extend his operations into Scandinavia, he found the going especially hard. In 1924, a Norwegian critic attacking Lever's penetration of Norway (he had just founded a small company there) referred to Lever as "a powerful and dangerous man. It is consequently exceedingly probable that if he secures a firm footing on Norwegian ground, he will be able to crush the Norwegian soap industry." Norwegian economic patriotism was easily aroused, as both British and Dutch intruders were to find.

Such were some of the problems of adapting products and selling methods of management originating in Britain to the needs and circumstances of other countries. Lever's overseas enterprises were not, however, limited to the promotion of his manufactures in civilized societies and advanced economies. They extended also to the purchase and production of raw materials, which he needed as a soapmaker and (after 1914) as a margarine manufacturer too. The more or less rational motive for his excursions into the South Sea Islands and West Africa was his conviction that he risked being "squeezed" (as he put it) on raw materials. And indeed the fear was not unreasonable in that pre-1914 age of trusts, cartels, and other forms of monopolistic practices. But Lever was also a man of his time—a Liberal, but also a passionate believer in Empire and the British mission in the outer world that lay beyond Europe. The early troubles that beset him were the result of disagreements with the governing authorities in the territories concerned or of labor problems which arose there. Between 1903 and 1913 the principal interest lay in the Solomon Islands where Lever's Pacific Company acquired plantations and trading stations. As was to happen in Africa, labor productivity immediately emerged as a problem. The declining native population had no excessive liking for work: as soon as they had satisfied their limited needs for imported luxuries they lost interest in employment.

The search therefore began for new recruits. "I do not see," Lever informed his shareholders, with his usual insouciant imagination in full flight, "why we cannot bring as labourers to these beautiful islands Hindoos from the teeming millions of India." But the government of India, alas, saw every reason. So did the Colonial Office which, like the government departments, was "very difficult to influence for the good and progress of those portions of the Empire which they feel a little in conflict."

His optimism that the Colonial Office would in time see his point was unfounded. Indeed, his quarrel with them was swiftly extended to African territory. Here Lever wanted to acquire land in order to introduce scientific cultivation of the oil palm and mechanical milling of the fruit. The government, however, was committed to the policy of not alienating native land and they rejected all Lever's advances, much to his chagrin: "I sometimes wish that all native chiefs in . . . Africa were made Dukes . . . we should then take the sensible view that this land was theirs for development and the advancement of civilisation and just as we will not tolerate a Duke keeping his land for his own pleasure . . . so I can never understand why a black man should be allowed to assume a different attitude and neither develop his own land nor allow other people to do so."

This liberal, simplistic view of economic development failed to commend itself to the Colonial Office and after a bitter and prolonged quarrel, Lever passed on from British West Africa to the Belgian Congo. Here, under very stiff terms, he succeeded in concluding a kind of treaty with the Belgian government to exploit a large area of natural palmeries in the Congo. The company was to provide from its own capital all the transport, services, housing, and welfare services for the native population. Lever was at once attacked by liberal opinion which still associated the Congo with all the evils of the preceding Congo Free State. He also faced daunting problems of tropical disease and especially labor recruitment and training. "This problem of labour," he wrote on his tour of the Congo in 1913, "has grown as an ominous dark cloud." He went on to elaborate with picturesque detail the backward-sloping curve that was showing itself:

"The native has few wants—a little salt and a little cloth are his indispensables. After this, beads, brass rods and other luxuries. Chief Womba at Leverville can be taken as an example. Twelve months ago he and his people were poor and few in number, and were keen to bring fruit. After twelve months or less of selling fruit, he is rich and lazy, has ten wives, and his village is about four times the size it was, but he gathers little or no fruit. . . . The palm tree is in these parts the Banking account of the nation and he no more thinks of going to the Bank for fruit for money when his wants and ambitions are supplied, than a civilised man would.

Eighteenth-century workhouse surveyors in Britain and even twentieth-century colliery managers were familiar with the problem.

These labor problems were not susceptible of an easy solution. To the Solomons he brought some tough Australian bushmen, accustomed (as he said) to a lonely life, resourceful and self-reliant. Both here and in the Congo, the fallout rate amongst European managers was (one suspects) high. But the best were very good indeed and exceptionally tough. One or two of those who prospected for Lever when the Congo was still a cannibal jungle were still hale and hearty in the 1950s.

Such were a few of the major problems encountered by Lever as he pushed his business outwards from Britain into the civilized and uncivilized world. The later Dutch partners in Unilever were meanwhile encountering their own problems. They were different in character and they are not recorded with the articulate and vivid detail which we owe to Lever's special genius; but they were serious and persistent. As we shall see, in both sides of the Unilever business they survive, even if only in vestigial form, almost to our own day.

Since Britain still stuck to free trade, the Dutch margarine makers did not need to put down English factories until 1917, when the war at sea made it impossible to continue their exports from Holland. Elsewhere in Europe, in Scandinavia, France, Belgium, Germany, they were already manufacturing locally to circumvent the tariffs.

Amongst the major problems the Dutch makers faced on their expansion into foreign markets were several which derived from the character of their product. First, margarine was a perishable food, highly vulnerable to off-flavors which could ruin sales, which were (in England and France anyway) in competition with natural butter. Second, the price was a matter of concern to growing millions of consumers, mostly from the poorest sections of the community. Third, as a butter substitute it had a direct impact on, or seemed to threaten it, the incomes of dairy farmers. These were considerations which powerfully influenced the competitive situation in margarine markets in many countries and the manufacturers' strategy therein.

The export business was itself subject to difficulties for the very reason that margarine was highly perishable. Tariff or no tariff, local manufacture would probably have come sooner or later. It had the advantage—which was to emerge in relation to many other projects—that local production management understood local tastes better than export managers. In Britain, customers liked their margarine salted (as they liked their butter). Continental customers generally preferred a neutral flavor, though one successful German brand was flavored with milk of almonds; they did not use it to spread on bread, like the English. Most continental margarine went into cooking or frying. And so on. Whatever the use, it was critical to slide the product through from factory to consumer with as little delay as possible so as to avoid rancidity. This was not easy: grocers were a leisurely race in those days. The makers therefore sought their answer through the grocery shop companies which were as much a feature of prewar Britain (and to a smaller extent other countries) as the supermarket is of the 1970s. Their energies pushed the new product hard. And in case they did not push hard enough, the Dutch makers bought their way into the companies and great battles ensued for the control of firms like the Home and Colonial, Liptons, etc.

This in turn created much controversy. Was there not a danger that the margarine companies, already showing all the signs of an incipient monopoly, might gain complete control over the price of an essential food? The controversy reached a pitch of new excitement during the 1914–18 war, when the Dutch were often accused by both Britain and Germany of soiling their neutrality. In Britain Jurgens were said to be providing hydrogen for German airships from their German factories—an early hint that while the multinationals' future might be profitable, it was also likely to be politically thorny. The makers did their best to draw a discreet veil over the whole matter of their retail connections, but never succeeded. And after the final merger, Unilever divested itself voluntarily of control over the shops. The concept of the vertical combine never materialized into a very satisfactory reality.

The many problems arising were tackled in different ways. Van den Berghs, a large family, sent some of their number to live in Britain and Anglicize themselves; others went to Germany and Germanized themselves. Jurgens seem to have been early to appoint English managers, though the family supplied some important staff in Germany. It was van den Berghs' English company which provided the model for the 1929 financial and organizational structure of Unilever.

Agrarian opposition to margarine arose and still arises out of the offended interests of the dairy farming community. Even in Denmark, where the farmers ate margarine and exported their butter, the manufacturers' situation remained delicate. Was it safe to advertise the awkward fact that margarine makers were also the largest makers of cattle cake for the farmer? It was certainly something to keep quiet about as long as you could in Holland, Britain, France and the United States. In many countries, agrarian lobbies saw to it (as they did in the United States and Canada) that margarine was duly and by law branded, either by coloration or compulsory shape, so that it could not be passed off as butter. In some cases mixing with butter was also prohibited. A little informal propaganda did no harm to the farmers' cause either. In New York, a helpful journalist observed that the curve of stillbirths rose with margarine consumption. Dark tales circulated in Britain that the London sewers were a profitable source of fatty raw materials. And so on.

Thus, until our own day, the margarine maker needed his wits about him. Politically, he was highly vulnerable to the attacks of those who scented an anticonsumer monopoly, an antiagrarian conspiracy, or a food scandal. Even in the 1960s, he was reminded with a rude shock how fragile was the reputation of his product, even though it was the first surrogate to be mass-made and marketed, and was now nearly a century old. Some poisoning cases in Holland in 1965 were said to be caused by a margarine made under a new process. Large sums of compensation were paid out before it was shown that no evidence whatever existed to justify any accusation against the makers.

MODERN TIMES

Many of the problems faced by the multinational Unilever of today in its overseas operations derive from those I have adumbrated for the early period. They arise from the nature of products and preferences, production problems, monopolistic situations, agrarian competition and opposition, nationalism, discrimination, xenophobia, and—above all—from government intervention in such matters as the price mechanism, import quotas, hard currency allocations, prohibitions or limitations on certain types of transaction, or all-out nationalization.

A glance first at the spread of Unilever business in 1949. Sales by regions are shown in Table 1.

TABLE 1

UNILEVER SALES BY REGION IN 1949

Region	£ (in millions)
Western Europe	334
North and South America	85
Africa, Middle East, and Australia	17
Orient	24
United Africa Group	144
Eastern Europe	0
Total	604 ±

Almost half Unilever's production was still in detergents and margarine. The depression of the thirties had been survived with relative ease in the west. Its main result was to spur on the concentration of production into larger plant units. In the postwar period, the concentration of production went on apace; the national brands which had ousted the old local brands now, in their turn, gave way to international brands, as competition, especially from the United States, intensified. The belief, strong down to the fifties, in local autonomy, began to give way to tighter central supervision (as had existed in the 1920s), as the volume of capital risked by decisions became far, far greater than ever before. Knowledge, including technical knowledge, had to be pooled. Thus what had been so far a loosely federated congeries of companies, growing together by a centripetal process, now found itself under inescapable pressures (especially the challenge of U.S. competition) to move toward a more truly and tightly integrated structure. Unilever's largest rival, Procter and Gamble, it may be remarked, had grown outward, centrifugally as it were, from the United States. Its problems were therefore different. How much Unilever's deeper roots in Europe were worth in hard cash is a matter of debate.

The solution suggested by events was a structure called "coordination," and the name reflected the need to compromise between the historic federalism of the old Unilever and the felt need for greater central guidance in the new. World policy, formerly on a regional basis, was now to be on a product basis, and a "coordinator" would take charge of over-all policy for each group of products—edible fats, other foods (including meats, frozen and canned foods, etc.), detergents, toilet preparations, chemicals, and other technical products. This, it was believed, would give a world company the necessary streamlining to meet competition from highly centralized rivals, while avoiding the alleged condition depicted in the large American company by one of its critics:

> Along these lines from toe to crown
> Ideas flow up and vetoes down.

The fact was that in a vast consumer organization catering for millions of customers, flexibility and local knowledge were still as vital as ever. This was the nub of the problem. Unilever bulged with examples of differences in consumer tastes which, if neglected, could prove catastrophic. It was especially true of the food industries, which were one of the areas of fastest growth and development in the postwar years. A sausage was one thing to the English: it was a different thing—many different things in fact—to Germans or Italians. Nobody in the world will tolerate an English sausage save its inventors. Conversely, only very slowly have the supermarkets overcome deep English suspicions about the contents of salami, etc. The large English minted pea outrages continental tastes; the English are not enthusiastic about *petits pois*. Ice cream is a different product in England, France, and Italy. And so on.

Similar problems existed in other fields. Atkinsons of Bond Street had been acquired by Lever's almost by accident. For some reason not wholly clear, it had never had much success in Britain. Yet in Mediterranean countries and Latin America its business had always done well (as a reference in Lampedusa's novel *The Leopard* demonstrates)[1] and in the sixties it flourished exceedingly. Even Europe was still far from uniform in its standards of living. Products which perfectly fitted the needs of the dollar socialism of Sweden were unsalable in the still primitive markets of rural Spain. And vice versa.

Meanwhile new technology had to be absorbed and disseminated. This meant especially the new nonsoapy detergents and frozen foods. The projection of both was a long and difficult task and the path of the innovators in Europe was strewn with catastrophes. Both processes, it need hardly be said, originated in the United States. American detergent manufacturers had a long lead over European competitors, whom the war had deprived of the necessary materials, scientists, and know-how. Moreover, detergent markets were governed not only by different standards of living, but by elementary facts like the hardness of water. In African, Asian, and South American markets, women needed high-lathering formulas for cold- and often soft-water washing. The maker could not always assume the existence of washing machines, just as the frozen food manufacturer was often in the dark as to how many refrigerators existed outside European cities. So while Unilever Birds Eye went ahead famously in Britain, there were heavy losses when frozen foods were introduced in Holland to face the traditional competition of plentiful fresh and canned foods. Here, as throughout the Continent, Unilever at one point withdrew from frozen foods altogether, only to re-enter later.

Such examples merely pinpointed the fragility of commercial knowledge. Even the appointment of management of local origin (adopted almost universally in postwar Unilever) by itself assured nothing in the complex and sophisticated world of new consumption. The capital at risk grew all the time. Hence the growing need for market research conducted on a basis as nearly scientific as possible to reduce the margin of risk. Hence the research and development work of the growing laboratories (detergents at Port Sunlight, foods at Colworth, edible fats at Vlaardingen, smaller establishments in a score of other countries) to improve products, reduce failures, lower costs, raise consistency, and generally ensure that consumers got what they wanted.

Concentration of production, already a leading feature of the oils and fats industries, now had to be carried further. Factory closure, or even the substitution of automatic for manual labor, is always fraught with risk. The more so if the culprit is a large business of foreign origin. So, even where worker organizations were not strong, Unilever attached critical importance to seeing that these consequences of technological advance were handled circumspectly and with tact, above all perhaps with good notice. Few problems have so far arisen, perhaps partly because labor in recent years has been in brisk demand. But the prospect of greater free-trade areas in Europe as a result of E.E.C. progress will bring further critical decisions and they will come at a time of rising unemployment. How many margarine factories can serve western Europe—two, three, four? Where shall they be located? Such decisions will, socially and politically, throw enormous responsibilities on to management, and if free-trade areas grow, a business like Unilever may have to learn how to backpedal on the painfully acquired experience of nearly a century of tariff-oriented decisions.

Agrarian opposition to margarine, which we have seen to be from the beginning a serious problem, is one question which has certainly dwindled in importance, and for an odd reason. In the United States, where the strongest lobby still maintained discriminatory laws against margarine in

1950, a revolutionary change came about as a result of the increased use of soyabean and cotton seed oils in margarine manufacture on a scale hitherto impossible, but now possible with a new technology. These products were grown in precisely those areas (like Minnesota) where dairy interests had been most vocal. While the North American farmer thus obtained an important stake in the prosperity of the margarine industry, other farmers in Europe, even in India, benefited from the Unilever demand for peas, beans, and other vegetables for freezing. But not all in the garden was lovely. U.S. exports of soya hit rapeseed producers in Germany and France. Growing use of margarine made Italian olive oil producers nervous. Hence the demand in the E.E.C. for a levy on margarine to protect butter, oil, and seed producers. Thus Unilever had always to maintain close and expert supervision of agrarian trends and policies in the world. You never knew where the next crisis was going to blow up.

Another technological bogey raised its head from time to time: the U.S. antitrust administration. This was something U.S. businessmen had to learn to live with and their task was made easier by the widespread American faith in utmost competition, from which even U.S. tycoons were not exempt. They might find any immediate manifestation of antitrust philosophy detestable, but they had been brought up to understand its ethos. It was less easy for Europeans who were often children of societies built on competition so imperfect as to be nonexistent. It was a hard lesson to learn (especially since the growing multitude of U.S.-owned companies in western Europe suffered no restrictions of comparable severity) that a non-American parent company was probably ill-advised, under any circumstances, to intervene in the upbringing or instruction of its American offspring. Lever's had learnt this lesson. The U.S. Lever Company was in all senses an American company and from it, under Countway's lead, Lever's in Europe had learnt a great deal. His retirement in 1946 left a gap not easily filled. It took years to stabilize management, but in the end it was achieved. Not too soon, for competitive pressures had never been harder. They produced one incident which demonstrated the crucial need for a type of expertise which could only be obtained (even then with good luck as well as management) in the United States itself. When Lever's acquired a special detergent from Monsanto, the Department of Justice instituted an antitrust suit against them for reducing competition. Lever's won, and they won by arguing that, far from reducing competition, their purchase had actually increased it. For the situation they had faced was one in which they and Monsanto were both losing money and would both have been vulnerable to take-over by a third party. A non-American lawyer might in such a case have been tempted to argue from standpoint of efficiency. Mr. Fortas seized on the one defense which was answerable in the U.S. context.

The incident highlighted once more the essential role of local expertise. But, in fact, the postwar decades illustrated continually, in developed and undeveloped areas of the world, its increasing importance. Antitrust law spilt over, for example, into the American zone of Western Germany. But it was in Africa and Asia that local opinion was most essential. The reason was always the same: the rising tide of economic nationalism and the type of program that followed in its wake. The international company might bring with it the technology without which a country could not develop, but it had everywhere to yield to pressure to conform to the immediate targets of government planning. Long- or medium-term growth had often to take second place to immediate crisis in countries racked by threat of civil war or on the brink of war with others. Import quotas for detergent raw materials were unlikely to stand high on government lists of priorities where ferocious balance of payment deficits had to be dealt with. Thus Unilever companies found themselves facing a variety of dilemmas. Hindustan Lever, now an Indian-managed and partly Indian-owned business of buoyant vitality, had to face cuts in its imports of oil seeds which severely cramped its soap sales, while its business in manufactured *vanaspati* was hampered by prohibitions on color and flavor to help the natural ghee producer. The Ceylon business faced crippling levels of taxation. The South American businesses were cursed with runaway inflation. Yet their problems were mild compared with those of Unilever in Burma. Here an agreement of 1950 with the government, under which a sizable investment was launched, was unilaterally and casually denounced and dishonored only five years later. The business in Egypt was nationalized in 1960 on Nasser's ukase declaring dividends on foreign equity to be an eternal strain on his people.

Examples could be multiplied. It is necessary only to summarize briefly the largest exercise in adaptation forced on Unilever by government pressure in Africa. Here, during the period of high prices and profits in primary produce from West Africa after the war—cocoa, palm oil, cotton, groundnuts—Nigeria, Ghana, Sierra Leone, Gambia all set up produce-marketing boards. Thus the largest traditional business of the United Africa Company, the subsidiary which accounted for a quarter of Unilever's world turnover, disappeared. The UAC did not, however, disappear. The import equivalent of its African produce export resided in a great variety of products—engineering, chemical and consumer goods—which it handled in association with European manufacturers and agents. The fifties and sixties saw a massive redeployment of capital formerly used in produce handling into manufacturing and assembly enterprises based on these earlier agency activities. Thus in 1949 UAC in Nigeria was concerned with banana, rubber, timber, and oil plantations. By 1965 there were between thirty and forty UAC businesses making or assembling vehicles, plastics, concrete, cycles, timber products, radio, paper, beer, etc. The pattern was repeated throughout West, and to a lesser extent, East Africa, and it involved ambitious and urgent schedules for training and retraining African management and labor for Africa's changing economic role. The integration of these training programs for Africa and Asia with those organized as a normal part of company development in the West was a matter of great consequence—and great expense. Thus the whole African situation illustrated the extension to the Third World of the process of import substitution and its attendant political problems familiar to Unilever from its European experience in the previous half century or more.

The organization of Unilever evolved to meet external as much as internal needs. In Lever's own day, management remained very much a personal dictatorship, reflecting Lever's determination, even after his company had gone public (1894), to retain ownership of all the equity and with it the personal control of operations and policy. Yet the system was neither illiberal nor inflexible; very much the reverse. His own convictions were Smithian and he constantly urged his view that the reins be kept loose. There should be, at home and abroad, maximum competition between operating companies. Any exceptional or urgent problems were decided between him and his local managers. As long as they retained his confidence they had a wide area of discretion.

In the postwar stringency (from 1920 until the mid-thirties), central control strengthened, until a Canadian executive complained in the 1930s that "You had to wire London before you were allowed to pull the chain." The Anglo-Dutch merger of 1929 brought in a vast empire of continental businesses. To manage the new world business, two identical boards were appointed, one for each parent company, and the finances of the two parents were linked by an agreement equating results for shareholders. Beneath the boards was an "inner cabinet"—the Special Committee of four—with plenary powers delegated by the full boards. This was limited to operating companies abroad by a Continental and an Overseas Committee. Between came roving directors ("contact directors") whose business it was to visit companies everywhere and report to the Special Committee on their condition, morale, profits, etc. In 1967, this system was modified again so that five committees (Continental, United Kingdom, Overseas, Tropical Africa, United Africa Group) reported to the Special Committee, but "coordination" was now made responsible to the Special Committee for many questions affecting production and sales of the five major different product groups. This meant that there was some diminution of national and group management authority, especially in continental Europe. The center, in fact, was once more linked directly to the local manager over most matters affecting his product. There was some modification, therefore, of the deliberate liberalism that had governed relations between headquarters and perimeter since 1945, summarized succinctly in the words of Lord Heyworth (chairman, 1941–60): "We run our business positively, keep it healthy and growing and let the chips fall where they may." Some of this liberalism had had to yield to growing pressures—for better capital control, more uniform procedures, more homogenous products, more competitive edge, etc.—but in many quarters there was still a healthy distrust of centralization, of blueprints, and of bureaucratic rigidity.

Imperial Chemical Industries represent, alongside Unilever, Shell, and British Petroleum, one of the largest aggregations of British capital, technology and enterprise of our century. (Their capital employed £1,581 millions, turnover £1,355 millions, profits before tax £200 million in 1969.)[2]

Even more than Unilever, ICI's origins were truly international. Its founders were Ludwig Mond, who was a German Jew from Cassel— brilliantly scientific, cultivated, congenial, patient, optimistic. His education reflected Germany's growing attention to science and technology. When he arrived in England in 1862, he brought with him intellectual equipment and an international outlook he could never have acquired in Britain. His partner, J. T. Brunner, was by origin Swiss. So were some of the scientific staff in Brunner-Mond's early days in Cheshire. Most were German and there was one very distinguished Hungarian. The process the partners set out to exploit was of Belgian invention, the discovery and property of Ernest Solvay, a chemist of that kind of genius which consists of an infinite capacity for taking pains. Solvay's work was to revolutionize the production of alkali, a major necessity to a variety of industries, especially to the makers of glass, soap, paper and textiles, and many others. In the 1880s (the age of "depression") its sales increased in Britain by over 55 percent.

The other major partner in the ICI was Nobel explosives. Alfred Nobel was by birth Swedish, but misfortune had drawn his father to Finland and Russia, where Alfred was educated. This did not prevent him from learning several other languages, including English, in which tongue he wrote a long and gloomy autobiography at the age of seventeen. After much wandering, research into explosives, especially nitroglycerin, and founding businesses in Germany, France, and America, he finally achieved his ambition: the foundation of a British factory—at Ardeer on the Clyde, at a discreetly safe distance from Glasgow (for dynamite was a perilously unstable substance). From this center Nobel was to expand his world-wide industry in explosives.

Finally there was the dyestuffs industry. The most original work on the manufacture of synthetic dyes was done in the 1860s by W. H. Perkin, an Englishman. But in spite of the vast demand from British textile makers, the industry developed fastest and in the largest units in Germany (and to a lesser extent Switzerland). It was in fact the formation of the great German dyestuffs industry I. G. Farben which was to trigger off the mergers which brought ICI into existence in 1926. The leading figure in the British industry over the preceding half-century was again a German Jew, Ivan Levinstein. "Saxon, or Norman, or Dane are we" sang the greatest Victorian laureate, but his own age matched its remote predecessors in absorbing new and dynamic streams of immigration.

The first point to be made about all these component industries of ICI was that only very exceptionally did they sell anything that could be described as consumer goods. The customers of the alkali and dyestuffs makers were other industries. So were Nobel's customers for industrial explosives—mining, railway, and public utility contractors mainly. But governments, too, needed explosives for army and navy ordnance and ammunition. This fact alone marks off the chemical industries from a large part of the oils and fats industries. True, as we have shown, soap-makers and margarine makers had to deal with governments about their raw material and other problems from time to time; but the tide which swung their boat around was mass demand, and their objectives were consumer relations and exploitation of the mass market. It was quite different with chemical industries. Technology and technical skill was certainly the *sine qua non* and recruitment of graduate scientific staff was from the first a major preoccupation at Winnington (Cheshire) and Ardeer. But the output of these industries was conditioned mainly by the needs of their customer industries, and this was not to be greatly influenced by advertisement or any of the arts of the market place. Technology could influence market price via cost, but hardly otherwise.

The power of the customer industries had one other important effect: their lobbying power was deployed to extend the life of free trade in an age when many voices elsewhere were clamoring for tariffs. Thus Brunner-Mond were able to remain for a very long time an exporting industry, based in Britain and little concerned with overseas factories. Contrariwise, the British dyestuffs industries were unable to convince government (against the powerful voice of British textile manufacturers) that they deserved protection against German low-cost imports.

It was very different with explosives. There were many reasons why governments everywhere wanted to foster local explosives industries. Even Britain, which had no tariff, had nevertheless stringent rules about the manufacture and carriage of dynamite, which made it of the first importance for Nobel to manufacture his explosives in Britain. And though the largest consumption of explosive in the late nineteenth century was peaceable, there was always the inescapable military value of explosive plant which no government could ignore. So gradually explosive industries grew in Britain, Europe, the United States, South America, Canada, Australia and South Africa, and to a lesser extent elsewhere. And all the time, manufacturers of different chemical products were tending to come together in larger units, largely because the scale of capital investment was growing rapidly, while human capacity to forecast and predict business fluctuations was not. Growing risks brought growing togetherness.

The world of chemical industry therefore became criss-crossed by a complex network of market-sharing agreements between British, German, Belgian, and American producers. The future ICI view was that the British Empire was a natural (though not always protected) market for British explosive producers. If Du Pont and the German producers were prepared to act on that assumption, they would be left alone to enjoy the American and European markets respectively. The alkali markets were divided between Solvay and Brunner-Mond in the 1880s on the basis (broadly) that Solvay took Europe, Brunner took the rest.

There were some areas like Canada, South America, and South Africa where joint enterprises sprang up. Du Pont and Nobel cooperated in the two former: in the latter Nobel had to combine with de Beers, who were too powerful to be ignored.

As time went on, the local plant became more and more the rule, and export trade the exception, even for alkali. The Dingley Tariff finished the Brunner trade to the United States. Trade to Japan, India, and China lasted much longer, though even here it came to be conducted through the so-called local, foreign merchant companies—partly for tax reasons, partly for prestige reasons in countries where "status" was very important.

The twenties and thirties saw economic rationalism and economic nationalism fighting against one another as one country after another raised tariffs and promoted local chemical industry. The "foreign merchant company" within the ICI organization often found itself the first victim of its own success. For the better it succeeded in promoting ICI exports, the more certain it became that it would give way to a local manufacturing plant. And as local industrial development went ahead, consumption of products like alkali and dyestuffs reached a point where the old consumers' lobby for free trade made way for the nationalist lobby for local production.

Within the ten years following its foundation, ICI therefore found itself faced with a world situation of increasing difficulty. As local competition or local pressure rose everywhere, the solution often seemed to be to placate governments (Chile was an example) by putting down a local plant. In some cases it was too small to be really economic. For this and other reasons it might be necessary to collaborate in a joint investment with Du Pont or the German industries—to all intents and purposes I. G. Farben. Other agreements with these giants of chemical industry were designed to meet the general fall in consumption, by a sick world industry and agriculture, of chemical products.

The result was a business which had to be carried on within a laboriously constructed framework of international agreements—with Solvay, I. G., and Du Pont especially. Much of it was imprecise and capable of being only imprecisely understood. Nobody could be clear, in particular, how far it was legally possible to enter into agreements with American producers without contravening American antitrust laws. And of course this applied to agreements covering trade and production outside the United States, as well as inside its boundaries.

Circumstances so pressing tended to produce a centralized and secretive management structure, for almost any policy move, whether it concerned prices or technology or markets, necessarily came within the scope of one, or more likely several, international agreements. And since the terms of all the agreements were confidential, only the small circle of top managers concerned with foreign operations could have access to the knowledge necessary to make any significant decision. The top management accordingly turned into a kind of endless international business diplomacy. The supreme exponent of this type of entrepreneurial expertise was Harry (later Sir Harry, later Lord) MacGowan, a Glaswegian who had had his early experience of business bargaining in the tough school (there was no tougher) of the Canadian explosives business. The business deal was MacGowan's forte, taking him to the top of ICI, where he survived, though not always without difficulty, from 1926 to 1950.

It was a curious irony that no one realized better than MacGowan, who was amongst its chief inventors, the fundamental weakness of this highly centralized system of management. During and after a visit to the Chinese business in the mid-thirties, MacGowan lashed the local management without mercy for its inertia, its timidity, its undue deference to London. But what else could he expect? The managerial psychology he was attacking was the almost inevitable consequence of the closely knotted intricacy of the world chemical industry which he more than anyone else had helped to construct.

So obscure did the outlook for ICI seem in the 1930s and so remote and unlikely seemed any solution of its complicated problems, that some of its top men believed that the only way out was to liquidate its foreign and overseas investments and concentrate on the home market. Overseas plant (it was argued) was often too small to produce any profits; when it did it was difficult to repatriate them and impossible to repatriate capital. Meanwhile these overseas infants demanded an inordinate amount of nursing. Even the profits from the export trade were often frozen, as in Germany or the Argentine Republic.

This cataclysmic pessimism was rejected, though its influence was perhaps reflected in the selling off (late 1930s) of some of ICI's smaller foreign investments. The major dilemma—how to reconcile necessary control from the center with that degree of independence essential to the efficiency and morale of local management—remained. It could only be resolved when the chemical industry emerged (as it was to emerge after the Second World War) into a clearer situation, less trammeled by secret diplomacy and restrictive agreements. The oils and fats industries, with few patents or agreements and therefore less secretive and less centralized, were able to devolve and delegate in an effort to meet their problems of international management. They also went farther and faster in meeting the demand of emergent countries that businesses in their territories should be managed by their own nationals. In both industries after 1945 the problem was not whether to delegate or not, but which areas of management could best be delegated and which still demanded a measure of central control.

Finally, it must be said again, even at the risk of repeating the obvious, that the evolution of these two great international business groups demonstrates clearly how the multinational business emerges as a necessary consequence of trying to maintain growth in conditions of economic nationalism. Mining or petroleum or natural gas companies must necessarily emigrate to the source of their materials and bring the product to market, wherever it is to be sold. Manufacturing companies to whom exports became a significant source of profit inevitably find themselves faced, sooner or later, with the alternatives of either putting down a local plant in this or that foreign market or folding up. And thereby hangs a long tale of management problems. Some are unique to one type of multinational, some to another. Some are common to many types of multinational but all of them pose the old conundrum—to centralize or delegate? To centralize what? To delegate what? Obvious as the logic of this is in the light of history, it still seems to be news to some of our economist friends, who persist in arguing as if direct overseas investment is a perfectly voluntary act, which a company can perform or not as it chooses. The history of the two firms studied in this paper suggests that such simplistic judgments fly in the face of the historic facts, and will continue to do so until that happy, but alas distant day when once again the world goes free trade.

How does the evolution of Unilever and ICI compare with that of the four great American companies analyzed by Professor Chandler?[3] I can only give a qualified answer; to be more sure would call for a closer discussion and definition of situations and terms. Broadly it looks as if the British or Anglo-Dutch companies follow the Chandler pattern, at any rate in general. Certainly their structure evolved as a response to the needs of business strategy. They too went through the appointed phases. They accumulated resources, they rationalized, they integrated horizontally, they integrated vertically—they also (consciously) dis-integrated vertically—they diversified, etc. Naturally, as between one company and another, then as always there were differences of chronology (as Professor Chandler remarks). In one respect the British record here is interesting.

The British companies lacked the great protected domestic market available to the U.S. companies. They were also very much less harassed by antimonopoly legislation. The continental markets were relatively near. The empire was far, but near (as it were) in spirit. These considerations combined to produce a precocious spilling over of investment overseas. It could perhaps be said that already, in their infancy, these entrepreneurial toddlers were stumbling into the neighbor's gardens almost before they were able to walk in their home nursery. In the case of the Lever/Unilever group, growth came by a centripetal as well as by a centrifugal process. Decentralization was therefore vital not simply at a late stage in growth but almost at the start. The difficulties of communications alone made it impossible to run (say) an Australian business from Lancashire or even an English business from Rotterdam. Language, taste, psychology all multiplied the problems of attempting central control.

Diversification likewise tended to come via acquisition and horizontal integration rather than via technological progress internal to the single firm—for many years anyway. This fact again emphasized the decentralized, almost federative character of such companies, or congeries of companies (for that is what they were). Any central authority just had to step carefully. Until the crisis of the early 1920s, the Unilever business operated pretty freely, as I have shown. Sheer financial pressure limited their freedom for the next twenty years. Then the War of 1939 rendered decentralization unavoidable. It continued as conscious doctrine until very recently when a total reorganization brought more control back to the center.[4]

I have explained earlier why ICI may be regarded in some senses as a highly centralized business. The hundreds of international agreements and patents by which it worked made it so. But this is not of course to say that a very large measure of decentralization did not exist so far as day-to-day management went and obviously even large issues must often have been settled locally. Indeed, physically, the ICI structure (of product divisions) closely resembles the reorganized Du Pont structure of "decentralization" as described by Professor Chandler. And both resemble the new Unilever "product" organization more than they do the old Unilever structure, which gave generously wide powers to national and even individual company managements.

Perhaps we might ask a few more questions about this "decentralization." How far did top management impose restrictions on the powers
delegated to lower echelons? Have periods of capital shortage tended to
be periods of a reversion to centralization or at any rate to greater re-
served powers for headquarters? Are there any signs of a neocentralization
in world business? How is decentralized organization standing up to the
stresses arising from the crucial character of single business decisions
which may carry multimillion dollar consequences? Would a 1972 version
of *Strategy and Structure* need any revision in this respect? Above all,
how do we reconcile our golden age of calculatedly liberal business administration with the Galbraith image of the twentieth-century business
juggernaut imposing its carefully planned and executed tyranny on a
submissive society that consumes what it is given?

A few general conclusions emerge from the foregoing. First, in the
seesaw battle about centralization versus decentralization which goes on
in every large corporation, the two factors which weigh in favor of the
former are capital investment problems and the ponderable importance
of those products which can be made and sold to a consistent formula,
regardless of place or time. In favor of maximum local option are (usually) all forms of social or personnel problems and marketing problems
arising out of products which have a character capable of modification
or substitution in response to local tastes. Yet to solve even this problem
of balance is not to solve all: for the most skillfully and tactfully managed
international business may fall victim in one place or another to xenophobia or the local brand of economic nationalism.

I will end with a personal impression. I have the feeling that under
the pressures I have mentioned the great companies are steadily becoming
more alike in their ethos and even organization, and for this there is a
plausible prima facie set of reasons. Diversification—into new products
and new countries—is constantly blurring the distinction between those
businesses which used to specialize in consumer goods for the millions
and those which made "capital" goods, or ministered to a handful of other
industries and governments. The great chemical giants now make tights
and pharmaceuticals. The detergent giants make complex chemicals used
by the paint, textile, and electronics industries. Thus each has to learn
(often painfully) the other's job. And thus the sharp image which their
creators stamped on their offspring becomes blurred. Their once well-
defined profile and special ethos fades. Their managers absorb the same
business education, the same concepts of management. They earnestly
search for every nostrum which promises protection against affliction and
stability in perpetuity. So the quest for private profit/public benefit produces that perfect model of anonymity, the corporate impersonality. For,

in the end, to sell all things to all men could mean to be all things to all men.

NOTES

1. At a comical point in the story (set in the Risorgimento), Prince Salina, a Sicilian nobleman, "plastered his hair with Lemo-Liscio, Atkinson's 'Lime Juice and Glycerine,' a dense whitish lotion which arrived in cases from London and whose name suffered the same change as songs."

2. I am indebted for most of the information about ICI to Mr. W. J. Reader's admirable first volume, *Imperial Chemical Industries*, vol. 1 (N.Y.: Oxford University Press, 1970). This takes the story down to the formation of ICI from constituent companies in 1926. The second volume is still being written and I have therefore been able to use ICI largely for purposes of comparison and contrast only.

3. Alfred D. Chandler, *Strategy and Structure* (Cambridge, Mass.: M.I.T. Press, 1962).

4. See: Charles Wilson, *History of Unilever*, vol. 2 (London: Cassell, 1954), pp. 384–88 for the views of Sir G. Heyworth (later Lord Heyworth) which are the quintessence of the decentralizing philosophy.

Comment

Mira Wilkins

Whenever I read the work of Charles Wilson, I am delighted. This essay is no exception. In my discussion, I thought I would try to take what he says about Unilever and ICI and to see whether his generalizations on these companies mesh with my own findings on the evolution of American business abroad. Second, I want to comment on the application of Professor Chandler's analysis of structure to the American multinational enterprise. In the process, I hope I can make an attempt to deal with some of the questions posed in the last pages of Professor Wilson's paper.

When Professor Wilson talks about his two companies—Unilever and Imperial Chemical Industries—he starts with their nineteenth-century multinational origins. But when we talk about the origins of American multinational corporations, we find no such mergings of Dutch, British, German, Swedish, and Swiss founders. The American "melting pot" did not seem to apply to leadership of individual corporations. To be sure a number of today's multinational enterprises had "foreign founders"—the du Ponts were French, W. R. Grace was Irish, George Merck was German —but I cannot off-hand think of a single U.S. multinational corporation that combined at origin the leadership of several nationalities, except possibly Allied Chemical, part of whose heritage bears a resemblance to that of ICI.

While at origin, and in their early history, a number of American firms borrowed the inventions of Europeans, the U.S. companies that earliest became multinational tended to be those that were most technologically advanced, whose domestic accomplishments far exceeded their foreign borrowings.

To be sure, small U.S. companies in the nineteenth century went abroad to find raw materials—to mine copper or to start sugar plantations—yet these nineteenth-century enterprises in general did not, like Lever, ransack the globe. Rather, these firms went to nearby areas—to Mexico, Canada, or the Caribbean. A few large enterprises participated in such activities. Amalgamated Copper Company—a predecessor of Anaconda—claimed in 1899 that it aimed to dominate the world's copper industry, but it came nowhere near that goal. Standard Oil by the late 1890s had begun seeking oil-producing properties abroad, on a limited scale and with limited success. United Fruit at formation in 1899 was growing bananas in a number of countries in Central America and the Caribbean. Here and there a truly worldwide hunt for raw materials in the nineteenth century stands out among U.S. enterprises. Thomas Edison, for example, had difficulty with lamp filaments. In 1880, he initiated a search for the best kind of bamboo for the filaments. He sent a representative to China and Japan, and another to Brazil; an expedition was also dispatched to Cuba and Jamaica. At first, Japanese bamboo proved most satisfactory, but Edison kept looking. In 1887 two men traveled throughout South America, while another circumnavigated the globe seeking, on Edison's behalf, the perfect bamboo. By the end of the 1880s, however, Edison had developed an artificial filament that substituted for bamboo fibers and offered excellent results. Edison's search, however, seems to have been a rare instance. Indeed, by the end of the nineteenth century fewer than a handful of U.S. enterprises had supply-oriented stakes in three or more foreign countries. I can actually identify only two such enterprises.

America was rich in raw materials in the nineteenth century. In the main, Americans did not have to go abroad to obtain them. Later, as our raw materials became more limited, multinational corporations in the United States did become concerned with foreign sources of supply. I have often wondered how this compared with European enterprise abroad and have on occasion gone so far as to hypothesize that European companies, because of shortages of natural resources in Europe, would early in their histories search for and make foreign investments in raw materials, and that they would tend to do this earlier than American companies.

Professor Wilson's comments on the predecessors of Unilever and ICI give only slim support to this hypothesis. Clearly the thrust of the early stakes of Unilever and of ICI's predecessors were market-oriented— although Lever's concern for and early investments in raw materials do seem to provide an element of support. Had Professor Wilson dealt with the strategies of Royal Dutch Shell, I suspect my hypothesis might have gained more confirmation.

By contrast with the limited multinational stakes of U.S. companies in raw materials, in the last decades of the nineteenth century numerous U.S. corporations sold their manufactured goods worldwide and a surprising number by 1900 had established foreign plants to sell abroad. These companies in the process of expansion outside the United States in many ways resemble very closely the predecessors of Unilever and ICI. It was marketing strategy that encouraged them to expand abroad. They too employed advisors, managers, and bankers of many nations. Their main investments were in Europe and Canada, where they utilized the capital and the labor of the nations in which they operated.

Some of the U.S. corporations that went abroad sold primarily to consumers, some sold to businesses and governments, and some to both.

Thus, in the nineteenth century, American Tobacco's foreign subsidiaries and affiliates sold to individual consumers. American Radiator sold mainly to heating and building contractors. Western Electric had foreign government telephone companies as large purchasers. General Electric sold lamps to consumers and heavy equipment to industry and governments. U.S. business, when it went abroad, clearly sold both consumer and producer goods—and sometimes the same company sold both.

Professor Wilson finds that the tangled roots of his two multinational enterprises help explain their later multinational growth. There are some U.S. companies with tangled roots that directly contributed to their multinational character. Polish-born Helena Rubinstein went to Australia, began selling and manufacturing there, then traveled to London and Paris and set up branches of the business, and then in time moved the headquarters of her multinational concern to the United States. So too, the Irishman W. R. Grace migrated to Peru, began business there, and in time became involved in handling operations that joined Britain, the United States, and the West Coast of South America; by the 1880s, W. R. Grace had transferred his headquarters to New York. Yet such ready-made U.S. multinational enterprises are exceptions.

Other U.S. companies were born multinational in a different sense. General Electric, for example, is similar to ICI and Unilever in that its predecessor enterprises had business abroad before the company was formed. This was also true of International Telephone and Telegraph Corporation.

On the other hand, the existence of dependent, or derivative, multinational ties at origin could impair the growth of U.S. international business. Allied Chemical's expansion abroad seemed to have been hobbled by its ties with Solvay, Brunner-Mond, and then ICI. In its early history, Merck & Co. only went to Canada; its German parent had the rest of the world for its business.

Some of my examples have strayed into the twentieth century, but to return to the nineteenth century, it is clear that in America as well as Europe, ebullient capitalism, to use Professor Wilson's well-chosen words, was not cramped by political boundaries. American business, not because of its European backgrounds but because of its domestic technological advantage, did seek and find world markets—and did invest abroad in reaching these markets. American companies with new technology and new products were the leaders abroad.

U.S. concerns decided to manufacture abroad rather than continue to export for the same reasons as Lever and the Dutch margarine makers—mainly to jump tariffs and other barriers to exports. They went abroad to get nearer to their customers. Foreign "political costs" (from those imposed by customs duties to those of host-country preference for locally made goods) as well as costs of transportation, materials of manufacture, and labor entered into their calculations, with the first two considerations perhaps the most important. In most cases, there seemed to have been obstacles to continued exports, then entry into foreign manufacturing, and then adaptation to foreign conditions. The strategies employed seem very similar to those Professor Wilson has described.

I think it is important to stress that in the case of the American multinational corporation, the early stages of this development occurred at a time when the Americans were a debtor nation in international accounts, not at a time when we were a creditor nation, as was the case in Great Britain. The latter stages came after World War I, when we were of course a creditor nation.

In Professor Chandler's superb book, as we all well know, he points out that as companies diversify and expand geographically, as their strategies change, they must, if they are to be efficient, alter their structures. In the process, many adopted a decentralized organizational structure, establishing product or regional divisions and a central staff.

Often, U.S. companies set up international divisions as the earliest of the decentralized "operating" divisions. Such a division, or international company (for the international unit in the early days was often incorporated), proved to be a way for an American enterprise to sort out its "foreign" administrative problems, to isolate them, and to give them specialized attention. Foreign activities seemed amenable to administrative unity. Generally, the international unit added a certain amount of staff activity, while foreign subsidiaries and affiliates carried on the operations.

As early as 1884, the electrical company Thomson-Houston set up an international subsidiary. It was ahead of its time, and when Thomson-Houston merged into General Electric in the reorganization of 1892–93 the international company disappeared. After World War I and in the 1920s, when Chandler's innovators were taking their important steps in decentralizing, a number of U.S. corporations established international groups or companies. After World War II, international divisions (as they more commonly came to be called) proliferated.

Recently, however, the international division has been found wanting by a number of companies. International divisions were established—as we have noted—to give specialized treatment to international business. Companies discovered that this served to isolate the international operations from the mainstream of company activity. Indeed, the international divisions were meant to isolate international business to give it greater attention. But in the 1960s a number of companies began to feel that their overseas subsidiaries and affiliates should be able to rely on the best resources of the U.S. parent—the financial experts, the engineering talent, the product planners, and so forth—and not just those individuals in the international group or division. In certain companies, the international division became increasingly superfluous as foreign subsidiaries and affiliates desired to go to the particular product divisions for information on products rather than to an intermediary, and as product divisions wanted to expand abroad directly, rather than having to go through an international division.

A number of U.S. companies have in recent years given up their international division, group, or company and have reorganized a grid, as it has been called, on a worldwide basis of product or region, or some combination of both.

There is no sense that these are final reorganizations, quite the contrary. Strategies continue to change, and so will structure. One company that discontinued its international division, its international group, and its international staff, and set up worldwide operations on a regional basis, assumed that the U.S.-based staffs would undertake a counterpart relationship with overseas affiliates. It found that while to a large degree this was accomplished, in some areas there existed, on the part of American staffs, "a natural resistance to adding to already heavy work loads." By 1972 this particular multinational corporation included on its central staff a vice president and assistant to the president in charge of operations in Europe in the company's principal product. The central staff also included a man with the title "executive director, international governmental affairs staff."

Another company—dating back to 1919—which had an international company division and then grew, in 1967 rid itself of its international group. Product divisions, manned by personnel who had no experience in overseas business, expanded abroad in their own products, with some really poor results. The particular company in question had by March 1972 reestablished an international group, with a vice president and group executive at its head and five vice presidents and general managers who headed various international divisions reporting to the group executive.

My comments so far have not come to terms with the question of whether the latest reorganizations involve greater centralization or decentralization. A number of people who have studied the organizational structure of U.S. international businesses have experienced difficulties with these concepts. Recently, one scholar told me he avoided the words entirely. The difficulties are not dissimilar to the ones with which Professor Wilson seems to be wrestling.

My reading of Professor Chandler's *Strategy and Structure* would give an evolutionary picture of the U.S. giant business evolving from a centralized to a decentralized structure. As he defines his terms, this seems legitimate.

Yet, if one considers only international business, I have found, as has Professor Wilson, that decentralization often starts very early with the existence of both spatial and political distance. In addition, as Professor

Wilson has pointed out, language, taste, psychology all multiply the problems of imposing central control.

Nonetheless, it is clear that at periods in their histories, U.S. companies have attempted to impose central control—especially in the areas of finance, production, and engineering; sometimes in the field of product design; to a far lesser extent in the fields of marketing and advertising, and to an even lesser extent in the field of labor relations. How do we form a composite index of centralization and decentralization? Which facet do we emphasize? How do we measure control? Do we trust the manager of the foreign subsidiary when he answers an interviewer's question that reads: "Are you completely, partly, or not at all controlled by your parent company?" To me such a question is fraught with the perils of ambiguity.

I have found, however, that parent company records do reveal a sense of the control exercised. We can by going through such records obtain the parent company's philosophy on the degree of control to be exercised at various times in the company's history. Professor Wilson poses the question, how far did top management impose restrictions on the powers delegated to lower echelons in foreign countries? This question would seem to get at the root of centralization and decentralization—the more restrictions the greater the centralization. But, what is top management? If top management—that is the principal officers of the American company—delegate responsibility for international operations to an international division, and then this international division puts great restrictions on the foreign subsidiaries, is this decentralization or centralization?

I prefer to look at the question in a broader context and ask, how far does the U.S. company—either directly through its principal officers or indirectly through its international division or other divisions—impose restrictions on the powers delegated to lower echelons in foreign countries? Looked at this way, a centralized international structure would be one where American methods were to a great extent imposed abroad. A decentralized structure would be one wherein the U.S. company would give the foreign subsidiaries and affiliates a large amount of freedom of action within the limits of the organization.

Sometimes centralization and decentralization in this context go together—with one foreign subsidiary tightly, and another affiliate loosely controlled. Often, there is considerable subtlety and a range in the degree of control, with strict control in one field and loose control in another. Yet, these reservations notwithstanding, I find there generally exists at any particular period of time an over-all philosophy of the U.S. company's management that tends toward centralization or decentralization. Indeed, I find myself very much in sympathy with Professor Wilson when he refers to a seesawing between the two. My own research would indicate that in the case of a single U.S. company's history there is an ebb and flow in the control pattern and there are distinguishable periods when the U.S. company's management feels a desire to impose American methods and tighten control, and then periods when there is confidence that all is going well abroad and that foreign managements of U.S. subsidiaries and affiliates are capable of running the business, with the result that there is a relaxation of control. Relaxation of control may also occur when all is not going well, and the U.S. company decides to develop domestic business and de-emphasize foreign activity. Then, when the U.S. company's management changes; when business overseas is in grave difficulty; when a new foreign expansion is contemplated, or for other reasons, there may again be a tightening of U.S. control. And the process is apt to repeat itself.

Professor Wilson asks in his paper whether periods of capital shortage have tended to be periods of reversion to centralization? I am not sure that I know what he meant. Was he talking about capital shortage in terms of the foreign subsidiary of the parent company? Or was he talking about capital shortage in terms of the international economy or the host country? If he referred to capital shortage in terms of the general economy (that is a time of general economic stringency), my research would indicate quite the opposite. In the 1930s, U.S. companies tended to relax their control over foreign subsidiaries. If, as his comments today seem to indicate, he is talking about capital shortages in terms of the particular foreign subsidiary, that the foreign subsidiary needs capital in order to cope with a particular difficulty or to expand, my own research would bring forth different results for different companies; in some companies, where there is a dependence on the parent company for funds, control tightens, as in the case of certain Canadian companies; in other U.S. cases, where the subsidiary is able to borrow in the host country and raise money through its own devices, the control of the U.S. parent company may lessen.

I do completely agree with Professor Wilson that capital investment problems tend to weigh in favor of centralization and when these have a high priority then centralization tends to exist, although this may be in a time of capital abundance on the part of the U.S. parent company, rather than in times of capital shortage. Likewise, if I understand Professor Wilson correctly, a company that has a homogenized product to market tends toward centralization. I also agree that the process tending toward decentralization is a growing awareness on the part of the parent company of social, personnel, and specific product problems distinctive to a particular foreign country. I also would add that changes in the parent company's management often have an impact on centralization and decentralization. A parent company's new management, convinced that its predecessors have done it all wrong, may change a company from centralization to decentralization or vice versa, just for the sake of innovation.

Professor Wilson poses the question, are there any signs of neo-centralization in world business? This it seems to me depends entirely on our definitions. Worldwide product and regional divisions or combinations thereof can easily be interpreted in Professor Chandler's terms as simply a different form of decentralization. On the other hand, if we look at control patterns, we may find greater centralization of business abroad in a number of companies. That central staffs play a greater role in international business in some companies may be interpreted to imply a greater centralization; but then again it may not. Perhaps too the technology of the modern age—the jet and the telex even more than the long-distance telephone—give an unprecedented opportunity for centralization, an opportunity that was absent in times past.

In closing, I would like to pose for further discussion more consideration of centralization and decentralization. Do cartel relationships really imply centralization as Professor Wilson suggests in his paper, or just a central framework with a high degree of decentralization? Are there comments that we can make on economic efficiency and innovation that relate to centralization and decentralization?

9. The Multi-Unit Enterprise: A Historical and International Comparative Analysis and Summary

ALFRED D. CHANDLER, JR.

Let me begin this summary of the several themes and messages developed during the conference by defining the nature of the beast—the patient as some have called it—that we have begun examining. It is the multi-unit enterprise. Such enterprises have consolidated under the control of a single office many different units, usually carrying on a number of different activities. Individually each of these units—factories; sales, purchasing, and financial offices; mines, plantations, laboratories, and even shipping lines— could be and often have been operated as independent business enterprises. United, they formed a single administrative network through which flowed orders, reports, information, and, of course, goods and services. A basic economic function of such a network has been to maintain a high velocity of production and distribution of goods and services through its many units. The increased velocity made possible the full use of the resources (men, money, and equipment) of the enterprise, and helped to lower its unit costs. While the reasons men created and continued to operate large multi-unit enterprises were often not those of maintaining the velocity of flow and so of lowering costs unless such velocity was achieved, the multi-unit enterprise has had difficulty in remaining a viable institution over a long period of time.

Once formed, such enterprises were under constant pressure to keep their accumulated resources employed. The creation of an enterprise involving many factories, offices, and mines required, almost by definition, the acquisition of a great deal more capital, men, and equipment than did a single-unit enterprise. The necessity to keep these resources employed created pressures to expand the activities of the enterprise in a number of ways. It purchased or built new units to assure itself of a steady supply of materials or outlets for its goods and services. It bought or otherwise obtained control of units carrying on similar activities so as to reduce the threat of overcapacity and, therefore, rigorous competition in a given market. The existence of excess capacity within the enterprise often moved it into the production of new products and services that used existing resources. Sometimes when changing markets or technologies made some of its existing resources obsolete, it entered into activities that, while unrelated to its current activities, promised a higher rate of return on investment.

If the addition of new units directly aided the enterprise in increasing the velocity of flow and lowering unit costs, the centripetal force that flowed through the enterprise kept it operating as a viable centralized administrative network. However, if the new additions produced goods and services for different markets and/or required new types of supplies or technical skills, centrifugal forces came into play that tended to pull the enterprise apart.

The requirements for keeping such an extended enterprise together normally brought structural reorganization. It led to a shift from a functional organization—production, sales, purchasing, and finance departments—to one that was oriented to products or regional markets. The new product or regional operating divisions included all the functional activities necessary to process and market a major line of goods. Their managers had full responsibility for coordinating the flow of raw and semi-finished materials from the suppliers through the processing facilities, and of finished goods to the consumers. Over these autonomous operating divisions a general office was formed which allocated the resources of the enterprise as a whole, evaluated their operating performance, set general policies, and determined over-all strategy. This type of organizational structure, depicted in Figure 1, has become standard for large, managerial, multi-unit enterprises in technologically advanced market economies.

Three important points need to be made about large, multi-unit enterprises, whether organized along functional or market lines. First, and again almost by definition, they have become managerial rather than personal enterprises; that is, they have become operated by managers rather than

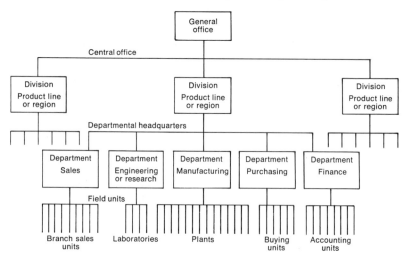

Figure 1. The Multidivisional Structure

owners. No family, not even one as prolific as the du Ponts, can provide the number of skilled and trained executives needed to manage the many offices, factories, laboratories, and mines involved. For a time, founders and their families maintained a place in the top central or general office. Managers who had risen through the ranks usually became better trained and developed more operating expertise than members of the family who came in at the top. So the managers came to dominate the enterprise. Moreover, because the operation of such an enterprise involved cooperative efforts of many administrators, consensus management usually became more effective than authoritarian control. In particular, top level strategic decisions involving large sums of capital and affecting the careers of many managers came to be made by several senior executives rather than by single individuals. Managerial enterprise thus encouraged consensus and group decision-making in a way that personal enterprise rarely did.

The two other points I want to stress are of particular interest to economic historians. First, the large, multi-unit managerial enterprise is historically a new institution. Second, this type of enterprise has become an engine of modern economic development. Public and military bureaucracies (i.e., multi-unit administrative hierarchies) have existed since ancient Egypt and have often been involved in economic activities. Yet until the mid-nineteenth century nearly all private, profit-oriented, economic enterprises were single-unit, personal partnerships. The very few multi-unit enterprises were much smaller than those of today and were still personally managed. They existed largely in commerce and finance, not in manufacturing. The Second Bank of the United States became the most powerful economic institution in the United States during the first half of the nineteenth century, and it did so precisely because it had branches and carried on a far greater volume of business than any other economic enterprise in the nation. Nevertheless, it had fewer branches and a much smaller volume of business than the Virginia National Bank, for example, has today—a middle-sized bank in a middle-sized state. The Second Bank carried on its $60 to $70 million business with twenty-five branches, while the Virginia National Bank has over eighty branches to handle its $600 to $700 millions' worth of business. The famous banking houses of the Peruzzi and Medici had still fewer branches and managers, and a smaller volume and velocity of business than the Second Bank. A look at the organization of the great trading companies, including the Hudson's Bay, the West African, and John Jacob Astor's American Fur Trading Company, shows that they were mercantile partnerships operating a handful of trading posts. Even the few large European shipping companies of the early nineteenth century were personal rather than managerial enterprises. The men at headquarters dealt directly with the managers of the units in the field. There was no middle or higher management, no managers who managed managers.

I am quite certain that as late as 1840 there were fewer salaried managers (who were not partners) in charge of a laboring group large enough to be formally subdivided in the United States than there are today in a single large enterprise. For example, the du Pont Company has ten thousand managers above the first line supervisor or foreman level. In 1840 the total number of plantation overseers in the United States supervising a working force of fifty field hands numbered about twelve hundred. The number of managers or agents of mills and mines handling a work force of the same number was about half that, while ship captains rarely had crews of more than thirty. Moreover, each manager was usually the only one in the enterprise. Managers worked closely with the owners. They were not linked to thousands of other managers by a huge administrative network. Their daily activities and lifetime careers had little in common with those of today's managers.

The coming of the multi-unit enterprise thus led to the creation of a new economic class to manage it. Certainly this new institution and new class have become exceedingly powerful in modern, technologically advanced, market economies. One reason for the power and the influence of the multi-unit enterprise and its managers is that they have been at the center of modern economic development.

Here I draw on Robert Averitt's distinction between economic development and economic growth. Growth, he defines as short-term expansion of gross national product. Economic development, on the other hand, is "a process of structural change." Such change, he continues, is "a long-run phenomenon, requiring the adoption of new skills, the accumulation of new knowledge, the use of new commodities, the creation of new materials, new markets, and new organizational forms." For Averitt, "The first principle of economic development can be stated as follows: development in an economic system is largely achieved by increasing the average velocity of production per unit of labor time." This increase in velocity, he points out, has come in what economists term the secondary sector of the economy. The biological nature of agricultural and other activities in the primary sector has put natural limits on volume and velocity of output. The personalized nature of the services provided by the tertiary sector limits increases there. On the other hand (and again Averitt says it very well): "The heart of the development enterprise resides in the secondary sector. Here the velocity of production is determined by mechanical, chemical, and electrical (including electronic) factors. Even the most primitive economy provides the characteristics necessary to sustain an on-going social life— food, shelter, clothing, transportation, communication. But when the commodities providing these life-supporting services are largely produced in the secondary sector, freeing their generation from biological constraints, the velocity of production can be increased, bringing the development multiplier into play." And it was in the secondary sector that the multi-unit, capital intensive, managerial enterprise came to dominate. It did so because it was there that it could best carry out its function of coordinating high volume, high energy-consuming production with mass distribution to concentrated markets.

These assertions about the historical role of the multi-unit managerial enterprise and its managers can be most quickly documented by making a brief review of its rise and spread in the United States. There such enterprises first appeared in the 1840s and 1850s on the new steam railroads. By assuring a much greater speed and regularity of the flow of goods, passengers, and letters, the railroads quickly triumphed over the canal and waterway. By 1870 institutional arrangements had been so perfected that cars carrying freight at a speed greater than ever before dreamed of could go from one commercial center to another in any part of the nation without a single transshipment. In these same years, the application of electricity to communication by means of the telegraph and then the telephone brought a wholly new level of velocity of messages and information within the economy.

The new means of transportation and communication quickly came to be operated by huge multi-unit enterprises. Largely because of the constant pressure to keep the resources under their control fully employed, the railroads created great "self-sustaining systems" reaching from the coast to major interior cities. By the end of the century twenty-five systems grouped into seven communities of interest operated two-thirds of the railroad mileage in the United States. As early as the 1870s the Pennsylvania Railroad had developed an administrative network that managed more than thirty-five operating units, each one of which was as large as many major railroad companies in the 1850s, and each of which was subdivided along functional lines. These thirty-five were grouped into twelve larger administrative organizations which, in turn, were managed by three great geographically defined subsystems. The general managers of these three reported to a general office that evaluated performance, set policies, and formulated strategy for the Pennsylvania system as a whole. When Western Union acquired, through mergers, a monopoly of the telegraph business in 1866, the company already operated 2,250 offices; by 1899 the number had increased tenfold, to 22,285. By 1887, just a little over a decade after the invention of the telephone, the dominant Bell System was handling over a million calls a day. By 1899 it was taking over five million calls. The creation of these huge administrative networks helped to make possible an expansion of the volume and velocity of transportation and communication to unprecedented levels.

This new velocity of transportation and communication permitted the rise of multi-unit managerial enterprises in American production and distribution. Between the 1870's and the end of the century such enterprises came to dominate industries that used energy generated from fossil fuels and/or produced standardized products for a mass market. In steel, copper and brass, oil, rubber, chemicals, glass, and complex machinery, especially electrical machines and automobiles, a few large integrated enterprises, competing as did the railroads in an oligopolistic manner, came in a surprisingly short time to dominate their industries. Ten years after Edison's first central power station went into operation, two enterprises towered over the electrical machinery industry: General Electric and Westinghouse. Eight years after the manufacture of automobiles had proven commercially feasible, the two largest companies were already Ford and General Motors. In the food industries, including sugar, beer, beef, bananas, and animal and vegetable oils, the large firm arose where heat was used in production and/or refrigeration in distribution. Similar multi-unit enterprises arose in retailing, where the pioneer department stores, chain stores, and mail order houses concentrated on scheduling the flow of a wide variety of goods to concentrated markets.

The multi-unit managerial enterprises came slowly and much later in those industries which did not require an intensive use of energy and/or did not produce for a mass market. In such industries the carefully directed coordination of flow from supplier to market did not quickly increase the velocity, and therefore did not provide the cost advantages that it did in railroads, telegraph, telephone, and the energy-using, mass-marketing industries. This was the case in the older industries—those with a history which was based upon biologically produced substances. In clothing, leather, furniture, and woodworking; in textiles, tanning, and lumbering; and in a number of food industries, small, single-unit, personally managed manufacturers who bought and sold through single-unit, personally managed jobbers and wholesalers continued to compete successfully with larger integrated enterprises in the same business. In fact they often did better than the consolidated firms. This was also true of machine-tool manufacturers and other producers who sold specialized products to the particular specifications of individual customers.

With the exception of the mass retailers, the large enterprise did not come quickly in the tertiary or service industries. (Like Averitt, I include communications and transportation in the secondary sector.) In finance, where legislation helped to prevent the growth of branch banking until well into the twentieth century, the large multi-unit enterprise appeared early only in life insurance. Here the nature of the business demanded a large marketing network. The actuarial requirements of a successful life insurance company made essential the sale of a large number of policies to people who had to be convinced that it was in their interest to give up present income for that which would only be available after their deaths. As the twentieth-century progressed, increasingly complex technology and increasingly concentrated markets encouraged the growth of the large-scale enterprise in these older industries. Yet even today, the biologically oriented primary and the service-providing tertiary sectors of the economy remain the strongholds of small business.

In the secondary sector, the large managerial enterprise continued to dominate and to grow in size. After the turn of the century such enterprises had started to expand overseas in search of markets and raw materials, often becoming multinational firms. Beginning in the 1920s and 1930s these same integrated empires began to diversify into new products and processes. These were the enterprises that after World War II created the structures depicted in Figure 1, with autonomous, self-contained product or geographical operating divisions to coordinate flows, and a general office to evaluate and plan for the company as a whole.

The demand for executives by the new intensive energy-using and/or mass-marketing enterprises led to the rise and then the professionalization of the new managerial class. American engineering and scientific schools first appeared in the 1860s and 1870s largely to meet the demands of railroads, telegraph, telephone, and factories for civil, electrical, and mechanical engineers. Then in the first decade of the twentieth century a number of business schools were founded to provide training in the basic activities of the multi-unit enterprise—production, marketing, and finance. In the 1870s and 1880s, railroad managers formed professional societies. At annual and semi-annual meetings railroad superintendents, accountants, passenger agents, and civil engineers read papers and discussed mutual technical problems and challenges. Similar associations were formed in the first two decades of this century by and for managers in the technologically advanced industries. With the rise of professional education and professional societies came the publication of a plethora of professional journals. The professionalizing of management, certainly a major factor in increasing productivity of American economic activities in the twentieth century, resulted from the operating needs of the new multi-unit enterprises concentrated in the secondary sector of the economy.

By comparing the development of similar multi-unit enterprises in different cultures the common characteristics of this all-pervasive, modern economic institution can be defined and evaluated. At the same time such comparisons can indicate how cultural and economic differences altered the structure and functions of these enterprises, the recruitment and training of their managers, as well as their modes of operation and ways of decision-making.

Let us begin with the British experience as analyzed by Peter Mathias (with comments by Barry Supple) and that of the British-based, multinational companies described by Charles Wilson (with comments by Mira Wilkins). A look at Britain can help to delineate common characteristics of the multi-unit enterprise. Then a review of developments in Western Europe, Japan, and Russia can help to reveal the impact of differences in cultural and economic situations on modern, large-scale enterprise and its managers.

Professor Mathias's paper focuses particularly on "the boundaries of an enterprise" and resulting management structures in four industries—beer, margarine, shoes, and groceries. In the first two the coordination of the flow through the multi-unit, multifunctional enterprise acted as a centripetal force that kept the enterprise together as a central administrative network over a long period of time. In the second two industries, expansion by integration failed to bring cost benefits through a more effective coordination of flow. Instead it created centrifugal forces that helped to pull the enterprise apart. The result was internal reorganization in the shoe industry, and, in the tea business, the spinning off of many acquired units.

The British brewing industry, as Professor Mathias has so ably documented in his *The Brewing Industry in England, 1700–1830*, was one of the very first modern industries. Production was fuel- and capital-intensive, relying on large quantities of coal, and distribution was primarily to the London market, probably the most concentrated market of that day. To assure continuing use of their accumulated resources, the large brewers moved forward to control retail outlets; and they did so before legal regulations on licensing became rigorously defined. They also moved backward to assure themselves of a steady supply of malt, hops, and other basic materials. By the mid-eighteenth century a few large enterprises dominated the industry, competing in an oligopolistic manner. Some of these firms are still among the leading brewers of the realm. While legal restrictions, which Professor Mathias discussed, reinforced the operating needs, the latter have provided the centripetal or cohesive force that have kept these large, multi-unit enterprises operating in much the same way for over two hundred years.

In beer the American experience provides a useful parallel. The American brewers did not attempt to take over retailing on a scale comparable to the British. However, as the railroad network neared completion and the process of refrigeration was perfected, brewers in Milwaukee and St. Louis began to sell to the larger national market. With high volume production, which again was fuel- and capital-intensive, and the careful coordination of flow through the massive wholesale network, Anhauser-Busch, Schlitz, Pabst, and Blatz, became and still remain leading brewers, serving national rather than local markets. Again the coordination of high volume flow encouraged the cohesiveness and longevity of the enterprise.

The margarine (and soap) story in Britain has similarities to that of beer. Its production was energy- and capital-intensive in a way that butter from biologically produced milk is not. It sold in a mass market. Soap had similar characteristics. The need for outlets brought margarine manufacturers into retailing (and soapmakers into wholesaling). The giant, multinational enterprise of Unilever had its beginnings and based much of its growth on the production and distribution of these two products. Here again the requirements for maintaining coordination of flow helped to keep an expanding enterprise a unified whole.

The history of shoes, on the other hand, differs basically from that of margarine or beer. Production was not energy intensive. Fuel was not used in the process of production, except for steam power. Machines were more labor- than capital-intensive. The market was large but affected by style and taste. In any case careful scheduling of flow which could be adjusted to changes in market demand did not give the large integrated enterprise a major cost advantage over the small single-unit producers, who bought materials and often sold their shoes through nearby wholesale jobbers, or dealt directly with small single-unit suppliers and retailers. As Professor Mathias noted, at the largest firm producing shoes in the United Kingdom, the centrifugal forces of expansion quickly prevailed over the centripetal. The manufacturing units in C. and J. Clark, Ltd., soon sold to outside retailers and wholesalers, while the retail stores and the shoe stores were buying from other manufacturers, and the shoe-machinery-producing units were selling in all parts of the world. As a result the enterprise was reorganized and became managed through quasi-independent autonomous units operating under the over-all direction of a general office, using a structure quite similar to that indicated in Figure 1.

In the Lipton grocery enterprises, the centrifugal forces unleashed by expansion through vertical integration brought an even greater dispersal of the enterprise. The production of many products on which Lipton concentrated—tea, bacon, butter, cheese, and flour—involved biological as well as mechanical processes. Here the enthusiastic but rather haphazard purchasing of plantations, supply depots, meat packing plants, and box and carton producers, as well as the buying of new facilities for the production of jams, jellies, biscuits, sugar, and chocolate brought no reduction of unit costs by improving the flow through many units. The resulting conflicts of interest and complexities of managing such a variegated business empire brought the spinning off of many units. Those that remained were operated as autonomous divisions, in much the same manner as C. and J. Clark, Ltd.

Again an American comparison is illuminating. The Great Atlantic and Pacific Tea Company was formed to serve much the same type of urban market as were the Lipton enterprises. It grew, however, more horizontally than vertically; that is, it expanded by increasing the number of stores to serve the same type of market. Its management concentrated not on a strategy of vertical integration but on carefully scheduling a high volume and velocity of flow through their stores. It moved into manufacturing or to control sources of supplies only as a last resort when the steady flow of such materials was threatened. Because in the grocery business suppliers were particularly numerous, this rarely occurred. The managers expected to make their profit on maintaining a velocity of flow, unlike Lipton, who instituted "new enterprise at every point in the business where he thought he could make a profit." Thus where growth for Lipton became a centrifugal force, it was for the A & P a centripetal one. The latter enterprise not only continued for more than a century as a cohesive organization; but it became a model in the twentieth century for a retailing revolution in the United States. Moreover, the American enterprises that concentrated on coordinating the production of one of the several that Lipton entered enjoyed a long and profitable life. Among such enterprises were Armour and Swift, National Biscuit, American Sugar, and Baker's Chocolate.

The British experience appears to reinforce the American one. The centripetal force that unified the multi-unit enterprise was its continued ability to coordinate effectively the flow of goods from supplier through the process of production to the consumer. Where expansion added new units whose activities could be fully integrated into the flow, the enterprise remained a cohesive unit. Where they could not be so integrated, they came to be administered separately (with each subunit oriented to its specific markets and suppliers), or (in many cases) spun off from the parent enterprise. In industries using energy- intensive and capital-intensive production and/or high volume distribution, the careful coordination of the flow achieved a cost advantage that provided the basic cohesiveness. Thus while I agree with Professor Mathias that one can think of successful examples of both integrated and nonintegrated enterprises in such industries as shoes, groceries, and clothing, I believe that this is as true for steel, chemical, rubber, oil, electrical and other machinery, elevators, cameras, typewriters, and automobiles, as for beer and margarine. In the latter trades a few large integrated enterprises have from the start dominated their industries in Britain, I believe, as well as in the United States.

It was in many of these same industries that modern multinational enterprises first appeared. They are still a rarity in shoes, clothing, lumber, furniture, and many foods; that is, in those older industries whose basic materials were biologically produced. Mira Wilkins in her excellent history of American multinational enterprise and in her comments this morning has described the pattern of growth of such firms in mechanical, chemical, and electrical industries. The stories of British-based Unilever and ICI presented by Charles Wilson have many parallels. The American enterprises that first went overseas were those that had developed a national and then an international marketing organization to sell relatively new, mechanically mass-produced metal products—sewing machines, harvesters, type-

writers, electrical machinery, and automobiles—or mass-produced cigarettes, matches, vegetable oil, kerosene, and rubber products. These new
international sales organizations were concentrated in the technologically
advanced urban nations of Europe. American firms moved into underdeveloped areas almost wholly to obtain assured supplies of raw materials.
The next step, which usually occurred because of tariffs and other local
protective legislation, was to build the processing plants to service the
marketing organizations. Then local managers began to look for closer
sources of semifinished and raw materials. Soon much of the coordination
of flow was handled by relatively integrated regional units, usually organized along national lines. These subordinate enterprises often depended
upon the parent for an assured supply of distantly produced raw materials.
This pattern of growth appears to have been much the same for European
as it was for American multinational companies.

As a result, multinational enterprises, both European and American,
tended to become federations of regional subsidiaries, enjoying what Lawrence Franko[1] has termed "mother-daughter relationships" with the parent
enterprise. Cartel arrangements to divide world markets, which were so
common before World War II among oil, explosives, and steel companies,
reinforced the pattern. Professor Wilson provided a good example of this
phenomenon in his discussion of ICI. In both American and European
multinationals, overseas activities tended to be supervised by an international division whose headquarters were housed in the general office building of the parent company. Many American firms after they began to diversify thus came to have product divisions which marketed at home and
an international division that supervised geographically defined autonomous
units abroad.

Since World War II, changing markets and technology have caused both
American and European multinational enterprises to shift from regionally
organized operating divisions to world-wide product ones. Increasing affluence in the United States and Western Europe and the lowering of trade
barriers, particularly with the coming of the European Common Market,
enlarged international markets and made them more competitive. The
failure to restore the older cartel arrangements after World War II further
increased competition. In the postwar years the technology of production
and distribution became increasingly complex and more energy- and capital-intensive. At Unilever the coming of detergents, frozen foods, and new
methods of margarine production were cases in point. That company's
response to these postwar challenges appears to have been typical also of
other European and American multinational enterprises. In Professor Wilson's words: "The solution suggested by events was a structure called "Coordination," and the name reflected the need to compromise between the
historic federalism of the old Unilever and the felt need for greater central

guidance in the new. World policy, formerly on a regional basis was now to be on a product basis and a "coordinator" would take charge of over-all policy for each group of products—edible fats, other foods (including meats, frozen and canned foods etc.), detergents, toilet preparations, chemicals and other technical products."

The function of the new coordinator was to assure continuing, close contact between suppliers, producers, distributors, and the ultimate consumer. "The fact was that in a vast consumer organization catering for millions of customers flexibility and local knowledge was still as vital as ever. This was the nub of the problem." By the mid-twentieth century coordination of flow thus meant more than just careful scheduling and adjusting the flow to short-term shifts in demand. It meant keeping tabs on changes in taste and style, on the actions of competitors often based in different nations, and on the activities of local governments. It was important in such coordination to maintain a continuing review of the new technologies of production and distribution. This was as true for enterprises manufacturing durable producers goods like electrical machinery and industrial chemicals as it was for those making perishable consumer products. Yet the central cohesive force remained the coordination of the processes of production and distribution with market demand.

Increasing homogeneity in the world markets and in the application of technology then has moved this coordination in multinational enterprises from a regional to a world-wide product basis. John M. Stopford and Louis T. Wells have documented this trend in American multinationals in their recently published *Managing the Multinational Enterprise*. Laurence Franko in a recent paper found the same trend in European multinationals. (See Table 1.) The standard multinational enterprise is coming to use on a world-wide basis the structure (delineated in Figure 2) that high technology-diversified American enterprise had used so effectively on a national basis. In both, the autonomous operating divisions coordinate flows in a broad sense to changing markets, while the general office evaluates divisional performance and makes policies and determines long-term strategies for the enterprise as a whole. In both the long- and short-term decisions, the market remains the nub of the matter.

If a review of the development of the multi-unit, managerial enterprise in Britain and on the world-wide scene helps to identify its common characteristics, a brief survey of its history in Western Europe, Japan, and the USSR can bring out differences resulting from operational differences in national economies and in culturally defined attitudes and values. The story of large business enterprise in Western Europe, including Britain as well as Germany and France, permits comparisons in an economic and cultural context derived from a common heritage. The Japanese experience, on the

TABLE 1

INTERNATIONAL ORGANIZATION STRUCTURES OF EUROPEAN COMPANIES ON THE FORTUNE 200 LIST AS OF DECEMBER 31, 1970
(PRINCIPAL ORGANIZATIONAL RELATIONSHIP BETWEEN PARENT AND FOREIGN MANUFACTURING SUBSIDIARIES)

Country of origin	Holding company	Mother-daughter	World-functional	International division	Worldwide product division	Area division	Mixed or grid	Unknown or no foreign manufacturing	Total
Switzerland		2			3	1*	2		8
Italy	1	1	1*	1‡	3*				7
Germany	2	10	1	3*‡	6		2	3	27
France	1	4*	2*	2	5			7	21
Holland		1		1	1		1*		4
Belgium and Luxembourg		2			3*			1	6
Sweden		2	1		4				7
United Kingdom§	3	5		13‡	8†	1*	16		46
Total	7	27	5	20	33	2	21	11	126

NOTE: In some cases these rough classifications are considerable oversimplifications of highly complex structures.
*In one case, the U.S. subsidiary does not follow the over-all reporting line.
†In two cases, the U.S. subsidiary does not follow the over-all reporting line.
‡In one case, the European Common Market is the "home market."
§Data for U.K. companies was compiled by Professor John Stopford of the London Business School. Both Royal Dutch Shell and Unilever have been included with U.K. companies.

SOURCE: L. G. Franko, "Organizational Change in European Multinational Enterprise," unpub. MS. Professor Franko is with the Center for Education in International Management. His study was supported by a grant from the Ford Foundation.

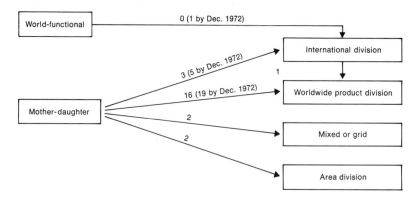

Figure 2. Patterns of Change in Organizational Relationships between Headquarters and Foreign Manufacturing Subsidiaries in Large European Enterprises, December 31, 1945, to December 31, 1970 (continental firms only). The expression "mother-daughter" indicates the existence of a personalized reporting relationship that runs directly from subsidiary to parent company presidents. All changes but three were observed to have occurred after January 1, 1968. This figure was based on incomplete data; information was not available on all organizational changes undergone in the 83 continental European firms in our sample at the time at which the figure was compiled. (Source: L. G. Franko, "Organizational Change in European Multinational Enterprise," unpub. MS.)

other hand, allows comparison of the development of this fundamental modern economic institution in a very different cultural context. Finally, an analysis of the operation of the Russian economy allows comparisons in managerial structures and in managerial recruitment and training where profit-oriented enterprises and a market economy do not exist and are indeed ideologically unacceptable.

In Western Europe the multi-unit enterprise appeared as soon as enlarged markets and large-scale exploitation of the fossil fuels permitted high volume production and mass marketing. Yet such enterprises long remained fewer in number and smaller in size than those in the United States. Until recent years their operation has been more personal and less managerial. In these countries the managerial class stayed small. Middle managers and the resulting management in depth was especially lacking.

Both the economic situation and culturally indoctrinated attitudes account for these differences. European countries had a smaller domestic market than that of the United States, and their businessmen always relied more than Americans on overseas trade. Moreover, in marketing overseas, European manufacturers depended on other enterprises—local exporters, foreign or colonial importers, or shipping and trading companies— to reach their point. Where they did move into marketing their own products abroad, they became multinational companies along the lines of Unilever and ICI. Hence European enterprises stayed small, often remaining single-unit ones carrying on a single function—production, marketing, mining, or shipping. This lack of vertical integration was one reason why the European producers long had a bias for manufacturing and engineering, and little concern with marketing. Such a basic structural difference in European firms and in many European industries meant that there was far less opportunity to coordinate the flow from supplier to consumer than in the United States. The failure to create large business administrative networks therefore lessened the need for middle managment. The management of production often involved only operating a factory, works, or mine whose manager, in many cases little more than a senior foreman, reported directly to the owner or members of the owner's family. The management of marketing enterprises remained in the hands of a few office managers assisted by clerks working directly under the guidance of the owners. The smaller number of managers, especially middle managers, meant there was less need to develop business education. There was less interest, too, in the forming of professional societies concerned with such managerial activities as accounting, marketing, and purchasing, as well as administration in general. In this way, the size and structure of the economies of Western European nations stunted the growth of the multi-unit enterprise and delayed the birth of a new class to manage it.

Cultural attitudes and values reinforced the impact of the economic situation. They did so by encouraging the continuance of personal enterprise. In the older, stratified societies of Western Europe, one of the firm's basic functions was to provide the income necessary to maintain family status. This goal remained more important than that of assuring dividends to a large number of nonfamily stockholders. Therefore European companies, including British ones, resisted expansion through the building or buying of new units or merging with others, for such expansion normally weakened family control. These owners had a strong dislike of competition. They preferred a more comfortable negotiated environment, and so encouraged cartels with other family firms to control competition within their industry and worked closely with their governments to obtain tariffs and other legislation to protect themselves from external competition.

In addition the authoritarian values that predominated in family life were carried over to the management of the enterprise. The head of the firm was normally the head of the family and was expected to be sovereign in both. As Hans A. Schmitt said in his reply to Wolfram Fischer's comments, extensive interviews of senior German executives indicated that they thought that they did, and certainly should, run their enterprises almost single-handed. Such cultural orientations further discouraged the recruitment and training of a class of professional managers by giving these men a low social status. They remained in a sense servants in a master's house.

For example, Professor Schmitt noted that Paul Reusch, "the major-domo of the Hankiel domain," was "strictly speaking . . . only a manager, a term invariably pronounced with a sneer by the people whose equal Reusch nevertheless became in his unique career."

Before World War II, both cultural and economic forces thus tended to cause the multi-unit enterprises in Western Europe to be operated at the top by small personal family groups who more or less directly supervised the work of the individual units within the enterprise—that is, the individual factories, offices, mines, and laboratories. James A. Laux has, by citing Oliver Gelinier, provided a useful picture of the traditional private French firm. "The traditional private firm described by Gelinier operated by customary and traditional rules but avoided written regulations which might limit the authority of top management. Desiring stability above all, it sought a protected or guaranteed market and found aggressive competition very distasteful. Top management centralized decisions in its hands and engaged in little consultation with subordinates. Those at the top expected loyalty and obedience from their subordinates even more than efficiency. The mobility of executives within or among firms was limited, and reactions to major changes outside the firm were muted and grudging. Traditionally, French management also shared the general European preference for problems of production and design rather than marketing."

There were, of course, important exceptions to this pattern. As Professor Schmitt implicitly suggested and Professor Fischer explicitly pointed out, the large multi-unit, managerial enterprises developed in Germany in the most technologically advanced industries, such as electrical, chemical, and metallurgical, much along the same lines as had their counterparts in the United States. By 1900, for example, Siemens had created a modern divisional structure similar to that shown in Figure 1 and relied heavily on professional managers. I suspect that the same was true for many of the chemical firms that came to make up I. G. Farben in the mid-1920s. In France, Pechiney had a comparable structure by 1948. Professor Laux indicates too that the automobile and chemical as well as metallurgical enterprises differed from those defined by Oliver Gelinier. Nevertheless the large integrated, diversified managerial enterprise appears to have been much more the exception than the rule in Europe before World War II.

Since the war, however, they have become increasingly the rule. The wave of mergers and reorganizations which began in the 1950s and accelerated in the 1960s brought both integrated and diversified enterprises to many industries throughout Western Europe. The increasing use of high velocity, capital-intensive production, often based on new chemical and electronic technology, and the expanding markets resulting from the new affluence and the lowering of trade barriers, all intensified the pressure to coordinate flow from supplier to consumer. Furthermore the increasing competition from American firms and the opening of the Common Market all but ended the prewar negotiated environments.

The enterprises that came to dominate nearly all capital-intensive and/or mass-marketing industries followed much the same organizational development. If they handled a single line of products they built centralized, functionally departmentalized structures. If they were handling two or more lines of goods they tended to adopt the divisional structure with a division to handle each major market. Such operating units became responsible for coordinating the flow and for carrying out all the activities involved in producing and distributing a major line of goods. The office at the top of both departmentalized or divisionalized organizations evaluated the performance of the operating units and determined strategy for the enterprise as a whole. Increasingly it was made up of professional executives with little or no personal connection with the owners. In many cases expansion, reorganization, and merger loosened the control of a single family or group. The German Versten and governing boards of large enterprises in other countries now made the larger strategic decisions through collegiate consensus rather than at the will of a single autocrat. Doctoral dissertations recently completed at the Harvard Business School document the growth of modern divisionalized enterprises in the United States, Great Britain, France, and Italy as well as Germany. Their findings are summarized in Figures 3, 4, 5, and 6.

The rapid spread of the large multi-unit enterprise, and particularly of its divisionalized version, have intensified the demand for professional managers in Europe. It has created for the first time a genuine interest in business education. In addition it has created a great curiosity about American management methods as the popularity in Europe of McKinsey & Company as management consultants attests. Finally the number of professional management societies is growing and attendance at their meetings increasing.

Since World War II then, European enterprise has become more managerial than personal. In both strategy and structure it has become closer to the large American firms. The continuing differences between European and American enterprises clearly reflect their past histories. Family ownership and control remain a factor in European companies while they have practically disappeared in the United States. The European firms still employ fewer middle and higher managers. The general office in a divisionalized firm is usually made up of the division heads and two or three general officers. The number of staff executives as well as general executives remains smaller than in American enterprises. The failure to use stock bonuses and options to set up internal reward systems suggests the continuance of family control and the view of the manager as a servant of the owners, while the less explicit use of statistical and other formal controls

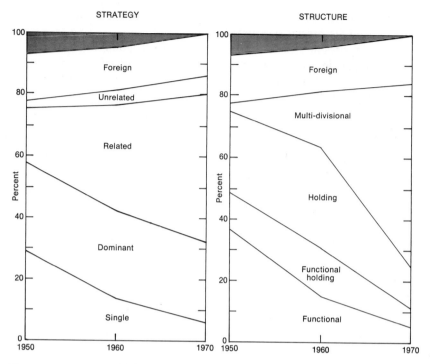

Figure 3. Great Britain: Evolution of Strategy and Structure in the Sixty-Six Largest British Manufacturing Firms, 1950–70. (Source: Derek F. Channon, "Strategy and Structure of British Enterprise" [unpub. Ph.D. diss., Harvard Business School].)

may indicate a continuing commitment to a more personal management. Yet despite differences in cultural values, in sizes and structures of economies, and the availability of natural resources, modern technology, affluence, and expanding markets have made the organization and operation of large multi-unit enterprises in Western Europe and the United States much more similar to one another than to those of business enterprises in either region that existed a century and in Europe even a generation ago.

If in Western Europe the organization of national economies and the impact of cultural attitudes and values held back the full fruition of modern enterprise and a class of specialists to manage it, both factors hastened the development of modern management and managers in Japan. There, the economic situation forced the Japanese to concern themselves more directly with the coordination of flows to markets, while cultural values encouraged the development of managerial attitudes and gave high status to managerial tasks.

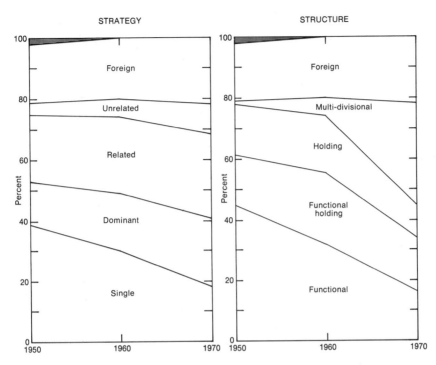

Figure 4. France: Evolution of Strategy and Structure in the Seventy-Nine Largest French Manufacturing Firms, 1950–70. (Source: Gareth Pooley-Dyas, "Strategy and Structure of French Enterprise" [unpub. Ph.D. diss., Harvard Business School].)

After the Meji Restoration, Japan made a far more conscious effort to industrialize than did the nations of Western Europe and the United States. The government took the lead in working closely with individual business enterprises in order to catch up with the West. In so doing the Japanese depended even more on the overseas market than did European countries. In meeting the challenge, Japanese businessmen relied from the start on large multi-unit enterprises—the *zaibatsu*.

The *zaibatsu* quickly developed modern management structures and professional managers. From the beginning their organization included a number of large units operating under the supervision of a general office that made long-term investment decisions. While the *zaibatsu* began as family affairs, they were soon managed primarily by full-time, nonfamily managers. Before 1900, Kozo Yamamura reports, the Mitsui *zaibatsu* had brought in an outsider, a president of a railroad company, to be its *bantō*, or *de facto* top executive. The many units within the enterprise were supervised by a committee which included, beside members of the Mitsui family,

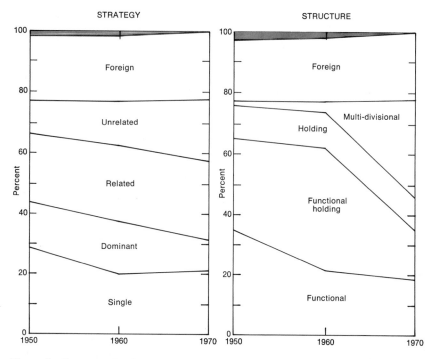

STRATEGY   STRUCTURE

Figure 5. Germany: Evolution of Strategy and Structure in the Seventy-Eight Largest
German Manufacturing Firms, 1950–70. (Source: Heinz Thanheiser, "Strategy
and Structure of German Enterprise" [unpub. Ph.D. diss., Harvard Business School].)

the senior executives of the Mitsui bank, coal mine, and recently acquired
textile, paper, mining, and shipping companies. The professional managers
at the top clearly outnumbered family members. Moreover, each of the
subenterprises included a full quota of managers. Thus the *zaibatsu* employed managers at the middle and senior level long before most European
enterprises.

Moreover, the different subunits in the enterprise supported each other
more effectively than did subsidiaries in most of the larger western multinational enterprises. The *zaibatsu*'s bank provided capital and its mines,
fuel. Most important of all, its trading company gave manufacturing units
in the *zaibatsu* direct contact with the overseas markets. These trading
companies with their "increasingly efficient network of trading posts around
the world" made possible the coordination of flows of goods from supplier
to consumer in a way which the Europeans with their independent manufacturers, jobbers, importers, and shipping companies could not match. In
fact the Japanese were probably in closer touch with market changes than

the prewar federated multinationals, such as Unilever and ICI. The Japanese trading companies provided a constant supply of market information as well as helping to schedule flows. Thus Professor Yamamura points out that "an export department of a large firm is often little more than a liaison office with the Mitsui Bussan or its competitors." Yamamura believes, and I would certainly agree, that the trading companies were "the key to the success of the Japanese firms in the international market." In fact, by the early twentieth century their services already "all but eliminated the differences existing between domestic and international trade."

The Japanese awareness of the value of defining organizational structures and developing management in depth is suggested by the rise of Matsushita Electric. Matsushita, who founded a small electrical appliance company in 1917, adopted in 1934, after a period of rapid growth, a modern divisionalized structure to handle four major product lines. After World War II, when the company had over forty thousand men working in seventy plants, it had built a divisional organization more sophisticated

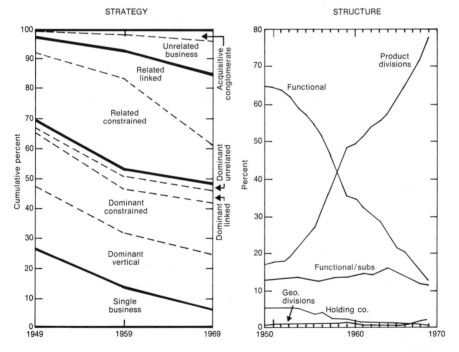

Figure 6. United States: Evolution of Strategy and Structure of the "Fortune 500," 1950–70. (Source: Richard Rumelt, "Strategy, Structure and Financial Performance of the Fortune 500, 1950–1970" [unpub. Ph.D. diss., Harvard Business School].)

than that of du Pont or General Motors. Thus in the development of new technologically advanced products, as well as in capturing overseas markets, the Japanese have relied on large managerial enterprises, with gratifying results.

Their organizational achievements have been aided by cultural attitudes and values that reinforced the commitment to managerial rather than personal enterprise. Group loyalties and group decisions have been valued. The enterprise came before the individual or the family. In Professor Yamamura's words: "The *uchi* counted, not the individual." Decisions were expected to be made by consensus, the *ringi* way, which was almost the antithesis of the decision-making process in the traditional European firm. Decisions in large multi-unit enterprises involve many interests and require implementation by many executives. Therefore, although the *ringi* system, with its requirements for formal written agreements from nearly everyone involved in a decision, was slow and cumbersome, it did help to assure that proper information and points of view were acquired and assimilated before taking the decision, and that the necessary teamwork and coordination was there to carry it out. In large managerial enterprises, such procedure would appear to have real advantages over management by autocratic dictates, autocratically enforced.

Although the Japanese do not put a premium on individual achievement, they do on an individual's status, or in Yamamura's terms "relative rank order." In Japan the rank order of a manager in a large enterprise has been high. Moreover, to the Japanese the most important ingredient in the success of a large enterprise was having "good men." And "good men" were defined as good managers and not as men from good families or even good schools. As was not always the case in Europe performance counted for more than birth. In Japan there were no sneers for the managers. Therefore the *zaibatsu* and other business enterprises had little difficulty in recruiting the most able graduates of the most prestigious universities. Because of their ability to recruit the best, Japanese business men have not felt the need to set up specialized business schools and professional societies. The ablest students to reach the top of a most rigorous educational system could be trained on the job.

The differences in the structure and operation of the large enterprises in Japan and the United States are less than those between comparable European and American enterprises. Again they reflect differences in their history. Moreover these differences are quite the opposite of those differentiating European and American firms. In Japan the problem is too much consensus and too little individual authority and responsibility. Professor Yamamura suggests that the *ringi* system is being modified so as to give increasing responsibility and authority to the heads of the operating divisions, leaving consensus group decision-making for financial and investment decisions. At the same time line and staff distinctions have become more precise and staffs, particularly at the top level, have been enlarged. All these changes have moved the Japanese enterprises closer to the organizational structure of large American firms. The weaknesses listed by Professor Yamamura—inflexibility, imbalance, lack of advisory staff, lack of communication between research and operations—appear to be as much inherent weaknesses in the structure of large managerial enterprises as reflections of culturally defined attitudes and values. Challenges created by such problems are in many ways less critical or difficult than those facing many European firms. Clearly the Japanese have developed large multi-unit enterprises to a high state of efficiency and created a remarkable set of managers.

Less than a generation ago Japan suffered a devastating military defeat; her physical plant was in ruins. In a quarter of a century the people of these islands, whose area is smaller than some American states and whose natural resources are far fewer than those of any major power, have created what is probably the most productive economy in the world. Its gross national product now surpasses all nations except those of the two superpowers. Surely a part of this achievement can be attributed to cultural attitudes that valued the work of managers and put a premium on traits essential to the management of highly complex, multi-unit enterprises. No nation appears to have been culturally better equipped to handle the managerial demands of modern technologically advanced urban economies than the Japanese.

In Russia the story could hardly be more different. There history and ideology have discouraged the development of the multi-unit enterprises comparable in function to those of the West and the creation of a class of managers to operate a modern technologically advanced economy. In the West and in Japan the cohesive force in the creation and continued operation of the modern enterprise has been the integration of the processes of production and distribution with the market—both the short-term coordination of flow and long-term investment strategy. In the USSR since the Revolution the coordination of the flow of goods and investment decisions have been in the hands of central political authorities. In their decisions market demand has been only one of several considerations. Revolution, war, purges, preparation for war, and again devastating war, meant that until the 1950s, the Russian leaders concentrated on building capital goods (including the basic transportation and communications network) and military equipment. They paid little attention to the production of consumer goods or, outside of the military area, to technological innovation.

Nor in the years before the 1950s did they specifically concentrate on building up a managerial class to run the economy. While the makers of the Revolution eliminated private personal enterprise, they were slow to recruit and train a new class to carry out the economic functions that such enterprises had handled. For one thing, Communist ideology had little place for factory managers and gave no attention at all to middle and higher levels of management.

To make matters worse, when Lenin and his associates began in the mid-1920s to become interested in the problems of industrial management, they became enamored of the managerial ideas of Frederick W. Taylor. The Taylor school of scientific management concentrated almost wholly on the factory. It said almost nothing about the operation of multi-unit enterprises, the coordination of the flow of goods from supplier to consumer, or even coordination of flow through a single factory. As Alexander Billon pointed out, the greatest defect of Taylor's doctrine was its emphasis on functional specialization and the resulting failure to consider the movement of goods from one subunit to another within the plant. For Taylor, managers became almost unnecessary. A planning board of functional specialists supervised the work of the specialized functional foremen. Such an organization was obviously attractive to the Soviets.

As a result of ideology, borrowed ideas and historical crises, the Soviets made few attempts to create multi-unit enterprises. Until the Khrushchev reforms, the Russian enterprise appears to have been almost always a single unit—that is, a factory, mine, shop, or store. Each such enterprise apparently reported directly to a ministry of trade or industry in Moscow, or in some cases in the capitals of local republics. In the mid-1950s 200,000 individual enterprises still reported to sixteen economic ministries.[2] If this was so, then an average of 12,500 enterprises reported to a single ministry. This is a most impressive span of control even where the enterprises were grouped for administrative purposes by regions, production complexes, or a combination of the two. Nevertheless, as Professor Billon reports, functional officials in Moscow or republic capitals dealt directly with managers carrying on the same functional activities within an enterprise. The one structural reform which took place before World War II, according to Billon, was to break this contact between the functional men in an enterprise and the ministry by giving the manager of the former the authority to control and coordinate all activities within his enterprise. This reform was achieved by setting up a clear-cut line and staff structure within both the enterprise and the all-union and union-republic ministries. The discussions about and the solutions provided to the problem of functional versus general line control were striking in their parallels to those concerning the same issues within the very first large multi-unit enterprises in the United States, the railroads.

Before 1957 then, the structure for the management of the Russian economy included the individual enterprises, the ministries, and two key central bureaus of economic control. One of these, *Gosplan*, basically determined strategic investment decisions. Using guidelines approved by the party leaders, *Gosplan* officials, working closely with the planning sections of the ministries and larger enterprises, decided on the allocation of capital and personnel needed to meet the over-all production plans. The second, *Gossnab* (Committee for Material-Technical Supply), formed in 1948, had the responsibility for scheduling and coordinating the flow of goods and materials through the economy from the supplier to the processing plant and then to the consumer. As Vsevolod Hulubnychy noted, *Gossnab* became the bureau most hated by Soviet managers. These managers must have attempted a variety of *sub rosa, ad hoc* techniques to effect the allocation of resources and to assure themselves of supplies and outlets, and at the very least, to coordinate their schedules with those of their suppliers and customers. In self-preservation they also must have learned how to affect the setting of output quotas and schedules for their specific enterprises.

Not only did the Soviets pay relatively little attention to building an organizational structure between the single-unit operating enterprise and the central control offices, but they also failed to make any special effort to create a large cadre of managers. Before the 1950s the lot of the Russian manager was hardly a happy one. He was carefully controlled from the top, closely watched by the party, and swiftly punished for failure, often beyond his individual control, to meet quotas set by the central authorities. Managerial positions were not the road to status and power in the USSR as they were in Japan and the United States.

Since 1957 the Soviet leadership has concerned itself more with the building of an intermediate structure between Moscow and the operating enterprises, and with training and recruiting a managerial class. As long as Russian production was concentrated on capital and military goods, the two-level system could work well enough. But when production capacity began to be turned to mass-produced consumer goods and when new technologies, particularly in chemicals and electronics, intensified the velocity and complexity of production, then the existing industrial organization began to falter. The 1957 changes under Khrushchev appear to have been an attempt to expand intermediate structures on a regional basis. It may not be too farfetched to see here a parallel to geographical decentralization instituted by the large American and multi-national enterprises earlier in the century. In any case continuing malfunctioning of the processes of production and distribution led to more basic reforms in 1965.

These changes as described by Professor Billon suggest that the Soviets since 1965 have been seriously attempting to build multi-unit enterprises. The production association has become a major administrative form. The consolidation of many single-unit enterprises into such associations has brought the number of industrial enterprises down from two hundred thousand to forty-five thousand. The resulting concentration and rationalization of production and distribution would seem to have many parallels to the merger movement in the United States at the turn of the century. At the same time "impressive experiments with organizational arrangements" have occurred in the ministries. The building of 2–3 and even 5–6 level systems suggests the development of a far greater field organization by the ministries. This and the creation of the production authorities indicate a rapid growth in the middle and higher levels of Russian management. A new interest in managerial education, including the setting up of management schools and the sending of experts to study the methods of Harvard and other American business schools reinforces this view. Moreover the 1965 reforms explicitly enhanced the power and prestige of the manager by greatly increasing his authority in the operation of the enterprise and by decreasing the number of direct controls placed on him from above.

Although the multi-unit enterprise appears to have grown rapidly in Russia since 1965, coordination of flow from one enterprise to another remains a critical problem. The fact that goals set for enterprises and internal incentives have been shifted from output quotas to sales volume and profit levels indicates an awareness of the importance of market demand in coordinating the flow, particularly in the growing consumer sector. So does the use of profit as "a tool in enterprise performance evaluation." Nevertheless, it seems clear that *Gossnab* still calls the tune. The response of a survey of 241 enterprise directors, cited by Professor Billon, suggests that *Gossnab* is still the most hated bureau. In that poll only 2 percent of the managers thought that their "material-technical supply" had improved since the 1965 reforms. Seventy-nine percent reported that they could see no change for the better. In listing the difficulties encountered in transferring their enterprise to the new operating conditions, these managers rated "unsatisfactory material-supply" at the top. The piling up of inventories of television sets, sewing machines and clothing, as well as the great washing-machine crisis, emphasized that the coordination of flow from supplier to consumer remained a basic problem in the Soviet economy.

As long as *Gossnab* and *Gosplan* retain their critical controls, the organization and operation of the Russian economy must be very different from that of the West. So too must be the structure of management organization and the role of the manager. In the Soviet Union, *Gosplan* and *Gossnab* continue to be responsible for the two basic functions carried out by the multi-unit enterprise in the United States, Western Europe, and Japan. Since *Gosplan* makes the strategic decisions (comparable to those by the general office of the large enterprise in a market economy) and *Gossnab*, those involved with the coordination of the flow (the task of the autonomous operating divisions), the Russian managers have far less to say in the making of the critical decisions in the management of an economy than do their counterparts in the West and Japan. Here then, is a basic difference between a market and a command economy. In the former, both the strategic investment and the day-to-day operating decisions are made on estimates of long-term and short-term market demand. In the latter the central authorities make both sets of decisions on the basis of criteria broader than the market.

Outside of Russia the large multi-unit managerial enterprise has become the dominant decision-making unit in the technologically advanced, industrial urban economies. Concentrated in the secondary sector of the economy, such enterprises have been the engines of economic development since the mid-nineteenth century. In so doing, they have taken on much the same form throughout the non-Communist world. At the top a small group of executives allocates the resources at the firm's disposal—capital, materials, and trained personnel—and monitor and evaluate the performance of the autonomous, self-contained operating divisions which handle a major line of goods or services for a major market. The rapid spread of this institutional form in all advanced market economies, as the papers and discussions of this conference emphasize, has raised many important questions. In these concluding remarks I will address myself only to those concerning its internal operations suggested by Professors Wilson and Wilkins concerning centralization and decentralization, and a basic one raised by Robert Averitt, concerning the large enterprise's continuing impact on its external economic and ecological environment.

The inquiries of Professors Wilson and Wilkins into the nature of centralization and decentralization boil down to asking what precisely have been the relationships between the general office and the operating divisions. The fundamental issue here appears to be that of control. Does the general office have sufficient control over the divisions to ensure that it can carry out its basic tasks? Does it effectively monitor the operating units? Does it really make strategy? Or has it become, like the board of directors, merely a ratifying and legitimizing body? The answer would seem to lie in the nature and sources of the information on which the monitoring is done and the strategy formulated.

My impression is that the general office does not really control the divisions, for the information on which it acts still comes largely from within. The staff at the general office level can provide data independent of the division managers, and the senior executives can go outside for consultants and experts. But I suspect that these executives rely primarily on information generated by the day-to-day operations of the divisions. One reason is that in the older, diversified enterprises, the executives in the general office normally are recruited from the top divisional management. They are familiar with these types of data and are sympathetic to the goals and objectives of the division managers. In allocating resources they do little more than approve proposals sent up by the divisional executives. Here they are on familiar ground. They tend to be uncomfortable, however, with proposals of the general staff or outside consultants to make strategic moves into areas where their divisions are not yet operating. So in reality, it is the more aggressive division managers who determine strategy, that is, the investment decisions. In evaluating performance, the general officers, given their training, are skilled in interpreting the data they receive from the divisions. Yet this information does come from within, so outside comparisons are hard to make. Moreover, because they were themselves recently division managers, these general executives tend to be sympathetic to reasons why performance has fallen off from that of previous years or from the forecasted rate of return on investment. Rarely do they take action to remedy the situation by removing managers or discontinuing lines.

The issue here is more than just one of internal management. If the general office made up of full-time executives has become a ratifying body, similar to the board of directors which has only part-time members, can anyone or any group really control the men who manage the day-to-day business of the large modern enterprise? Could government regulating agencies or even government-appointed boards of directors do any better? Could they independently generate the information necessary for control?

Even if they could not, outside boards, whether private or public, could at least provide viewpoints and outlooks differing from those of the divisional executives. Such boards might be more objective in the evaluation of performance and apply broader criteria in the making of strategy. Possibly this is one long-term advantage of the recent conglomerates which have grown up through the purchase of enterprises in quite unrelated businesses. Their governing executives have fewer personal ties with and different career patterns from their subordinates than do the executives in the general offices of the older, high technology, diversified enterprises. Such general executives can give more concentrated time and obtain more specialized information than can large institutional investors—the managers of investment trusts, pension funds, and so forth—who are the only stockholders in a position to exercise control.

The possibility of public control does seem difficult to achieve. The experience of all non-Communist nations maintaining a market economy is that government can indirectly affect decisions as to coordination of flow and strategic investments by altering market demand and capital supplies through regulatory bodies, legislation, tariffs, and monetary and fiscal policies. But rarely have they taken over the actual decision-making as to strategic investment and coordination of flow which remains based on managerial perceptions of long- and short-term market demand. Only in Russia and other Marxist states does the actual decision-making power on investment and flows lie outside the managers of the multi-unit enterprises. The Russian experience testifies to the difficulty of managing a highly technological, increasingly mass-consumption economy, when such basic decisions are made without reference to the market mechanism.

Yet Professor Averitt's evaluation of the impact of the modern multi-unit enterprise on the external environment emphasized that public oversight of private enterprise must continue to be of public interest. Since World War II, economic development has become a basic concern for many nations, and clearly so must be the activities of an institution so central to economic development and growth. Moreover, the very success of these enterprises in generating change has raised a host of new problems. Their effectiveness has created an imbalance or bias in favor of the secondary sector. Mass-produced goods come relatively cheaply. Services remain costly and difficult to obtain. In the United States, as Averitt points out, government subsidies have become increasingly necessary in education and medicine in the tertiary sector, as well as in the primary sector's major industry, agriculture. This same pattern appears to be occurring in Western Europe.

More serious has been the impact on the ecological environment. The high velocity, energy-consuming processes of mass production and mass distribution have vastly intensified the depletion of natural resources, while at the same time, spewing out huge quantities of nonbiological wastes. In Averitt's words: "The development multiplier seems to be turning cancerous." Since the instruments for high velocity production and distribution are world-wide, so are the evidences of the cancer. The Rhine is as polluted as the Delaware; the air of Tokyo is of poorer quality than that of Pittsburgh. It is difficult to see how an institution whose whole purpose has been to assure high velocity production and distribution can be used to slow down the rate of structural change and growth in societies committed to affluence and modern creature comforts. This is particularly true if the operating managers, who are not subject to over-all controls, continue to make decisions on the basis of consumer demand.

Obviously the problems of corporate control and industrial pollution can only be raised and not answered by a conference such as this one. The knowledge, however, of how the most powerful institution in the modern economy came into being, spread, and continued to grow, should be of value to businessmen and public officials seeking such answers. It can at least point to the extreme naiveté of some of the answers now proposed. The problems must be viewed as central to the rapid industrialization and urbanization of the modern world and not as local evidences of the activities of unthinking men.

For this reason the approach used by this conference has as much value as the findings presented and the questions raised by its participants. It has helped to place this critically important modern economic institution in a broad historical and international setting. The papers and discussions not only say much about the rise of modern business enterprise, the coming of modern industry, and the process of economic development, but they also reveal changing relationships between classes and economic groups, and they suggest the interrelations between political processes and economic change. Collectively they point to the organizational and technological imperatives of modern economies. They suggest ways in which organization and management affect economic productivity and growth. They help to show the strengths and weaknesses of different industrial strategies and structures. Finally, they provide an insight into how culturally defined attitudes and values hasten or retard economic development.

The conference thus provides an impressive challenge to economic and business historians. Its scope should be enlarged. If each of these papers were developed into a full-scale monograph for each of the seven topics, and if a standard set of terms, concepts, and questions were framed for the writers of each monograph, the result would greatly increase our knowledge of the rise and operation of modern technologically advanced economies. Such knowledge would be of value to businessmen and public officials as well as historians, economists, sociologists, and other scholars. In such an enlarged research project, business historians are especially well-equipped to make contributions. I do hope that some will respond to the challenge so effectively presented by this conference.

NOTES

1. "Organizational Change in European Multinational Enterprise," an unpublished manuscript by Lawrence G. Franko of the Center for Education in International Management. Professor Franko's study was supported by the Ford Foundation.

2. I have relied here on Merle Fainsod, *How Russia is Ruled* (Cambridge, Mass.: Harvard University Press, 1963), pp. 333–53, 422–41, to supplement information provided by Professors Billon and Hulubnychy.